SEEING GOD
SEEING YOU

This Is My Gospel

Ronnie Worsham

ISBN-13: 9781731038968

To Treva and Kelley,
my mom and dad

CONTENTS

PREFACE

U ltimately, the gospel, if it is to be anything to us at all, is to be very personal. Each believer's story is a unique living sermon about the gospel of Christ. That Jesus died for the sins of the world is incredible; that he died for my sins is even more so. Yet it is true for each believer! The apostle Paul wrote to Timothy, "Remember Jesus Christ, raised from the dead, descended from David. *This is my gospel*" (2 Tim. 2:8, italics added). Each of us must take personal possession of the gospel in our own lives as well as the responsibility for its proclamation and advancement.

Understanding the gospel as it appropriates to our individual lives is a lifelong experience. Each step of the way, more of its depth and scope can be understood, believed, and appreciated. Each new day with its new insights gives us a newer and more powerful reason to worship our Savior and Lord Jesus Christ.

In that vein, *Seeing God Seeing You: This Is My Gospel* is my understanding and personalization of the gospel. We all think and process differently. For over forty-five years of my adult life, first as an unbelieving seeker, next as a new believer, and then as a called evangelist and pastor, I have vigorously pursued God. I am a melancholic man and a thinker, both for better and for worse. I have analyzed, reanalyzed, and likely overanalyzed at times the principles of the Bible and how they apply to and affect me.

I am a skeptic when it comes to believing good things pertaining to me, and the gospel is the best thing of all! I simply cannot begin to understand why God called me, a weak, humble believer, to be with him and serve him. I certainly cannot even begin to understand why he called me to carry this message in such a profound and important way. I know for sure that "I'm not here because I am good, but because he is very, very, very good!" Suffice it to say, the gospel as applied to me is extremely difficult for me to believe. I still carry only a mustard seed of faith in it as it pertains to me. I have much more faith as it pertains to everyone else, though!

The more I have come face-to-face with God, so to speak, the more sinful and guiltier I realize I was, and beneath the covering of Jesus's blood, I still am. It has been only in getting out of myself and looking through the lens of God in the Bible and seeing how God sees me that I can bridge this horrendous guilt and shame gap that exists before me and approach him with any measure of freedom and confidence (Eph. 3:12).

So I offer this volume to others who struggle the same as I do with seeing how our loving gracious Heavenly Father sees us. Although I have continued to edit and change it for quite a few years now, this volume represents in fact the first manuscript I ever wrote. But for some reason, I have not until now felt ready to publish it. Through it, my hope and prayer is that others too can find help in "repenting and believing the good news," as Jesus first called us all to do (Mark 1:15). Also, please note that all quotations are in the NIV, 2011, unless otherwise noted. Any alterations I took the liberty to make to the biblical quotations, such as italics and brackets, are also noted.

INTRODUCTION

I found a mirror in the darkness,
The lighting was dim, so I drew very near,
I saw two eyes looking right through me,
Filled with light and ever so clear!

The eyes were not mine; I was filled with wonder;
Who through the darkness was looking back at me?
Was it a mirror or was it a window?
I paused to ponder: what did they see?

My wife, Tana, and I have been together for a long time. We actually were friends and playmates back in grade school and then on in junior high and started dating when we were in college, having been married now for forty years. We are still playmates. At the time of this writing, we have four wonderful children together and two grandchildren. We know each other really well. And then again, we don't know each other very well. There's this big problem we have—she is a woman, and I'm a man.

One day, sometime back, we were having this "discussion" where I was trying to convince her of some important reality—I am sure mine. She, of course, took just a feminine moment to read my mind and then informed me what I was thinking—obviously a womanly ability. I told her, "You've been reading my mind for all these years, and you are almost always wrong." I'm sure that fixed everything! Well, maybe not. But what it did do was trigger me to think again about objectivity and subjectivity and how we all look at things. It especially reminded me how important it is for us to see things through God's eyes—the only truly objective view of anything. Reality. However, it is a fact that I am much more effective at correcting my wife's thinking than my own! Just don't ask her. I'm only kidding, of course, and she won't get mad; she'll just get even!

Objectivity is thinking about things from an external perspective, assuming that all truth does not pass through us. Objectivity assumes there is reality outside of us that is independent of our perception or our opinion about it. It is using accepted facts and information independent of self. On the other hand, subjectivity is processing information internally, from a personal perspective. It is using ideas and information from the perspective of ourselves. It assumes that reality is ultimately somehow dependent on our perspective and opinion.

And the reality is that we humans are all terribly prone to be subjective—seeing the world through our own paradigms and lenses. However, the more we are able to break out of this bad habit, though, the more objective we can be, and the better we will be at honesty and truth. The better we will be at seeing and dealing with reality. Even then, however, our objectivity will face the obvious human limitations of our own skewed human lens.

To be truly objective, we have to work very hard to get out of ourselves and see the world as it actually is—to see reality, to seek and discover mere truth. As mortal humans, we are just not naturally good at this. We do not trust others very much that they will tell or show us the truth. I think we intuitively know that everyone else is subjective too and that some are downright dishonest. As I have counseled and studied people all these years, and studied the work of others in this field, I have come to recognize that because of our subjectivity, as well as our less prurient nature, we humans tend to be a pretty deceptive species!

Also, because of our subjectivity and limited personal experience, each of us can become quite myopic, that is, shortsighted and narrow-minded. We have our noses wedged so closely into the bark of our own trees that we cannot see, let alone comprehend, the massive forest in which ours grows! Objectivity requires us to see reality through the greater context. To do this, we have to strain to learn and to get outside of ourselves. We have to admit how limited we are and to surrender control. We must dare trust other authorities and their information. We must learn to interpret us in view of all of us.

But because of our natural proclivity toward subjectivism, humans tend to be quite selfish and self-centered. And in this fallen world, it causes the world outside of Christ to end up being a giant con game where everyone gives only to get something back in return, hopefully more than given. It is, in a large part, a dog-eat-dog barter system, because it is impossible for fallen ones, void of the Holy Spirit, to give expecting nothing in return, as Jesus would have it (Luke 6:35). Thus, in the sinful world, deception, lying, and subterfuge are essential qualities of the best players.

That's where God comes in. Here is a "person," a being, who is complete within himself and who needs nothing and wants nothing. He *is* the truth. He is a giver, not a taker. He can give to us expecting nothing in return because he needs nothing *from* us; he only wants good things *for* us! He is a God of grace (the Greek word for "grace" means gift). When we, as humans, interact with other people, we generally assume that they expect something out of the exchange, just as we usually do. And likely they do. Hence, we do not trust them to be completely, or even very, objective (or objective at all) in their view or interpretation of us and the situation, because they are likely not very objective. They cannot be completely objective. But God can be completely objective. God *is* completely objective.

As we grow from infancy, we gain most of our self-view from our perceptions of others' views of us. In reality, what others actually think about us is not what affects us; rather, how we *perceive* that they see us is what affects us. These perceptions of how we think others see us, be they negative or positive, are blended together and averaged out in a way with those of who significantly impact our lives, carrying a greater weight. Particularly harmful views, whether communicated by words or actions, especially coming from key people, can scar us for life, because they drag down the average of our perceptions, as we are constantly and intuitively measuring it. This is why bullying, especially among the young, can be particularly damaging.

In contrast, if we generally perceive others' views of us as positive, we will more likely have a relatively healthy self-esteem. However, that still is not enough to meet the human need for self-worth. When our self-worth is dependent on mere humans, we become humanists. Although we generally will not realize it, let alone admit it, we ultimately end up worshiping and serving humanity, beginning with ourselves.

Even "feel good" books and articles fall short of salving our wounded egos, as they are still written by other people. We know that no human beings are completely objective. We just instinctively know it, and it doesn't take much effort to expose it.

But when our self-worth is dependent on God, rather than our human social orders and their "popularity games," we realize that at our worst we are priceless to the objective, divine appraiser of human value—God himself! I have an adage I teach and live by— "You can't get where you need to go until you truly know where you are." It's like the map at the zoo or amusement park. You know where you want to go. You can even locate it on the map. However, you cannot figure out how to get there until you figure out where you are at the present. So you gaze up at the map in wonder at the utter reality of the message informing you that "You Are Here!" Is it not funny, and even ironic, that you are standing in a spot and there is a map in front of you to tell you that you are "Here"?

Of course, you know you are standing here. Duh. But your perception of "here" is still subjective, not objective, and you just do not know where "here" is relative to anything else. Your initial perception of your own location is subjective and limited. Unless we make the effort to do otherwise, where we perceive we actually are at any given moment is relative only to the immediate surroundings and bears little on where we might in reality be relative to the bigger picture.

So, lost in a zoo or amusement park, one looks around close by and perhaps sees a large oak tree over there, a bench here, and the lion exhibit nearby. However, none of that gives one the objective perception of the location relative to the bigger picture, and more specifically relative to where we want to go. Thus comes the need for the map. Objectivity. Actuality. Reality. Once you figure out where you actually are, and not just where you might "feel like" or "think" you are, then you can chart a course to where you really want to be. I think that may be why, as the proverbial story goes, a guy does not want to stop and ask for directions or maybe even take a look at a map (although my map illustration breaks down a bit in this modern era of smart phones and ever-with-us GPS, I hope you get my point). To ask for help, we would thus have to admit we do not know where we are and thus do not know how to get where we would like to go. Because that might wound our silly human pride!

At the core, pride is the ultimate cause of human lost-ness! Literally and figuratively.

It's this way with life. We need a map. We need a map drawn out by someone with a correct view of the big picture. A map that not only helps us determine where we need and want to be, but a map to show us where we actually are—not where our intuition tells us we might be or where our prideful stubborn heart deceives us into thinking we are. Sadly, our personal feelings, apart from a solid knowledge of God's truth, are more often than not wounded, skewed, thrown off, deceived, and sometimes just "plain shot." At best, they are subjective and thus not really trustworthy at all.

We need a mirror that reflects to us what we really look like in the setting around us. We need objective eyes to look at us and reflect back what we look like to others. As a conversation with my wife might go, "Honey, does this tie look okay with this shirt?" The nice reply might be, "Hmm, how about this blue one?" Simply put, we benefit greatly when we receive feedback from another with a more objective, knowledgeable, capable point of view—and in my case with colors, ties, and my sweet wife, *much* more knowledgeable and capable. We have to work for objectivity in a world of the subjective. Part of what makes us so deceptive, as humans, is our lack of objectivity.

Often, we would have decided a long time ago where we wanted to be. We wanted to be happy, fulfilled, saved, and so forth. We wanted to feel loved and appreciated. We wanted to be successful. We wanted to be a good mom or a good dad. But we usually have pretty vague ideas about what any of that really looks like beyond what we have seen and experienced. When we start out, we certainly have no good and concrete view about what we ought to look like when we get to where we are designed to be going. But still no doubt, most of us have spent some time thinking about where we want to be, albeit often not very specific about it, and wondering how to get there. We may have often grown weary and discouraged even thinking about it. Too frequently, we may have just sort of given up and let life happen to us through our day-to-day, reactive decision-making. And the sad reality is too few really think much at all about the eternal implications.

However, I believe the real problem is not that we are incapable of getting where we want to be. The real problem is that we never figured out where we actually were in the first place. Perhaps we were afraid to admit it and thus made ourselves blind to any honest suggestions about our situations. Perhaps we received bad information and feedback from those around us, because they did not know much themselves, they were too biased, or they were afraid of our responses if they told us what they thought. But whatever the reasons for our failure to see ourselves as we really were, from the very start, the courses we charted were seriously flawed, thus doomed.

Only God can save us from this existential lost-ness that came over humanity in the fall. He fully and completely sees the big picture as it actually is. He sees us as we really are. He is the ultimate magnifying glass and the consummate mirror. If we will seek him, his are the eyes we will see peering out of the marvelous light into our present darkness. Jesus stated it clearly—"I *am* the truth" (John 14:6, italics added). He is the standard. He is the cornerstone. He is the benchmark. Thus, if we want to see ourselves as we truly are, we need to look at his template and portrait as well as his map and see where we are, at present, in relation to him, who is the perfect model. "YOU ARE HERE." It is then through his lens that we can thus *see God seeing us.*

It is only when we fix our eyes on the Holy One of God that we are ready and able to chart a right course. That is what this book is about. It is about gaining some perspective on how God sees us. God is more beautiful than a million sunsets. His love is unlimited. His power is immeasurable. His grace is unimaginable. In fact, God is infinite in all that is good. God is omnipresent (fills the universe), omniscient (all-knowing), and omnipotent (all-powerful). The creation declares all of God's invisible qualities (Rom. 1:20). Yet many don't believe this—either that God exists at all or that he is in fact good, loving, and aware of us. But I believe the creator, God, Yahweh, has made himself known to the creation and that we can see him and come to see how he sees us!

Most importantly, this Creator God, in fact, wants a relationship with each of us. He wants us each to see how he sees us personally. The Bible in general, and ultimately the gospel specifically, describes and demonstrates how God sees humanity.

In the words of the apostle Peter, "We also have the prophetic message as something completely reliable, and you will do well to pay attention to it, as to a light shining in a dark place, until the day dawns and the morning star rises in your hearts" (2 Pet. 1:19). Note again, you will do well to pay attention to that light shining into your own heart. It will bring unimaginable light to your darkest places.

Questions for Reflection and Discussion

1. Thinking back over the course of your life, how would you say you have generally felt God has seen you or felt about you? Why?
2. What was your "spiritual location" when you started your walk with Christ? If you are not a Christian, where would you say you presently are in regard to spiritual matters?
3. How does your perception of how you believe God sees you, for good or bad, affect your spiritual walk?
4. How might your view of where you actually were in the beginning have been skewed, and how might that skew have negatively affected your spiritual journey to this point?
5. When beginning and traversing our journey with God, why are our perceptions of how others see us (especially the views of our parents, caregivers, friends, and loved ones) so critical to our perceptions of who we are and of our intrinsic value?
6. How does seeing God as he really is help us to see ourselves as we really are?

CHAPTER 1

AND IT WAS VERY GOOD

Sometimes everything seems all right,
As if everything's going our way.
Everything is seemingly perfect,
One big bright and cloudless day!

I remember well when our first son, Brandon, was born. I felt like one of those dogs might feel when they keep tilting their heads back and forth from one side to another as if trying to figure something out. I could not seem to wrap my mind around it at all. Here was this little guy who was *my* son. I still felt the same way when my second and third sons, Kale and Casey, were born. Then my fourth, my only daughter, Brianna, was born. Oh my goodness. These were *my* children. My sweetheart's and mine. Probably as virtually all parents, I cannot say our beginnings were completely unselfish and just about having kids. Our desire for marriage and intimacy and family are not just about making babies and helping them to grow up happy and fulfilled—we need and want something out of it ourselves. Our mating instincts are powerful, often spontaneous, and sometimes not too well thought out. They can often even be completely selfish if we are not careful. But even in our basest human motivations, by God's design we continue to perpetuate our species.

We wanted children badly though, and like most couples, we had discussed it fairly early in our relationship, even before we were even married. I am the youngest of eight children. I was sociable and loved my siblings. Initially, I wanted lots of children, but after the third and then the fourth, my expendable energy decreased, my eagerness for more kids waned quite a bit, reality set in, and our pocketbook was about shot. My wife was an only child. She wanted several children too, but she'd never been around babies growing up, so the stark reality of the challenges of raising babies and the challenge of raising three and then four kids was a reality check for her too.

So after being married about three years, we had our first child. It was a boy. *And it was very good.* In fact, the whole experience seemed "magic"—supernatural—from the positive pregnancy test to the delivery—even in spite of the "morning" sickness stage early on (rather sometimes it seemed to be the "all-day" sickness stage) and the discomfort stage in the home "stretch" (if you know what I mean)!

The book of Genesis is the Bible's story of how God brought his children about. Seven times in chapter one, in this beautiful, seemingly poetic story of creation, we are told that God looked at what he had made to that point and saw that it "was good." The final time, as if to punctuate humanity's importance to creation and after completing his work by making humankind oversee the earth, we read, "God saw all that he had made, and *it was very good*" (Gen. 1:31, italics added). In light of humanity's responsibilities in the world, as well as our bearing God's image here, only after Adam and Eve were created did God see his work for the first time as "*very* good." However, that statement only becomes understandable—through God's eyes—when you understand the rest of the story.

Woman and man together are the joint image-bearers of the very substance and nature of God. The reason God wants us to imitate Jesus is that he is the exact representation of God (Heb. 1:3), and when we are imitating him and behaving as he did, we are being who we really were designed to be. We are re-conforming—being transformed by God—to our original mold and design. The Bible reveals that ultimately this whole universe was created for God's plan through and for his children (Col. 1:16). Paul tells us that God chose us before the creation of the world (Eph. 1:4). So even before he created it, he had us in mind. Just like people who want to be parents, I remember thinking about being a dad and the kind of father I wanted to be a long time before I even got married. In fact, I remember thinking about being a dad even when I was quite young. During our engagement period, I prayed about it and began planning to be a good dad.

When I saw my first son, it became my own reality that "it was very good."

I was watching a documentary on the "Big Bang Theory" a while back and was reminded how amazing the creation really is. I studied science back in college, even before the Big Bang theory fully "banged" into the middle of the scientific mainstream. Initially for me, some bitter life experiences along with my study of the physical sciences, psychology, and philosophy spelled the ultimate demise of my little country-church, country-boy faith. I had no real basis for any of my beliefs in God, Jesus, or the Bible, that is, other than it was what I had been taught amid quite a few other things I had also been handed and subsequently rejected. The unanswered questions simply drove me to unbelief.

By the time I was twenty or so, I did not disbelieve per se, because I just had no reason to actually believe. But later it was also science, psychology, and philosophy that served to drive my new, more informed faith. Contrary to the experience of many, I found that the study of these secular disciplines led me to faith in God, rather than away from it. Logically, I simply could not believe what I would have to believe to *not* believe in God. In my way of thinking, it takes a much longer leap of faith to *not* believe in a creator than it does *to believe* in one. And I think there are definitely compelling reasons to believe. And in my estimation, whether we like it or not, everyone lives by faith, whether they recognize or want to admit it or not. The real question is: what is each of us living by faith in?

I also cannot accept some of the simplistic and, to me, illogical assumptions of a large portion of Christianity either. In my experience, the louder and more forceful people are in their own assertions, and the more critical they are of others' beliefs, the less logical and compelling their own arguments seem to be. I believe truth sets us free and allows us to think freely, critically, and creatively about the scripture without fear of retribution. Seeking is thinking. Seeking opens our minds rather than close them. Seekers don't grow less and less open and unwilling to continue learning; they grow more open and eager to continue growing in the truth, wherever it is to be found. Mature disciples are humble, not arrogant. Mature disciples engage new and possibly more insightful ways of understanding God and the Bible. No one has a monopoly on the truth, and I decided two decades ago to mostly disassociate myself from any persons, churches, or organizations that sought to dictate to me what I had to believe to be a part of their circle or community, especially those who seem to think they have a monopoly on God and truth! Jesus is Lord, not any human or human institution. Jesus is my only Lord, and I think it should be that way with us all. As Paul said, "We make it our goal to please him" (2 Cor. 5:9). The true prophets will lead you to *him* (Christ); the less than honest ones will always lead you to *them*.

The truth of God is, in fact, offered to each individual who accepts Christ and without any required vote of approval from other humans, including churches and other centers of church influence (John 1:12–13)! And if I sound a little irritated on this, it is because I generally am. In my eager search for the pure truth of Jesus, I feel I personally fell victim to it myself, and sadly more than once. I know many others who unfortunately have been trapped by it as well. Please note, I certainly do not think everyone who subscribes to an overly literal or "patternistic" view, as an interpretive method, are necessarily closed-minded, too controlling of others' faith, or condemning of others. I know many who hold strong fundamentalist or more conservative views of the Bible who are not this way. But a significant number of people who write and lead from such views can seemingly try to theologically "strong-arm" others who do not happen to agree with them on their ideologies. I believe those who claim to hold the exclusive rights to the truth and the kingdom keys are the very ones who do what the Pharisees and teachers of the law were doing—forming a human barrier in front of the ever open and inviting gates into God's kingdom. Jesus described these sorts, saying, "Woe to you, teachers of the law and Pharisees, you hypocrites! You shut the kingdom of heaven in men's faces. You yourselves do not enter, nor will you let those enter who are trying to" (Matt. 23:13). They inadvertently set themselves up as lord!

So do your own thinking and don't let anybody or any particular ideologies tell you that you have to believe their interpretations of what the Bible is saying in order to be right, faithful, or committed or even be able go to heaven and so forth. Read it for yourself and ask God to guide you. Of course, use more learned people's insights and writings; just don't take anybody's work as gospel other than that in the scripture.

Also, as I will discuss later, be wary of humanistic "scientism"— the modern "religion" of science, which would have you believe that science has all the answers because it involves only reason and works only with the "facts." It is in fact patently *not* a fact that science works only with facts! And it *is* patently a fact that there is plenty of emotion and subjectivism involved in at least some of it. I believe many atheists and agnostics are in actuality emotional unbelievers and not intellectual ones! In thinking and understanding, as in all human endeavors, I believe the proverb on remaining balanced rings true, "It is good to grasp the one and not let go of the other. Whoever fears God will avoid all extremes" (Eccles. 7:18). You certainly do not necessarily have to take radical, extreme views of science or religion to believe strongly in God and his principles.

Anyway, the Big Bang documentary I just mentioned was recounting that science suggests that the entire "universe" began in a super-dense mass, almost infinitely minute, that came into being from pure energy. It was said to have been almost immeasurably hot and dense. Energy was converted to matter through the process of fusion. This is how stars are powered. This fusion is the opposite of what happens with the atomic bomb where matter is turned into energy, called fission. Arguably the most famous equation in the world is $E = MC^2$ (E = energy, M = mass, and C = the speed of light). Albert Einstein is most notably connected to the revolutionary discovery of the mass-energy equivalence, which, in effect, asserts that the mass of a body is a measure of its energy content. I believe it brings the concept of a creator God back into the science equation. In fact, for my own part, I believe it necessitates a belief in the unseen or the divine!

The Bible, I believe, tells us that God was the energy supplier behind the Big Bang, or whatever you want to call the initiation of the creation. That God was the energy that became matter, I suppose, is a fair way of thinking about it, as we read, "In the beginning, God created the heavens and the earth" (Gen. 1:1). But please note that this is not at all to insinuate a pantheistic view of creation—that the universe is somehow a manifestation of God himself. And the Bible also tells us God is the energy that sustains it all—"sustaining all things by his powerful word" (Heb. 1:3). He creates it and he sustains it.

Ultimately, science tells us, our mass—our physical existence—has an equivalence of energy. Just perhaps this energy equivalence is our own spirit itself. Of course, for believers that equivalence is rooted ultimately in the original power source himself—the Creator God. Jesus said he was the alpha and the omega, the beginning and the end. As hard as that is to believe, it at least makes sense, unlike some of what is suggested, even by science. We also come to know through the gospel that God is the energy that regenerates us from our own fallen state and separation from the divine. He does this by saving us and reconnecting us to God, plugging us back in, so to speak. He puts his own Spirit in us to enliven our spirits that have been dead from a lack of power. He regenerates us. He re-energizes us.

So the ultimate power source—God—created all matter from energy in order to provide a physical home, a workroom, and playroom of sorts, for mankind—and for the universe to ultimately be a temple for him as well as for those who accept Jesus as Lord. While you may feel small—a mere speck of a person on a mere speck of a planet in a universe vast beyond comprehension—you are not small to the Creator Father.

Being the youngest of eight in a backwoods country family, I know about getting lost in the shuffle. When I was a child, we attended a small church near our house where there were probably only fifty or seventy-five members. Thus, my family of eight or nine constituted a big part of the church! One Sunday morning when I was only five, I was outside playing around the church building after services when I saw my family driving off. Without me! There were not many people there, and thus there were not many cars parked outside. The parking lot was quite small too! How could they miss me? I took chase, just knowing they would see me through the rearview mirror and stop and get me. Our family could be brutal in teasing, taunting, and humiliating, so my immediate assumption was that they were just messing with me.

No. They drove to the highway, never looking back and never stopping. They went home. Yes, I was five. So I can relate to Jesus being left unnoticed in Jerusalem by his family when he was twelve.

The preacher took me to my home after a few more minutes of "fellowship," which for my part involved me standing around waiting, a bit scared and in disbelief about being left behind. It was a pretty memorable experience for me. I was the baby! In fact, looking back, I *was* still practically a baby! It was a very odd experience. I was a "momma's boy," and my mom was normally a brooding hen. But I still got lost in the shuffle. Not a single one of them had noticed that the baby of the family was not in the car or present after they got home. I am sure they would have noticed when there was an extra piece of fried chicken at Sunday dinner that day (we called the noontime meal "dinner," and it was usually a big meal). My brother just older than I, and the closest one to me, claims he knew I was not there and was glad I had been left (again, the teasing). When I walked in the front door, they still had not noticed I was missing. I honestly remember feeling pretty unimportant. Even embarrassed. Although as I grew up, I could process it better and know that my mother and my whole family loved me a lot. However, the experience definitely left a small impression on my heart about how any of us can get lost in the human shuffle. Even with those who love us dearly!

It is not that way with God though. God knows us in the womb, "For you created my inmost being; you knit me together in my mother's womb" (Ps. 139:13). The Bible asserts that the physical and spiritual development of each one of us is directed by God himself—"I am fearfully and wonderfully made" (Ps. 139:14). God "knit" us together in our mothers' wombs in a fearful and wonderful way. Of course, it is a natural human process. But remember, the Bible tells us that the "natural" processes themselves were created by and are sustained by God. There is not a dual physical and spiritual universe in the Bible's way of explaining it. They are merged and intertwined. They interact.

And as far as our conception, gestation, and birth are concerned, even a shallow study of the reproductive process can make one wonder how any of us was ever even conceived, let alone born. Talk about working with bad odds! But in spite of those odds, due to the hand of God, the human population multiplies at an unbelievable rate.

So reconciling what Genesis (the written revelation) tells us with what our best science tells us (the revelation of creation itself), God supplied the original energy that created the world. He also is active in the process of forming each of us in the womb and sustaining those of us who are finally born. Further, as previously noted, he sustains the whole universe with his powerful word—his immeasurable power. It all means that you and I—all of us—were made by acts of the Creator's will and that we live on by his will. We are not a cosmic incident or accident formed as a result of chemical and biological evolution, as science confidently claims but without any real foundational proof. Instead we were lovingly and intentionally designed and created by an unbelievable intelligence. We are infinitely significant to God, as dearly loved children are to their earthly parents.

Jesus said, "Are not five sparrows sold for two pennies? Yet God forgets not one of them. Indeed, the very hairs of your head are all numbered. Don't be afraid; you are worth more than many sparrows" (Luke 12:6–7). Did you get that? You are worth more than many sparrows—a lot more in fact. God is quite aware of and concerned for each of us. We are priceless to God. Again, Jesus said concerning sparrows, "Not one of them will fall to the ground apart from the will of your Father" (Matt. 10:29). And we are worth much more than they. God is said by the Bible to be omnipotent, omnipresent, and omniscient, and yet he cares deeply about the least among us. God is also most loving. The nature of the world manifests these virtues of God—his eternal power and divine nature (Rom. 1:20). So God has got it all covered—both for now and for later.

Simply put, God will not forget you! You matter to him far too much for that to happen!

Although God has created physical processes, and in my estimation even randomness as a part of his creation, he still oversees it all. He is sovereign. It turns out the way he wants it to. He predestined it that way. He sustains the universe with his powerful word. He can intervene wherever and whenever he wants. However, it seems he generally lets the universe run as he designed it, on its own well-planned, intricately designed course. There are as yet unexplained physical forces that seem to hold it together, such as gravity and whatever else it is that holds the universe in place. But in this vast universe of space and time, God forgets not one of us. Not one of us falls to the ground in any way apart from the will of our Father.

God made you as part of the crown of his creation—humankind. You are part of the very purpose of the creation. You were chosen before the creation itself. When God looks at you, he sees his creation as "very good." In fact, he sees those who are "in Christ" as "holy and blameless" (Eph. 1:4), and he decided to do so from the beginning. We, both male and female together, bear his image—"In the image of God he created . . . them" (Gen. 1:26–27). And it was very good.

The world, including your own family, may "drive away" and forget about you, or just drive you away, because the world struggles with its own limitations and mostly with a selfish, humanistic focus. God is not limited or selfish though. He will not forget about you. We, however, often seem to forget about him!

In his eyes, we are "very good." And he has very, very good vision—way beyond simply 20/20.

Questions and Thoughts for Reflection and Discussion

1. How can seeing how God saw us and his creation from the beginning help us see how he sees us now, even in our present fallen state?

2. How might seeing the creation, and thus ourselves, as highly planned by God, rather than seeing ourselves as simply an evolutionary cosmic incident, affect our views of how God now sees us?

3. What was your faith growing up like, and how has adulthood affected that faith?

4. Why might it be true that everyone lives by faith in something or someone, whether they like it or admit it?

5. What are some of the things people live by faith in other than the divine, such as money, possessions, or other people?

6. How can knowing God, as he actually is, solve our fears of abandonment and insignificance, and how will that affect the quality of the lives that we live here?

CHAPTER 2

AND THEN AGAIN: WHEN IT WAS NOT VERY GOOD

Life is strange and funny in ways.
It seems that when all is sunny and good
It can all turn on a dime—in an instant,
Into a dark and desolate mood.

It does not seem like so long ago that I started reading the Bible while I was in college, although at the time of this writing, it has been forty-five years! The book of Genesis amazed me then and still does. I suppose I had read the Bible a bit as a child while doing my Bible class lessons for church, filling in the little blanks in the lesson booklet with the "correct" answers. However, I remembered very little by the time my college years arrived. From those early Sunday school classes, I really could only recall reading some from the gospels and from Acts. I also had sketchy memories of a few of the famous Old Testament stories.

The Bible I was using when I first started reading was a King James Version that I had borrowed from a generous family who had invited me to their church and into their home. It was the family of my brother's girlfriend and then soon-to-be wife. Unbeknownst to them, the fact that I finally accepted their invitation grew out of an inner faith crisis of my own. As I mentioned previously, I had lost my childhood faith concerning the Bible and even my belief in God. I was actually fairly unsettled by it all. I had not spoken to anybody about it, as my family did not really talk much about religion other than for the adults to engage in an occasional inane argument over doctrines. And we sure were not very vulnerable about personal things when we actually did discuss them. I also knew if I told them about my doubts that it would not be met with approval, and I still sought their acceptance. Also, I had an older sister who was vocal about her skepticism about God, and that had not gone over very well with the family, so I just kept it to myself.

What finally triggered my search occurred in a physical chemistry class during my junior year of college. The professor, who it turned out was a Christian, was discussing the theory of relativity and such and simply mentioned something to the effect that, scientifically speaking, it was not at all implausible that there existed an omnipresent and eternal spirit-God. That's all. Apparently, I simply had never intellectually made the connection between science and faith. They were each processed in a different part of my brain and dealt with in a different part of my world, I suppose. But here was a man, a scientist, whom I respected, who was correlating science and faith. I decided I would like to read the Bible and see for myself what it said.

I was still a pretty backwoods boy. In retrospect, it amazes me how little I knew about life and the world at that point in my life. I did not even know where to get a Bible and did not know whom to ask. Do not get me wrong, I was a pretty bright kid, but just not very knowledgeable about lots of things, due to how small my world still was. So after one of a few "big Sunday dinners," sitting in this Christian family's living room, I spotted a stack of Bibles on the lower shelf of their coffee table. With some naïve trepidation,

I asked if I could borrow one (I had no clue that they had purchased these generic American Bible Society Bibles in order to give them away). Of course, they said, "Sure!" And voila, I had me a new hardbound copy of the King James Version of the Bible. The "authorized" one! I had not a clue.

The King James Bible was all I had ever heard or read, so I was not completely shocked by the language, but rather just expected it. But I still had a big problem understanding it. I was trying to grow beyond the Okie vernacular I had learned, and so getting from "cain't" to "canst not" and "dudn't" to "doeth not" were far reaches for me. I had to read with a dictionary handy at all times, and thus it was slowgoing for sure. But I persevered and slogged my way through it.

But even with the slow going, it did not take me all that long to get to Genesis 6. As the narrative flowed, in only five chapters, God had created the whole world, put humankind in the garden home in Eden, banned them from their garden home and sent them "east of Eden," cursed Cain for the murder of his brother and sent him even further away, and taken Enoch to heaven for his faithfulness to God. Then there were those odd, baffling texts, such as the one about giants and angels and such.

At the start of Genesis 6, the Bible simply says, "The Lord saw how great man's wickedness on the earth had become, and that every inclination of the thoughts of his heart was only evil all the time. The Lord was grieved that he had made man on the earth, and his heart was filled with pain" (Gen. 6:5–6). Wow. That fast, huh? From God's perspective, his creation crown, humankind, had gone from looking "very good" to *not* looking very good at all. In fact, humankind looked very bad to God now.

I was hooked. The Bible had me.

It at least proposed an explanation for the roots of so many things, and for me, it seemed to be in simple, frank terminology and stories, albeit in the odd language in that KJV translation I was reading. Then there were the ancient cultural practices and mores to deal with too. Sure, it did not satisfy some of the scientific questions very well, if at all, but it was not written first to and for scientists, and I knew that even then. And it did not reconcile to some of my own lines of reasoning, when I tried to read everything as completely literal. However, many of its revelations certainly did appear to me as more than simple, insightful human notions. I quickly understood that the Bible was written to be read by all— educated and uneducated, intelligent and not so intelligent, rich and poor, and also by country boys.

I mostly understood what the Bible was saying; simply put: God made it, man messed it up, and God was in the process of repairing it. There was and still is plenty of confusion and mystery in it for me. But there was and still is plenty that I actually could and still can understand. Most importantly, it is information about the foundational and vital things of life. Unlike reading textbooks, scripture had heart. It had not just the fingerprints of fallible humans on it; it had the handprints of God on it. The Bible certainly showed plenty of insight into science, psychology, sociology, philosophy, and so forth that were not only profound during the time it was written, but in ways even more profound in my more modern world. But still, those things were not what the writers were directly addressing. They were writing to communicate what was underlying all of it and where it all came from.

So I discovered that God had quickly, in that it was after only six chapters, decided things did not look "very good" concerning humanity anymore. This brings up an important theological discussion that has deeply divided Christianity from its early times. It has to do with "depravity"—the effects of the original sin (of Eve and Adam in the garden) on all humankind. The position held in Reformed theology originates from Augustinianism (from the theologian Augustine). It is also called "total or radical corruption" and other such things.

Augustine developed a view of original sin that asserted that because of the sin of Eve and Adam in the garden, every human was and is totally corrupt and completely unable to choose God, except by the grace and action of God alone. John Calvin further developed the underlying concept during the early Reformation. He accepted too the idea that man was totally corrupted (depraved) by sin and could not by his own freewill choose God. His view was that certain people were predestined by God before the creation to be saved, and thus others were not. This is called double pre-destination. So as the thinking goes, in his own timing, God then extends his efficacious grace (grace that cannot be resisted—irre-sistible grace) to those so predestined. This is obviously a very, very simplistic explanation of the views of some serious theologians, but it can aptly, I think, serve our purposes here.

Total depravity does not assert that men are as evil as possible but that sin just completely corrupts us. It is said to be the same as with how a few drops of poison completely contaminate a glass of water.

However, others countered this with an opposing point of view. In fact, Augustine is said to have developed and written his view in response to a monk, Pelagius, who believed that man was not so totally corrupted by the fall and was capable of choosing God by his own volition. He even dared to insinuate, against the tradi-tional or orthodox positions of the time, that man was still some-what "good" after the fall. The Christian "authorities" of the day considered Pelagius as spiritually treasonous, as it has seemed to be in every generation of the church, God forbid anyone dare dis-agree with certain church power centers of the day! Thus Pelagius was labeled a heretic by the official church. He lost.

This debate has raged on over the centuries, often with great vigor. And if the right people (or wrong ones depending on what your views are) ever read what I have written here, the assumption might be made that I am supporting the views of Pelagius, which

I am not. I am only in great generalities explaining the evolution of the views involved, which bring us to where we generally are at present, along with some sidebar commentary to encourage us to be more open-minded, more collaborative, and less quick on the trigger toward one another. By the way, I have been called lots of things and wonder what label this new one might be—a "Pelagian"? Christians are in fact like every human family—we can just seem pretty crazy sometimes! By the grace of God however, we in most cases still find ways to love each another though.

So what does all of this have to do with seeing how God sees us? Well, lots. First, it makes us think in terms of God seeing some as "chosen" and others "unchosen," some as able to accept Christ and others as unable to, and some created for salvation and others created for destruction. Second, one of these two opposing views underlies most of the theology that we hear and read about. One side believes there are some people who cannot choose God at all and thus remain corrupted in God's sight for their lifetime and on into eternity. The other side agrees that man is in fact corrupt, and his only choice at redemption is to choose God. But the latter group believes that man through God's grace actually has some choice in the matter. There are many in the middle of the two extremes. No matter what one's viewpoint ends up being, each position can be seen as at least somewhat biblically plausible, I believe, for truly open-minded, sensible people. But both of the opposing views, in their efforts to convince men to turn away from sin, have at times unleashed a barrage against the other that I believe leads only to hopelessness for many caught in between struggling to even understand what the real fight is over.

I do a lot of counseling, and somewhere at the root of most of our mental and emotional issues is the problem of how we see ourselves. Ultimately, our self-view emanates directly from our view of God and how we perceive him to see us. Of course, a lot of that is formed in us by the way we perceive our parents and the way other significant people see us. Thus in trying to help people deal with their life issues, correcting their view of God, as well as helping them think more clearly about the impact others have had on them, becomes mission-critical in their learning to adequately cope, heal, and grow.

I certainly do not intend to wade much further into this discussion. I consider myself a minister and pastor, not a "theologian," per se. I do believe that "un-forgiven" sin causes total separation from God. However, I also believe that since we are all image-bearers, we do retain the ability to do good, even if such good cannot merit any forgiveness for our sins, of course. Part of that good capability is that men can seek God—"God did this so that men would seek him and perhaps reach out for him and find him, though he is not far from each one of us" (Acts 17:27). I believe however that God retains the right and ability to take even that opportunity away from individuals if he so chooses (Heb. 6:4–6). That you just do not "mess around" with God is the point here.

The reality is that no one can turn to Christ unless God enables him to do so—"I told you that no one can come to me unless the Father has enabled him" (John 6:65). I believe that God responds to our seeking. "Seek and you will find" (Matt. 7:7) and "For the eyes of the LORD range throughout the earth to strengthen those whose hearts are fully committed to him" (2 Chron. 16:9). God has this world under his control, and our role is to come to sufficient faith to not just trust him when we understand and agree, but even more so to trust him when we don't understand or agree.

So to continue my thoughts on the Genesis narrative, sin ran rampant in emerging humanity; that is, it got very bad very fast, because, as the apostle Paul wrote, "Bad company corrupts good character" (1 Cor. 15:3). Any of us can attest to the truth of that statement. Thus, as a few turned evil, human character became utterly corrupted quite quickly. "Every inclination of the thoughts of his heart was only evil all the time" (Gen. 6:5). Very bad, very fast. Quite a strong indictment, I think.

God loves us unconditionally and saw our original creation as "very good"—"God so loved the world" (John 3:16). He hates the sin that corrupts and destroys us—"For the wrath of God is revealed from heaven against all ungodliness and unrighteousness of men" (Rom. 1:18). And he sees the sin that corrupts this world as very bad and intends to be rid of it—"so he condemned sin in the flesh" (Rom. 8:3). In a beautiful, divine mystery, God atones the sins of those who come to him in faith based on what he accomplished through Jesus and his cross sacrifice. God's atonement is "covering over" or "making up for" our sin. Somehow, he does not see our sinfulness when we are a part of Christ's body (Rom. 8:1). In fact, "He chose us in him before the creation of the world to be holy and blameless in his sight" (Eph. 1:4). Note: it is in *his* sight that we are holy and blameless. Even after we are saved, we still commit sins and are prone to it (1 John 1:8–10). However, when we connect to and are "in" Christ, God chooses to *see* us as holy and blameless. His choice. His plan before he even created us.

Simply put, God can do things we cannot only *not* do; he can do things we can't even *imagine* doing (Eph. 3:20–21). Paul tells us, "God . . . gives life to the dead and calls things that are not as though they were" (Rom. 4:17, NIV, 1984). The more recent and probably more accurate translations reads, "God . . . gives life to the dead and calls into being things that were not" (Rom. 4:17, NIV, 2011). But nonetheless, what is being said is that God makes us a "new creation" (calls into being things that were not) in Christ and sees us as holy and blameless, when in our present reality none of us actually are, in our own right.

It would be as if someone you dearly loved went out and developed extremely bad body odor, bad breath, and became caked over with excrement (just bear with me a bit). It would likely, even in the long run, not change your love for the person. But it would make it extremely difficult, perhaps impossible, for you to be very near them or perhaps even in their presence, let alone embrace them. You might advise them to "take a bath and then come back to hang out." Much like a loving wife might do when a sweaty husband comes in from a day of dirty yard work. Because of the female's "nature"—generally a strong sense of smell and sight—the condition might ultimately make hubby so repulsive as to cause an essential avoidance by the wife! At least until he showered!

Well, it is the same way with God and us. Sin gives us an impossibly undesirable spiritual "odor" to God because of his own holy, spiritual nature and sensibility (Isa. 59:1–2, 64:6). For those who are called, and answer that call, God has provided a spiritual cleansing "bath" for us in the blood of Christ—"But you were washed, you were sanctified, you were justified in the name of the Lord Jesus Christ and by the Spirit of our God" (1 Cor. 6:11) and "Get up, be baptized and wash your sins away, calling on his name" (Acts 22:16). Now none of us can possibly accurately imagine what that "looks like" in the mind of God, but that is how the Bible says he does it. We are "washed in the blood of the lamb," as an old hymn goes.

You see, God is a God of grace. A lot of grace. He is extremely generous. Grace (*charis* in Greek) means free gift. The Bible says that God "lavishes" his grace on us in Christ (Eph. 1:7–8). He gives us tons of gifts, and his greatest gift to us is the mercy he has on us in our sinful condition. He forgives all our sins—"he has rescued us from the dominion of darkness and brought us into the kingdom of the Son he loves, in whom we have redemption, the forgiveness of sins" (Col. 1:13–14). He washes away the excrement and removes the odiousness from the ones he loves and calls, so that he can "be in the room with us"—so we can be in his glorious presence. He "smells the odor no more." He sees the filth no more. Even though the odor is still there, he smells it no more. He doesn't see the excrement. He sees us as clean and fresh—holy. He sees us as blameless. He sees us as sinless. If we can "get that," we see God seeing us! That is truly good news!

And from the way I read it, God wants to call all of us into his presence. Paul says that God "wants all men to be saved and to come to a knowledge of the truth" (1 Tim. 2:4). Peter wrote, "He [God] is patient with you, not wanting anyone to perish, but everyone to come to repentance" (2 Pet. 3:9). God is waiting and desiring that none of us live eternally away from him. All of humankind bears God's image, because we all have his DNA. All of us. We "look" like him. Sin corrupts our God-nature just as rust corrupts iron. But just as cleaning and oiling can stop the oxidation cycle of rust on iron, the blood of Jesus can stop the corrupting cycle of sin on us, and it can indeed renew us. In the end, God will, in his own way, redeem the whole world—"For the creation was subjected to frustration, not by its own choice, but by the will of the one who subjected it, in hope that the creation itself will be liberated from its bondage to decay and brought into the freedom and glory of the children of God" (Rom. 8:20–21). I do not mean to imply everyone will be saved, because sadly the scripture seems to indicate otherwise, but only that God will redeem creation. I know personally that I am looking forward to "a new heaven and a new earth!" (Rev. 21:1). Amen!

God paid the ultimate price so that our sins could be removed and so that the sin cycle could be reversed. He did it through the sacrifice of his own son, as Paul wrote, "God made him [Jesus] who had no sin to be sin for us, so that in him we might become the righteousness of God" (2 Cor. 5:21). God sent each of us a very important message of how much he loves us, how he saw us at our beginning, and how he wants to see us now through Christ's eyes— "God so loved the world . . ." He also wants us to be a living letter to others who have not yet seen how God sees them (2 Cor. 3:3).

You are created with the very image of God himself. You "look" like him, just as our children often "look just like us." Even if they are misbehaving, and perhaps even more so when they are misbehaving! Even if they leave us and go into a life of evil, they will still bear their parents' image in some perhaps corrupted but still unavoidable ways! They bear our resemblance because God designed it that way by designing us the way he did. We are priceless to him, even at our worst, as a child is to a deeply devoted parent. "God demonstrates his own love for us in this: While we were still sinners, Christ died for us" (Rom. 5:8). While we were God's enemies, Christ died for us (Rom. 5:10). Jesus said that to die for another was the greatest love that exists (John 15:13). I do not think many would argue about that either.

Oh, if we could all come to see and trust how God sees us in Christ! It would remedy all the self-worth issues that lie at the root of so much of our inner suffering, emotional disorders, and dysfunction. It would transform the way we see each other. It would alleviate the slavish search so many engage in looking for love and validation from other similarly struggling, misguided humans. The loving and merciful nature of God is the core of the gospel message. That he calls us, died for us, and wants to forgive us is the outcome of that message.

Seeing God seeing you? If you are not saved, God sees you as impure and tarnished gold nugget waiting to be cleaned and made beautiful. We are fairly useless to him in such a condition, but priceless in potential value when restored. He wants to fix that for you and for himself, by the way. If you are saved, God sees you as a bright, shiny, priceless gold nugget that is of great use to him and his purposes.

Questions and Thoughts for Reflection and Discussion

1. Why might it be important to see how God went from seeing creation, humankind included, as very good to seeing humanity as not very good, at least in their thoughts?
2. How do you see the corrupting influence of sin robbing humanity of our original likeness of God?
3. Why do you think God didn't just destroy all humankind in the flood rather than starting over and seeing the plague of sin just continue on?

4. How do you think God can see us as holy and blameless when we clearly are not?
5. What do you think God is doing to finally fix creation for good?

CHAPTER 3

OH MY, THEY WERE NAKED!

Embarrassment is a great human dread,
Being caught off guard in our folly and sin,
When others suddenly see clearly on the outside,
What was formerly hidden within.

I can remember being naked as a child. I was unashamed. With my large family of seven brothers and sisters, it was no big deal. I was the youngest in the family, and I really had no privacy. I took baths with my brother, and early on, there was a sister thrown in there as well. And I shared a small bedroom and a double bed with two older brothers. We only had one restroom in the house, and anybody who wanted to could come in when I was in there. I was the youngest and had absolutely no seniority.

Unlike a lot of people I know, I have some memories from very early in my life. It has been both a blessing and a curse. I remember when I was surely in my twos that an older teenage girl from next door came over and for some reason wanted to give me a bath (nowadays that would in itself perhaps be seen as a little sketchy).

She was a friend of the family. Well, my mom let her give me the bath. I remember it was in the kitchen sink of our old house, so given the small sinks in those kinds of houses, you can imagine how little I had to have been to get in it. I can still actually feel the kind of embarrassment I felt when I heard her ask to do it. But in my home, led by a very domineering father, there was little chance to say "no" to stuff, and certainly no fits could be thrown. Even if you cried, you'd be embarrassed and called a big baby and, sometimes, even worse! But that's the only time I remember feeling embarrassed about my nakedness early on.

But as with most everyone else, preadolescence and junior high brought on this great tsunami of embarrassment and even shame. My closest brother, who was a year and a half older and one grade above me, and I went through puberty later than most of the other guys. The others in our classes were brutal in their name-calling and joking. And, the joke was *on* us and not *for* us. It would very much be considered bullying today. And there were always others in the same boat. Even coaches got in on the "fun." It was not fun to us though even though we laughed and played along as a deflection. It was inwardly frustrating and humiliating.

Junior high especially can be brutal for kids, because it consists of a bunch of young, insecure people who are in a situation sort of akin to that of Adam and Eve after the fall. Their sexuality is waking up, and they become much more aware of theirs and others' bodies, and a deep shame or embarrassment tends to set in. And the shame can be about just about anything. Preadolescents and adolescents become very fear driven, especially fearing what their peers think and say about them. So at that early stage of life, we all learn to hide in our own emotional and psychological "bushes." And our self-styled kid coverings we make for ourselves—the deflections we utilize to try to protect our inner psyches—scarcely cover this pervasive shame and embarrassment.

Thus, many of us learn quickly to close ourselves off physically and emotionally to most others. And if we don't, we make ourselves very vulnerable to getting hurt by stupid and insensitive peers and others who might just "out" us about something embarrassing. And at that age, anything can be embarrassing! With all this comes all the other challenging things about puberty—awkwardness, acne, increased sexual curiosity and desire, and sexual identity issues. Our psyches and self-esteems can take a real battering. So we simply try to hide.

Being naked is a funny thing. I mean, beneath the clothes and all, we are all "naked" all the time. But our nakedness is hidden from others most of the time by the clothes we wear. Our nakedness is never hidden from God though. What are we so ashamed of? By the law of averages, we all, by genders, have the same things, and it all looks and works about the same way! Boy, do we have "hang-ups" about our bodies though? Lots of hang-ups and the accompanying shame.

I have been counseling in various capacities for a long time. For some reason, people just tell me things—"things they've never told anyone else"—as I have regularly heard in various ways. Opening up about body hang-ups is one of the most difficult things for most to do. Many simply will never do it, and our shame remains locked inside us with this evil lie that batters us relentlessly. In reality, many times these kinds of hang-ups are the real root causes of so many other issues. This or that is too small, too large, too misshapen, and so forth. Now in reading this, many will immediately think of sexual organs, breasts, derrieres, and such. But just as significant are those concerns about such things as height, weight, hair color, body hair, and body proportions, as well as facial attributes such as noses, eyes, and ears. I think everyone understands. And these embarrassments about our bodies take root in our psyches and personalities early on and affect everything we think about ourselves! For example, a feeling of inadequacy or unsightliness physiologically inevitably affects our social interactions. Our perceptions of these social interactions then affect our overall self-perceptions. Our self-perceptions then play into everything else about us.

Sadly, our feelings of inadequacy and embarrassment about our "nakedness" are largely based on our own misperceptions about how everybody else looks and feels and how we might in reality look to others. Just as our perceptions of how God sees us are often skewed and are sometimes incredibly wrong, our perceptions of how others really see us are the same way. And even if we are right about some negative way in which they see us, if their view is not coming from God, they are wrong anyway!

Living in the flesh, outside of a close relationship with Christ, we tend to measure our value based on our perception of our social position. We even project it all onto God and assume he sees us like we assume others do. But when we born again and become increasingly God-focused, we start getting God's view of us right. And when we finally start to get our self-image from God instead of from the world, then we can start getting our view of others right—most importantly in realizing they are not God, are not good evaluators of human worth, and are likely just as "embarrassed about their nakedness" as we are. Only the gospel of Christ reveals the real truth of our true, underlying looks and true value to God. His view is very good.

The gospel gives us the correct view of God, *and* the truth about God views us—it lets us see God seeing us. He is a God of love. He is in fact love. He loves us all and considers us worth the highest price he could pay—his own Son, Jesus Christ (John 15:13). In seeing how God sees us, we come to see ourselves as loved and priceless rather than as unloved and worthless. When we see ourselves as God sees us, we begin to see others as God sees them too. This is why we have to "repent and believe the gospel." Repent means to "change your mind." We change our minds from seeing things from a human point of view to seeing them the opposite way, from God's point of view. Our viewpoint of others' and our worth determines so much about the quality of our life and how we live it out.

Sadly though, our words and language reflect our "un-dealt with" shame in many ways and on various levels. We even use certain words as cover-ups (fig leaves and bushes, so to speak)—verbal "clothing" to hide our shame we feel about our naked inner selves. As adults, these words can be even more embarrassing when applied to ourselves; however, we often continue to teach them to our children! We use words such as "pee-pees" for penises and vaginas. We might just call them our "privates" or speak of things "down there." For shame! To jest a bit, I fear that some of our shame might be that the actual "correct" words for these things often sound weird and sometimes pretty awful. Who thinks these scientific words up? The actual words really do often sound nasty or gross for some reason! Perhaps it's just our early hang-ups about what they refer to. Maybe it is all just part of this shame.

The Bible describes this, telling us that after their sin something strange and sad happened. "Then the eyes of both of them were opened, and they realized they were naked; so they sewed fig leaves together and made coverings for themselves" (Gen. 3:7). What happened? How could they not have realized they were naked before? Why did it matter afterward? Why did their sin make them ashamed of their bodies? In the original sin, why did humanity's God-given sexuality become a source of shame and embarrassment? Because of the shame over their nakedness, God himself kindly and lovingly made them decent coverings for their bodies. He does the same thing for us in our sinful shame today, covering over our sins with his blood that flows from his love and mercy.

Before the sin, "the man and his wife were both naked, and they felt no shame" (Gen. 2:25). Why before they sinned did they feel no shame in their nakedness? They had been sexual from the beginning, because they had been given the command to be fruitful and multiply themselves. Clearly their sin and shame were not involving their sexual intimacy itself. So they were not ashamed of being naked together prior to the fall. When they sinned, their eyes were opened and they realized they were naked. They were suddenly embarrassed in front of each other, when they had already been seeing each other naked from the beginning. They make inadequate cover-ups for themselves and hid in the bushes from God. That is quite an odd scene and thought—people hiding in the bushes from God. When God calls them out, they report that they were afraid of meeting up with him because they were naked. God then asked them the question, "Who told you that you were naked?" (Gen. 3:7–11). Apparently nobody told them that, but for some inherent reason, in their sinful condition, they realized it and got embarrassed and scared. We have been hiding our nakedness in fear and embarrassment ever since.

Clearly, this depiction of sin's origination has metaphorical and allegorical meaning concerning much more than embarrassment over our bodies. Our deeper inner nakedness, hidden beneath our often deceptive, always careful behavior and communication, is what really horrifies and controls us—our spiritual nakedness. It has this ugly corrupting sin all over it. We are inwardly dirty and stained, and we feel it deeply inside. But the gospel can remove our fear and embarrassment by removing this sin corruption. As God did for humankind from the beginning of this embarrassment, God has made for us a more adequate covering for our spiritual nakedness. Not so we look better to him, but because in our sinful condition we are fearful and embarrassed. He did it to save us from each other and ourselves. No covering can ever completely hide us from God's eyes. He made us naked in the first place.

There is then a direct correlation between the shame sin brings about in the nakedness of our physical bodies and our shame in the nakedness of our inner selves. Genesis shows us the former, as just pointed out. Likewise, Jesus points to the latter in his admonition to the lukewarm Laodicean church in the book of Revelation. He says, "I counsel you to buy from me gold refined in the fire, so you can become rich; and *white clothes to wear, so you can cover your shameful nakedness*; and salve to put on your eyes, so you can see" (Rev. 3:18, italics added). He is obviously referring to their spiritual nakedness and shame.

In the first situation, the Lord recognized their new reality, and so he made Adam and Eve some decent clothes to actually cover their bodies (fig leaves were not cutting it, I suppose). Sadly they could not even get that right. And come to think of it, we still cannot seem to get the modesty part right. Hmmm? We read, "The Lord God made garments of skin for Adam and his wife Eve to adequately clothe them" (Gen. 3:21). Considering some of the skimpy modern styles, God may need to act again to help us out. Maybe hand out some adequate coverings at the beach, at the pools, fitness centers, and parties!

We just seem to keep trying to go back to the inadequate fig leaves to try to cover up our deeper inner shame or maybe intentionally *not* cover it up! But in doing so, we are trading one kind of shame, the one we should not have to feel, for another kind of shame, the kind we should feel but too often don't.

Just as God had to step in and make them some real clothes to cover their physical nakedness, God had to also step in to make available to humanity coverings for our spiritual nakedness. For some reason, tied up in his very nature in the spiritual realm, God cannot "look at" our spiritual nakedness in our sinful condition. It is a mystery to us concerning him. However, in some way, Jesus and his blood literally "covers over" (atones) our sin before God's eyes so that he sees us as holy and blameless. But the sin is still there; we feel it and struggle with the shame of it. There is indeed shame associated with all sin. The shame is not God's though; it is ours. We are the cause of it; he has the only remedy.

What is it about the original sin that brought on this shame? I think it is at least partially about purpose—whether we will be givers or takers. God is a God of grace. Remember, grace means gift. Thus God is a giver. He needs nothing and is the giver of everything. We are made in his image. Thus we are designed to be givers. However, when sin entered the world we became "takers"— consumers. Our God-given, God-purposed, pure sexual appetites and desires suddenly became selfish mouths we would be driven to feed throughout human history. Societies and individuals always tend to become more sex-driven and sexually impure as they move away from God. Heck, even with God in our lives, the church itself is wrought with too many examples of sexual excess, immorality, and abuse. Rather than giving our bodies to our mates, as we were designed for, we become focused on getting somebody else's body for ourselves in a "devil's pact" with another selfish taker. We are prone to use our appetites and pleasure capacities to serve ourselves in spite of what it might mean to us, to others, and to God, when in fact our sexuality was, is, and will always be a gift and a desire to be enjoyed within the acceptable bounds of God, not an absolute need or entitlement. But after the first sin, humans became consumers—selfish, self-centered, and bent on pleasing themselves. In our fallen state, we made that which was about God about us. Sadly we still do.

The world was created to be about God though. God created it for himself (Col. 1:16). But in the original sin, it became about us in our own mortal way of thinking. We tried to make ourselves the center of it all. We tried to be self-reliant rather than God-reliant. It was the start of humanism. We made it that way because of the choice of sin—the tasty but toxic fruit of "Tree of the Knowledge of Good and Evil." Even the things that are otherwise "good" have become tainted and poisoned by sin. We made our bodies, designed to fulfill God's purposes, instruments for pleasing only us. We consumed the things of God—"holy things"—for unholy purposes. At its core, that's what sin is.

Of course, God saw it for what it was. Ugly. Selfish. Self-serving. Harmful. Deadly. And he saw us for who we were and still are. It was shameful. It still is shameful; at least beneath the covering, he has so mercifully made for us in Christ.

I was talking to a good friend some years back, and we were joking and discussing the toll the years had taken on our bodies. In jest, he said that when he was a younger man, when he would get out of the shower, he would "take a peek" at himself to see how he looked. We both had a good laugh when he said, however, he did that no longer, as it was pretty discouraging! I agreed wholeheartedly. I am not sure this shame about our aging bodies, brought on by human vanity, is the same thing as the original shame, but it grows from the same source—our pride. That is primarily why we see aging as such a curse, when we make it all about us, rather than as God sees it as a crown, when we understand that it has always been about him. How we see our bodies is a powerful thing. It is a huge component of our self-esteem—our sense of our very worth! Our bodies are a gift designed to be a temple for us to dwell in with God. Our bodies are intertwined with our souls and spirits and in some ways reflect us outwardly as spiritual beings.

Sadly, sin brings the same kind of ravages to our spiritual selves as aging and misuse do to our physical bodies. It can be scary to even take a peek! I think that is one of the big reasons so many Christians are so unwilling to confess their sins to one another, as James so wisely instructed (James 5:16), and which is such an important part of bringing healing from sin's effects. It is just hard to face the reality of what we do and even more so what we often desire and are capable of doing. We become out of touch with reality at the most basic level—our physical selves—and thus we are out of touch with reality, at least to some significant degree, in every area of our lives.

One of the sadder, yet more heartwarming, Bible stories is that of the Old Testament prophet Hosea. He was to be a living illustration of God's relationship to Israel. He was instructed to marry a prostitute named Gomer, which he did. Hosea and Gomer had three children while married, although the text leaves open the possibility that other men may actually have even fathered those children during her marriage to Hosea, as God later calls them "children of prostitution." Talk about stigmatized!

After some time of marriage, Gomer finally leaves Hosea for another lover. I have been counseling others for over thirty-five years and have had far too experiences helping individuals deal with marital infidelity. I have sat in such situations when a woman informed her husband she had had an affair. I have seen husbands' hearts torn apart by an affair of their wives. I have had to witness wives' lives devastated by unfaithful husbands. It is most painful to watch! It even can get worse. Everyone who counsels and pastors has plenty of experience with it. This is nothing new. But nothing is much harder for one to get over than the unfaithfulness of a mate. In an instant, the love of one's life—the apple of one's eye—can suddenly become repulsive. A sacred trust is broken forever. The marital bond is adulterated. So quickly perception of a mate can change, going from seeing them beautiful to perhaps even completely repulsive. Talk about shame!

Hosea was later instructed by God to go buy Gomer back from her latest owner and lover. Literally. Not only was Hosea to take his adulteress, prostitute wife back, he had to *buy* her back. God wanted Hosea and us all to get the point. God loves us enough to go to these kinds of ends for each of us. In fact, he has already bought back each and every believer from our prostitution to the world, and he is equally prepared to buy each and every person outside of Christ who humbles himself and comes to him in faith.

The text of Hosea only gives enough details to make God's point about his relationship with Israel. But I picture this horrifically sad scene of Hosea seeing Gomer again—a sad, broken-down, badly used woman. Probably battered and abused. Sad. Depressed. Ashamed. Likely hardened. A living human example of a soul that is dirty and stained by the devastating corruption of sin bearing its fruit in us.

Imagine Hosea's pain. Imagine Gomer's shame! Heck, imagine even his *own* shame! Both must have felt a painful mixture of all kinds of emotions and thoughts. This story then is a lasting metaphor for how it was with God taking Israel back one more time, after her latest stint of adultery with the nations around her and their idol gods. Hosea's story is a metaphor too for Christ's relationship with us, the church, his bride. Imagine God's pain in seeing us after we have prostituted ourselves to a world equally bent on simply consuming us for its own pleasure and ready to cast us out when it is through with us. To think that we actually sell ourselves to it and submit ourselves to its ungodly use and abuse! Sadly our counseling chairs are full of spiritual Gomers trying to figure out why they are so broken.

It doesn't even require many acts of unfaithfulness; it only takes *one single act* of adultery to devastate a spouse. Multiple affairs bear an even more tragic emotional and spiritual cost.

It was the same for God and humanity in the original sin. One act of sin changed everything! Sin corrupts and devastates humanity and the world we live in. It is contagious, and it spreads to us all. It is unavoidable.

In considering the bigger picture, God's ultimate purposes in the creation and humanity are really a divine mystery to us. Although some is revealed to us along the way, and much is revealed by Christ himself, we are ultimately left only to speculate based on bits of information, observations, and various hints given in the scriptures. We know it is all happening by his plan and on his schedule. We are told that our fall into sin was not a surprise to God. We know too that God intended for this world to assuredly declare his divine nature (Rom. 1:20)—certainly his love, justice, and his mercy. We also know he chose us from the creation of the world to be holy and blameless in his sight (Eph. 1:4). Good news for sure. But we are incapable of understanding all of this at the deepest levels.

I still do not know, at the core, why sin causes us to be so ashamed of our bodies. None of us really do. I do not fully understand why sin made us so very aware of our bodies and why it creates all these incredibly powerful hang-ups. I don't completely understand why simply covering it up makes the difference it does, knowing we all know fully well what generally lies beneath. I can't figure out why we are so obsessed with the looks of our coverings to boot, other than for attracting suitors and seeming impressive.

I know in the beginning God recognized it for what it was and covered up their "shameful nakedness." I know God wants us to have our shameful spiritual nakedness covered as well. I know Jesus's blood somehow does that for us in the spiritual realm. I know his sacrifice not only demonstrates God's act of grace to forgive us but also gives us the permission to forgive ourselves. And to forgive others.

I am so, so glad about that!

One day sin will be forever banished. And thus shame will be forever banished. I suppose we will run around on the streets of gold completely naked and free and not one bit ashamed. Perhaps again completely unaware of it. Like little three-year-old children right out of the shower running naked and free! Unashamedly so. Woo-hoo! We will not need to be ashamed. Free at last, free at last!

No one will be a consumer anymore either. No more will any of us be lurking and looking, as our original ancestors, for that which is "good for food and pleasing to the eye, and also desirable for gaining wisdom" (Gen. 3:6)—the fruit of the Tree of the Knowledge of Good and Evil. We will be content forever with the eternity-giving Tree of Life—Jesus Christ himself—growing out in the open in the revitalized formerly lost Garden of Eden, the coming New Heaven and New Earth. The eternally available, fully accessible fruit will be free for all living there.

So God has got us covered for now. As Christians we are not shamefully naked in his realm. He is making it such that we will not need covered again in eternity—"I go to prepare a place for you" (John 14:2). "For now we see only a reflection as in a mirror; then we shall see face to face. Now I know in part; then I shall know fully, even as I am fully known" (1 Cor. 13:12). He has got it all covered for now, and he will uncover it all again in the end. Shame will be no more.

Through Christ, we will be returned to the perfect place again where "the man and his wife were both naked, and they felt no shame." No one will need to ever feel shame again! Hallelujah!

But for now, in Christ, God does not "see" you naked, so do not get all embarrassed and go hiding from him. It's a good idea to talk to a trusted pastor, counselor, or mature friend about your own body hang-ups that bog you down and help empower some of your other life struggles. Or they will continue to wreak havoc on your inner self.

It's also even more important to talk to a trusted spiritual advisor about your deeper inner spiritual and emotional shame. Maybe you don't yet realize that through Christ the stain is fully removable.

Questions and Thoughts for Reflection and Discussion

1. Why do you think nakedness brings such shame and embarrassment to us, when we all know what each other has beneath our clothing anyway?
2. Why do you think we are so worried about what others think of our bodies?

3. Why do you think we often care so little about what God thinks of our inner selves?
4. How much do you think should be taken literally and how much metaphorically of the Genesis account of the fall of humankind into sin in the Garden of Eden? Why does it matter?
5. Why can talking to others about our shame help bring healing from its sinful effects and negative consequences?
6. Why do you think marital unfaithfulness, along with other forms of relationship unfaithfulness, is so devastating to individuals in particular and humanity in general?
7. For those who have already accepted the gospel of Christ, how does the gospel address our deepest shame and how does that impact everything else about us?

CHAPTER 4

SEEING GOD SEEING YOU THROUGH HIS MAGIC MIRROR

I looked in the mirror to inspect my appearance,
Saw an image of me like I'd never seen.
I looked perfect and beautiful and new again.
I was glowing, not dirty but clean.

Then in the mirror I looked directly into two eyes,
But they were not my eyes, but those of another,
Not the sad, deluded eyes of one fallen,
But the knowing, caring eyes of a Father.

I remember when I was a child trying to look into the mirror in our bathroom. We were a fairly poor country family with only one bathroom. At our place, there were certainly not a lot of amenities and all. Believe it or not, there was not even a multicolored plastic child stool for me to stand on at the sink (no, we did not have a vanity but just a sink with pipes exposed beneath)! So much for any sense of entitlement back then! What does a kid need to see anyway, huh? We had one of those little square medicine cabinets with a mirror on it mounted over the sink, projecting out from the wall. There was a single light bulb on the bathroom ceiling. And not only was the mirror too high for me to see into, the bottom few inches of the mirror were also corroded, as mirrors can get on the backside of the glass that causes the reflection. It was clouded and marred by age and use. So when I could finally get high enough to look even partially into the mirror, the part I could see was still pretty useless. Needless to say the time I decided, when I was around five years old, to trim my hair in the front, well, the "do" did not turn out so good, and my mom was not very proud of me. Talk about shame . . . Of course, my older siblings were supportive and encouraging and didn't dare tease me and add to my shame. Not!

But that is my first memory of a mirror.

When I first read Paul's metaphor about seeing a poor reflection in a mirror in a verse cited in the last chapter, I got it. He wrote, "Now we see but a poor reflection as in a mirror; then we shall see face to face. Now I know in part; then I shall know fully, even as I am fully known" (1 Cor. 13:12). The day finally came that I grew up enough that I could actually see a good portion of my face in the mirror without any assistance. I could see face-to-face. The day has now come however that I do not want to look anymore! Some time back, I made the mistake of looking at something on my face in my wife's magnifying make-up mirror. Yikes! Talk about aging and sun damage! I haven't made that mistake anymore. Looking in a regular mirror with less than perfect near vision is much more merciful. I'll stick with that.

That mirror mirrored my personal development in growing up and aging as well. I often felt I was fairly unwanted and unliked as a child. I wasn't "old enough or big enough to do this or that or to understand one thing or another." I sometimes felt that I must be stupid and ugly and incapable. I got teased constantly. We all did. I felt weak and helpless. In reality, however, I did not see myself as my family actually saw me. I saw them through the skew of the human condition—mine and theirs. They have told me over the years that they thought I was smart and cute. But I absolutely did not get that at the time. I think little kids are pretty incapable of processing much of that, especially when there's not a lot of support on the backside of it all to shore up a child's emerging self-esteem. Perhaps they were secure enough in their own self-esteem and assumed that I should be. But I was a very sensitive kid with an already bruised ego, and I simply could not handle much of it. Perhaps some of them weren't as sensitive and were just oblivious. Or perhaps they were terribly insecure themselves and joined in, finding in some way that to put down and tease someone else temporarily salved their own inner angst.

On top of that, I was the eighth child. Actually I was the tenth, as my mom had a set of twins after my oldest brother who had died at birth. Having that many babies is surely hard on a woman's body. But as the story was told, my mom had a lot of trouble birthing me, so my dad used to say things along the line of "You liked to have killed your mom when you were born." How does a sensitive little momma's boy process a statement saying that he somehow almost killed his mom? My dad also would tell me occasionally that they hadn't planned to have any more kids and that I was a surprise. I cannot remember what I was thinking when he would say those things, but as a pastor and a counselor, I am sure it figured in greatly to my often felt sense that the world would be better off without me. Sadly still, when I go through a bout of fighting off depression, I feel those old feelings. In fact it is that feeling that tells me for sure that I am getting depressed. (I have written a book *Fighting and Beating Depression*, which tells about my experiences with depression all the way back to my childhood and discusses what I have learned about beating it.)

But as a five-year-old, I was incapable of effectively processing all the physical and verbal assaults against my self-esteem. I sometimes wonder how it would have affected me had I known they loved me, liked me, and wanted me. Thankfully, in the end, we all survived the poor judgment and dysfunctional behavior. We love being together and often reflect back on the dynamics of our lives back then.

Seeing how God sees us is not an easy task. It's a faith task. When we are young, we mostly do not worry quite so much about how we look. We may look in mirrors, but our perspectives are very limited. As I have already noted, we draw much of our self-perception from how we perceive that our parents and other key people see us. Babies study the faces of their moms and dads. Those early days are spent with the brain programming itself to interpret what it sees. Lots of mimicking the facials of caregivers go on. A child's study of parents' facial expressions, voice inflections, and other communications is a critical part of a child's development. Only with the onset of maturity does one begin to develop any true objectivity and understanding of self-perception apart from that of their caregivers. The perceptions of those important to us are most powerful during those early developmental years! They may be less so later as we mature, but they still remain powerful for our lifetime.

As with infants, it is exactly the same after our rebirth into Christ. We have to look at and study the face of God as seen in Jesus and the church in order to develop our spiritual brains. We must come to see ourselves as God sees us! But if we don't focus on Jesus consistently, we will never develop well inwardly and spiritually. The Bible says, "Therefore, holy brothers and sisters, who share in the heavenly calling, fix your thoughts on Jesus, whom we acknowledge as our apostle and high priest" (Heb. 3:1). That's it: fix your thoughts on Jesus. And keep them there.

Children quickly learn to recognize the faces of their parents and loved ones. Children learn the voices of those who care for them, protect them, sustain them, teach them, and interact with them—those they depend on for their very growth and survival. And even in the womb, babies are learning and beginning to respond to the familiar. We never lose that as we grow up, especially if our parents were loving and protective. It must become that way with God for us. We must learn to recognize his "face" when he shows up. We must learn the distinctive sound of our true shepherd's voice when he calls us. We must see and experience with our minds and our hearts his invisible qualities through the home he created for us. We must learn to trust him and to follow him faithfully. It is essential that we learn about the "Presence of God"—how it looks and feels when he is near, as Jesus himself said, "All who love me will obey my teaching. My Father will love them. My Father and I will come to them and live with them" (John 14:23, Easy-to-Read Version), and as Isaiah wrote, "Seek the Lord while he may be found; call on him while he is near" (Isa. 55:6).

Jesus calls himself the Good Shepherd of us as his sheep and says this to us: "The gatekeeper [God] opens the gate for him [the good shepherd Jesus], and the sheep listen to his voice. He calls his own sheep by name and leads them out. When he has brought out all his own, he goes on ahead of them, and his sheep follow him because they know his voice. But they will never follow a stranger; in fact, they will run away from him because they do not recognize a stranger's voice" (John 10:3–5, brackets added). Jesus becomes real and experientially present in us and with us when we are in him.

So we must strive to learn his voice, and that takes earnest spiritual listening. We must recognize his face, and that takes earnest looking and seeking. As with the book title by Francis Schaeffer, *He is there and He is Not Silent* (Tyndale House, 1972), the creation reveals God's invisible qualities—his eternal power and divine nature (Rom. 1:20). And as the psalmist said, "The heavens declare the glory of God; the skies proclaim the work of his hands" (Ps. 19:1), the creation declares the heart and personality of its creator.

Our accounts of Jesus give us a clear mind's eye picture of what he looks like in our human form. We should study creation and the gospel and "listen" carefully to them with our hearts, our minds, and our bodies so that we fully inculcate the gospel message into the very core of our spirits and become aware of his constancy with us and in us!

I heard a preacher speak one time, saying that as we grow older, if you will notice, there is a principal of "tagging up." Perhaps it can be seen as a way of "recharging" our emotional batteries. Feeling safe again. Gaining a sense of being moored safely somewhere in this world we have grown up in. To explain, as children grow and become more mobile, they will begin to crawl or toddle away from mom or dad. However, just as quickly children will usually return quickly to them. Often they will crawl back and literally get in mom's lap or drape their arms over their dad's leg. If they cannot find a parent, then the crying out for them starts. All of us as parents at some point have heard a kid crying and shouting "mom" or "dad" in some public place, and we instinctively look for the tot. But once tagged up, a child will most assuredly shortly go to explore again. Then back to tag up again. Parents are our home bases. And on our bases, we feel safe.

Even as adults, we still feel the need to "tag up"—to go back where we came from. We go off on our exploits, but we regularly feel the yearning to "go home." We want to again see our parents, other significant loved ones from our childhood, the places that were significant to us and again relive the sights, sounds, and smells that shaped our early development. Be back on home base where we feel safe.

Unfortunately, sometimes tagging up may not be so helpful for some. Perhaps home base was never that safe, or it became unsafe at some point. Either way, the believer learns to make God the home base and to tag up with him anytime and anyplace we need to!

A few years ago, I took a trip back to my home state of Oklahoma, where we hold our summer camp for our church elementary children. The small "town" where I grew up was easily accessible on the trip. It was hardly a town, even though it had a name, had a post office when I lived there, and had some houses strewn up and down an oiled, gravel county road. It was home though. So on the way back to where I now live in Texas, I decided to go by and "tag up." I was a bit charged that summer morning as I drove alone in my thoughts down those familiar roads and drove into the grassy place that had once been our gravel-covered driveway. It was a bright summer morning. My thoughts gravitated only toward good and pleasant memories. The bad memories were in the background.

I sat for a few minutes in the air-conditioned comfort of my car, still insulated from the already hot summer day, and just looked around. Soaking it all in, the scene was haunted and eerie and exhilarating at the same time. The house was gone, and all that was left was the concrete front porch that I could remember sitting and playing on. This was the front entry to our house. But I could see it all clearly in my mind's eye and feel the waves of feeling rippling inside of me. But all too suddenly, that concrete porch that welcomed guests into our home became in my mind's eye the hard, cold, concrete porch I remember standing on, watching my mother be taken away to the hospital for the last time, and my dad telling my brother and me she would never be back home. Words that can cause an adolescent kid an emotional heart attack. I had one that day.

As harsh as that pronouncement was to us, he was right; she would never return. The place was haunted. There are obviously countless more memories than that—the good, the bad, the ugly, and just the plain old normal stuff. It all seemingly wafted through my mind and heart in such a brief moment. The yard was about an acre when we lived there. It had seemed so large back when I was a kid, yet it looked so small to me that day as an adult. My world had obviously expanded greatly. An acre didn't look so big anymore. A world that had seemed so big and so all-encompassing suddenly looked so small and isolated, as it had really been all along.

After looking around, feeling the sentiments, and poring over innumerable memories, I opened my door and got out. In contrast to the cool comfort of the air-conditioned car, the late-morning heat and humidity of that June day was already stifling. I began walking around what had been our yard and decided to walk out to where our dirt basketball court had been. I had spent countless hours on and around that court. As I was walking that way, however, I snagged a head of "stickers," as we called them, in my sock. They stung pretty badly so I bent down to remove them. While I was bent down, in broad daylight in the heat of the day and out in the open, a mosquito wandered by and decided to secure a blood meal and go lay her eggs. Again, this was in the middle of a hot day! Mosquitos like that are supposed to me resting during the day and biting mainly at daybreak, sunset, and in the night. That mosquito was as desperate as I, I suppose. It was tagging up on me!

I was hot. I still felt the sting of the grass burrs. Now my arm began to itch, as I've always proven to be a very attractive mosquito bait, as well as being pretty reactive to the anticoagulant that they inject while they suck your blood. My arm itched a lot, as I had so often experienced in the woods of Oklahoma growing up. I guess I felt tagged up enough. I was quickly reminded why I had looked so forward to getting out of there! Life had metaphorically been like that for me in that place, especially during my last years at home—just not very fun much of the time. But it was still where it all started for me, and I needed to be reminded that it was all quite real. I didn't make any of it up, not the good or the bad or the ugly. None of it. It was all real. It all had happened pretty much as I remembered, and I was shaped by it. It was and always will be home base, for good and for bad.

It reminds me of the opening lyrics to James Taylor's 1968 hit song, "Carolina in My Mind." The song reflects on the singer's own homesickness for his home in Carolina while he was overseas performing. The lyrics say, "In my mind I'm going to Carolina. Can't you see the sunshine, can't you just feel the moonshine? Ain't it just like a friend of mine to hit me from behind? Yes, I'm going to Carolina in my mind." Sometimes the friend that is your original home—home base—can slip up on you and hit you from behind. That can be a good thing; it can be a bad thing. It depends how you are remembering it at the time.

To continue my tagging up story though, just to make sure I was fully tagged up, I then drove by my old country school. I attended the same school from grades one to twelve. Probably at least half of the fifty-two students in my graduating class had attended most of all the twelve years together. It was summer, so no one was on the school grounds and everything was locked up. It was primarily brick and rock buildings surrounded by gravelly grounds. I knew it was going to be really hot. But I decided to jump out and quickly look into the windows of the old gymnasium where I had also spent many hours. I'm sure the adage rings true of my play there, "The older I get, the better I was." But I do have some good memories connected with it, along with some very bad ones. There was some sparse high grass beneath the windows, and I got another set of stickers in my sock as I waded through to look in! So after tiptoeing to look in the gym windows, I went back to the car, opened the driver's door, and sat sideways to get the stickers out before I got in. As I raised my foot up to get the stickers out of my sock, I felt the stretching of a large wad of gum that now had me connected by the sole of my shoe to a patch of hot asphalt parking lot under me. Oh my; oh me!

Suffice it to say, I had fully tagged up! After getting the stickers out and, as best as I could, removing a big wad of hot, gooey gum from my shoe, I immediately turned in my seat to face the windshield, closed my car door, cranked the AC, buckled my seat belt, and headed for my most blessed home in Texas. With my air conditioner on as high as it would go, I turned up the music, and I "ran" the rest of the bases all the way back to my new home base and my sweet wife. Safe! And I was so very elated to return to my very cool, comfortable home, a yard without stickers, and in a city miles away from my original home base. I have remained sufficiently tagged-up for quite a few years now.

Do not get me wrong; I love Oklahoma. I love all my family and friends with whom I shared it and many who still live there. I cherish countless wonderful memories of fun, family, and friends. But still it may now be true for me, as it was for the character George Webber in Thomas Wolfe's *You Can't Go Home Again* (okay, just go look it up!). Hey fellow Okies, it was just the stickers, the heat, the humidity, and the mosquitoes that drove me away this last time. I still love you and root for your teams. I'm just illustrating a point and not nearly as "home on the range" as I once was!

So where am I? Oh yeah, suffice it to say we seemingly need to tag up no matter what our experiences were with home and family. We just need to occasionally hit the "reset" button inside of us. We need to see and even study the faces again, though older and marked by time. We need to hear the voices again. We even need to figuratively remember and sense any ghosts that live there. We need to see where we came from and remember what it was like, why we mattered or did not seem to matter then, and most importantly, why we matter now. We need to feel the security that comes from "home," or perhaps feel the insecurity associated with it in order to help dispel it. We will never of course matter to anybody more than we matter to truly loving parents and siblings! No one on earth can love us quite as completely and in the same way a mom does. No one in this world can quite feel toward us the way a good dad does. Some, as well, need to again revisit the pain of the losses of childhood and perhaps remember that any abandonment and rejection that may have occurred was simply not our fault. We sometimes need to go back in order to move forward. We need to remind ourselves that we have grown from victim to victor!

It is pretty much the same with us spiritually. Just as when we were young children, and the mirror was too high and may have been cloudy, it is that way with all things spiritual. We first see through the bottom of the mirror through the eyes of our moms and dads—our "fathers," believing and accepting as truth what they tell us about our world—the physical world and the spiritual one. Our caregivers' communication of their own often skewed perceptions of the physical and spiritual worlds may be more non-verbal than they are verbal too. They also may be more subjective and presumptive than objective and accurate. We heard what our parents said. We spoke as they spoke. We used the very words they taught us. We even mimicked their nonverbal expressions and gestures. For most, we likely still do to some degree.

Thus, for the rest of our lives, their voices will resonate in our hearts and minds and will come to bear in how we perceive ourselves in the world around us. We see as they taught us to see. That is a good thing with those things that are right, good, and functional, especially if we investigate and own them as truths for ourselves. However, the things that were wrong, or those things about which we made incorrect assumptions, will prove harmful and destructive to us if we do not replace them with better thoughts, beliefs, and subsequent behaviors.

It is just a fact—we will have childish ways when we are children. We cannot do otherwise. These childish ways are important to our early growth and development. We need to crawl to best learn to walk. We need to string syllables together such as "goo-goo" in order to learn to string words together into sentences. We need to explore to learn to find our way ahead. We exercise our imaginations in order to develop our speculative and imaginative capacities. We need to see, taste, hear, smell, and feel in order to learn to interpret our sensory perceptions. We need to be "read" by our parents in order to learn how to read and understand ourselves. We need to play and make-believe. We need childish ways. But if as adults we are still doing some of those things, it gets a little foolish and perhaps just downright weird! And possibly quite unhealthy. We must finally "put the ways of childhood behind" (1 Cor. 13:11) in how we think about God and the creation, how we think about ourselves, and how we think about others. We must learn to see reality as best as we can. We need to learn to see as God sees.

I think many and possibly most would agree that as children we do have a natural spiritual proclivity to us. We have spiritual instincts just as we have physical ones. They are in fact not segregated for us. It is we who unwittingly segregate the physical and the spiritual. As with the rest of our capacities, these have to be developed and honed though. However, our spiritual instincts will surely wane as we are corrupted by the sin nature we inherit and are afflicted by. But we are not designed for that; rather we are designed so that our spiritual selves grow intertwined with the rest of our whole self. We are spiritual beings, yet for far too many, our spiritual selves have been starved out early in adolescence. We don't sense it anymore because it is weak or dead. But still, we bear the very image of God himself, and God is Spirit. At our worst, we still "look a bit like him," so to speak.

Just as our bodies grow and develop, and we know there is something wrong if they fail to do so, it is the same way spiritually. We are designed to grow spiritually and see spiritual things in mature ways. But because of the curse of sin, we must be "born again" to be enabled by the Spirit to actually "see" the kingdom of God. Jesus said, "I tell you the truth, no one can *see* the kingdom of God unless he is born again" (John 3:3). Further, God then reveals himself and things about himself to us by the Spirit—"However, as it is written: 'No eye has seen, no ear has heard, no mind has conceived what God has prepared for those who love him'—but

God has revealed it to us by his Spirit" (1 Cor. 2:9–10). God reveals spiritually what we cannot physically "see." But this spiritual vision is not possible without God's redemptive work in us and on us through Christ and the Holy Spirit. Apart from his work in Christ, we can neither see the spiritual, even with the powerful eyeballs he has gifted us with, nor can we perceive it with the incredible minds he made for us. Paul wrote, "The person without the Spirit does not accept the things that come from the Spirit of God but considers them foolishness, and cannot understand them because they are discerned only through the Spirit" (1 Cor. 2:14).

Without the Holy Spirit, we are like babies with blurry vision still trying to interpret the reflections we are seeing. We have to learn to see, that is, develop our visual and mental acuity to sense, contextualize, and interpret what is visible to us. Our emotional, mental, and spiritual "vision" is blurred by infancy and the world itself, as well as skewed by our inevitable fall into sin's grip. It happens to everyone—"all have sinned and fall short of the glory of God . . ." (Rom. 3:23). Thus, when it comes to the things of God, we must have the Holy Spirit in and with us to learn to see and interpret the spiritual, because "they are spiritually discerned." Without the Spirit, we may see blurry images of the spiritual, but we do not have the spiritual acuity to make much sense of any of it, and thus, it is "foolishness" to us.

God's Holy Spirit is the anointing that we are given in Christ that enables us to see—"you have an anointing from the Holy One, and all of you know the truth" (1 John 2:20). Thus, it is the Holy Spirit that we are to be led by—"those who are led by the Spirit of God are sons of God" (Rom. 8:14). The Holy Spirit guides us on our way and teaches us how to walk in Jesus. John further writes, "As for you, the anointing you received from him remains in you, and you do not need anyone to teach you. But as his anointing teaches you about all things and as that anointing is real, not counterfeit—just as it has taught you, remain in him" (1 John 2:27). The

Holy Spirit searches our minds and God's mind and intercedes in communication and interpretation.

Further, Paul writes, "In the same way, the Spirit helps us in our weakness. We do not know what we ought to pray for, but the Spirit himself intercedes for us with groans that words cannot express. And he who searches our hearts knows the mind of the Spirit, because the Spirit intercedes for the saints in accordance with God's will" (Rom. 8:26–27). The Spirit matures us spiritually and allows God to see within us. And he helps us to see how God sees us. The Holy Spirit is just as natural as the world around us. It is because our spiritual acuity has been blinded that we cannot spiritually sense him—"The god of this age [Satan] has blinded the minds of unbelievers . . ." (2 Cor. 4:4).

Thus, to look into the eyes of God—to look into the mind of God—one must have Christ's mind. And in Christ we are given his mind and his perspective, as the apostle Paul writes, "'For who has known the mind of the Lord that he may instruct him?' But we have the mind of Christ" (1 Cor. 2:16). And to really even begin to see ourselves in the kingdom light, we must first be reborn—born of water and the Spirit—"I tell you the truth, no one can enter the kingdom of God unless he is born of water and the Spirit" (John 3:5).

God gives us his mind when we change ours—literally when we repent. Repent means to change our minds. It is in our conversion that we receive his Spirit. We change our minds (repent), then are born again, and we receive forgiveness and his Spirit—"Repent and be baptized, every one of you, in the name of Jesus Christ for the forgiveness of your sins. And you will receive the gift of the Holy Spirit. The promise is for you and your children and for all who are far off—for all whom the Lord our God will call" (Acts 2:38–39).

We literally are spiritually reborn of water and the Spirit. It's the covenant promise given to everyone whom God calls to himself and who by faith accepts Christ as Lord and Savior. Paul wrote, "So in Christ Jesus you are all children of God through faith, for all of you who were baptized into Christ have clothed yourselves with Christ" (Gal. 3:26–27).

Further, as believers, his transforming power is unleashed through the changing of our minds, as Paul wrote, "Do not conform any longer to the pattern of this world, but be transformed by the renewing of your mind" (Rom. 12:2). We fight the spiritual battle first in our minds with the weapons he arms us with, beginning with his Word and his Spirit. Through them, we are able to take captive untrue and unhealthy thoughts that ultimately come from Satan and through which Satan is able to separate us from God and cause us to stumble in darkness. So we are told, "The weapons we fight with are not the weapons of the world. On the contrary, they have divine power to demolish strongholds. We demolish arguments and every pretension that sets itself up against the knowledge of God, and we take captive every thought to make it obedient to Christ" (2 Cor. 10:4–5).

Through God's Spirit, we are able to see into the mind and heart of God. Through the Spirit, we are able to see into and operate in the spiritual realm. Through the Spirit we are able to see and make sense of the things of God. Through the Spirit, we are able to finally grow tall enough to see clearly into God's mirror and see ourselves face-to-face. Through the Holy Spirit Jesus has poured out on us, we are able to *see God seeing us*!

God's mirror is never marred by time and use. It is clear and bright. However, our own vision and the haze of this sinful world may blur what is reflected back to us. The gospel of Christ will help correct our vision though. And in correcting our vision, he can lead us victoriously on a life-saving course.

Questions and Thoughts for Reflection and Discussion

1. How do you see that the dark, damaged mirror of this present world blurred your early vision of yourself, that is, your self-perception?
2. How do you see a poor self-image as having damaged you or others?
3. How does seeing God directly through the image of Christ correct our self-perceptions?
4. How do you interpret the statement that as Christians we have the mind of Christ?
5. What are implications of this reality?
6. What do you see as the steps or the process of changing our thinking and conforming it to the way it's supposed to work—the way Christ taught us?
7. How do you think seeing ourselves as God sees us changes our lives?

CHAPTER 5

WHAT GOD SEES: MAN LOOKS AT APPEARANCE; GOD LOOKS AT THE HEART

We see each other on the outside.
It's all that we can view.
But the eyes of the Creator who made us
Sees inside us—all the way through!

Humans look at other men's external appearances, because that is what we have been given the ability to see. As mortal beings, we cannot literally look into others' hearts. God can though. And God does.

Samuel was the last of the judges of Israel, and he was a true man of God. He was not only a judge; he was a prophet as well. After God rejected Saul as king, he appointed Samuel to go to the family of a man named Jesse and from among his sons anoint a new king. But he did not tell Samuel up front which one it would be. God does that to us all sometime—tells us to do something and then makes us work our way through before finally telling us what's up! When Samuel arrived, he saw Jesse's son, Eliab, and was impressed by his physical stature. Judging by outward appearance, he quickly assumed Eliab was to be the new king.

However, God addressed the issue with Samuel, who, even though he was a prophet, was still prone to judge by outward appearances, unless of course God revealed the inside of things to him. God said, "Do not consider his appearance or his height, for I have rejected him. The Lord does not look at the things man looks at. *Man looks at the outward appearance, but the Lord looks at the heart*" (1 Sam. 16:7, italics added). Although to the father and brothers, David apparently seemed the least likely among them, it was he who had been preselected. God had already searched for and found the man he wanted even before he sent Samuel. Samuel had stated the principle himself when he told Saul God was rejecting him as king, saying, "But now your kingdom will not endure; the Lord has sought out a man after his own heart and appointed him leader of his people, because you have not kept the Lord's command" (1 Sam. 13:14). God picked a man with a heart like his own. He still looks for that in us.

God looks at the heart.

What is the "heart" in this context anyway? Well, it is obviously part of the brain, as the word of God judges its thoughts and attitudes—brain functions (Heb. 4:12). The "heart" in biblical terminology is what controls behavior. Jesus said, "What comes out of a person is what defiles them. For it is from within, out of a person's heart, that evil thoughts come—sexual immorality, theft, murder, adultery, greed, malice, deceit, lewdness, envy, slander, arrogance and folly. All these evils come from inside and defile a person" (Mark 7:20–23). It is a very powerful thing within us, this heart of ours!

The heart is the "wellspring of life" (Prov. 4:23), and it can also be the source of our undoing. It is the eyes of our hearts that must be enlightened to be able to see the reality of the blessings God gives us in Christ (Eph. 1:18–19). It is that part of us that ultimately defines who we actually are and how we behave and live. However, unfortunately, it is notably deceptive and difficult to understand (Jer. 17:9). As we too often do with others, we can obviously even fool ourselves concerning who we are—what we really think and feel. And we can fool ourselves in regard to others the same way. It is only by watching the overall outcome of another's life that we can reasonably discern the sincerity of their heart and life. To counter a fleshly drift toward hypocrisy, we must pursue integrity so that what is said and done on the outside is completely consistent with what is thought and felt on the inside.

I sometimes ponder what the heart actually "looks" like to God. What is it that God "sees"? Of course, our ability to see physically derives from God's ability to see spiritually, because, as I keep noting, this physical world emanates from, and mirrors, the spiritual world. Remember, Paul said that God's power and divine nature can be seen through the created world (Rom. 1:20). Thus our own ability to see reflects in various ways God's spiritual ability to see. Just as we see by interpreting light reflected back to us off objects, God sees by shining his own light on us and having it reflected back to him from within our hearts. He thus sees into our hearts. Jesus of course is that light (John 8:12).

God's Spirit works inside of us to search our hearts and minds. In some way, he bears testimony to each of our individual child-to-father relationship to God, as the apostle wrote, "The Spirit himself testifies with our spirits that we are God's children" (Rom. 8:16). Just as one might examine a new or a classic car—looking under the hood, kicking the tires, slamming doors, and so forth—God examines us. "I the Lord search the heart and examine the mind . . ." (Jer. 17:10).

So there can be no pretense before God. We cannot hide anything from him, and we cannot manipulate the facts. We cannot deceive him with our subterfuge. Our facades are transparent to him; our deflections useless. He knows. "God is greater than our hearts, and he knows everything" (1 John 3:20). The apostle John describes Jesus's ability to truly know us, saying, "He did not need man's testimony about man, for he knew what was in a man" (John 2:25).

God's word lays bare our hearts before him. As just mentioned, his word is what judges our very thoughts and attitudes, and it will judge us in the end (John 12:47–48). His word is the "sword of the Spirit" that "penetrates" into our hearts (Eph. 6:17; Heb. 4:12–13). His word makes us clean on the inside (John 15:3). His word helps keep us from sin (Ps. 119:11). It is not the words themselves that do all this, nor it is the rules or laws. It is something much deeper. Jesus is the Word (John 1:1). The words *from* God found in the Bible are as agents of the Word *of* God, Jesus, and they are power by the Spirit of God, given to us by Jesus when we believe (Eph. 1:13). And through the word and the Spirit, it is Christ himself who lives within us—"We will come to them and make our home with them" (John 14:23) and "For it is [not your strength, but it is] God who is effectively at work in you, both to will and to work [that is, strengthening, energizing, and creating in you the longing and the ability to fulfill your purpose] for His good pleasure" (Phil. 2:13, Amplified Bible). Jesus sees all—"Everything is uncovered and laid bare before the eyes of him to whom we must give account" (Heb. 4:13).

When I was a young child, there was a song that was occasionally sung at our church, the theme and title of which, although I've never known the words, I seem to have always had a haunting memory. It was called "There's An All-Seeing Eye." That was a scary visual for a young boy who was often focused on less than ideal imagery and bent on mischief. The chorus went: "Watching you, watching you; Ev'ry day mind the course you pursue; Watching you, watching you; There's an all-seeing Eye watching you." There was such a sense of foreboding in those lines. I think I came to imagine this stern and perhaps angry God watching me and waiting to punish me, like a couple of my junior high teachers seemed to do sometimes. I have often heard variations of this same sentiment from others as well. There is indeed an "all-seeing eye" watching us. However, the eye of God is from the heart of a loving father watching out closely for a precious child, not from the heart of some lurking predator God determined to find some reason to abuse or punish us.

When my daughter was quite young, a young girl was kidnapped from a playground where soccer was played, in a very nice suburban area in our city. She was found murdered a short time later, her body dumped only a couple of miles from our home. The killer was on the loose for a time afterward. The schools, city, and parents were obviously coaching kids on being very careful, so, unfortunately, my daughter was forced to hear some pretty scary realities both at school and at home.

One of those frightful nights, I was putting her to bed and saw just how scared she was to be left alone in her room. She slept upstairs, and our master bedroom was right at the bottom of the stairs. We had a good security system. We always locked the doors, and I often rechecked them when I awoke at night. We lived in a very safe neighborhood in a city known for its low crime rate. Our city had a good police force. We had done all that we could to secure our children's safety. I asked her if she was scared, and she replied yes. I asked her if she had noticed when we were out somewhere or at home that we would scarcely let her out of our sight day or night. I asked her if she had noticed how her mom and I were very careful with all of our children, especially knowing where they were at all times. She said she did.

I then asked her if she could trust me to watch out for her. She said she could. I said something to her like, "Sweetheart, your job tonight is to go to sleep, rest, and not worry about your safety. It is Daddy's job to make sure you are safe. And I do it very well. I promise." Any loving dad can relate to the passion and intensity behind such a promise. God gave Israel the same kind of promise: "Be strong and courageous. Do not be afraid or terrified because of them, for the LORD your God goes with you; he will never leave you nor forsake you" (Deut. 31:6). And through the apostles, Jesus gave us a similar promise saying, "Surely I am with you always, to the very end of the age" (Matt. 28:20).

I wanted my daughter to have as much of the innocent carefree childhood as I could give her in a world gone mad and seeming to get madder! She, of course, could not know the prayers her mother and I prayed over her most nights even after she was asleep. She could not have known how regularly I awoke in the middle of the night and walked out into the house to make sure the alarm was set correctly and that all was still well. She could not have known all those times her mother or I walked quietly up the stairs late into the night to look in on her and her brothers, as much for our own sense of security as for hers. Their security was more important to us than our own. We did it with all our kids their whole lives. Although they are all adults now and can take care of themselves, and now find them more and more watching over and protecting my wife and me, I still prayerfully and thoughtfully hover over them, ever watching, always hoping, and constantly being vigilant for them.

I'll always be their dad, and loving dads just do that kind of stuff, because we learned it from our heavenly dad, and in the same spirit of a child, we cry out to him, "Abba, Father" (Rom. 8:15). I have long told my kids to do the same toward me—cry out for me—telling them, "If you need me, call me; if you need me really badly, call me really fast!" And I mean it from the bottom of my heart!

My wife and I are "all-seeing eyes" when it comes to our kids. Certainly we do not have the omnipresence, omniscience, or omnipotence of God. None of us do. We surely cannot guarantee our loved ones' absolute safety the way God can ours. However, what we can guarantee is that we would lay our lives down in a heartbeat for the well-being of our beloved children and two wonderful granddaughters (to this point). We are their fans, not their critics. As God does us with his all-seeing eye, we constantly watch over them to protect and save them, not to punish or condemn. God is our fan, not our critic. It is we who become his enemies through faithlessness, disobedience, and unbelief, not he who becomes ours! It is humanity who turned on him, not he who turned on us. God is a faithful God, even when we are not. He has promised us clearly that in the end he will give us what we in life have chosen from the two choices he offers us all—to be with him forever or to be without him forever.

As loving parents, we are prepared to lay down our lives for our children just like God already laid down his for us. As God with us, we wish only the best for each of them. But as loving parents, we ultimately give them their freedom to choose. Enslaving them or attempting to somehow program them to be robotic lovers and followers of us is not love at all. The love of God, by definition, requires will and choice by the one giving it; therefore, to allow us to love as he loves, God gives us the freedom of choice to love him or not love him. Thus, we do the same for those we love.

God is watching us to protect us. He will protect us in this world according to his will and plan. That does not mean no harm will ever come to us though. Jesus said, "I have told you these things, so that in me you may have peace. In this world you will have trouble. But take heart! I have overcome the world" (John 16:33). He also said, "Do not be afraid of those who kill the body but cannot kill the soul" (Matt. 10:28). God assures us he will protect us in eternity from all harm and pain, even though we must sometimes suffer now for a little while (1 Pet. 1:6). We as parents know that our children have to go out and play and learn and in doing so will be hurt sometimes, possibly seriously. We know that to overprotect them is to do the worst damage of all to them. The world is full of potential perils, but it is also even fuller in potential blessings. To experience these blessings, we must face and sometimes endure the perils that exist. God allows *us* to face them, even though he gives us careful instructions and the presence of his Spirit so as to minimize and mitigate the serious risks. So must we let our children. Even the facing them and the suffering involved in experiencing them, God will turn into blessings (Rom. 8:28).

When God watches us, he watches out for our hearts. That is, because who we are on the inside is who we really are and ultimately determines what we do. We can appear to be one thing on the outside and be someone completely different on the inside—in ignorance, because of external pressures, or on purpose as hypocrites. However, inevitably whatever is on the inside will be revealed outwardly.

In our church, we have a motto: "To build from the ground up and from the inside out." Jesus said we should first clean inside the cup. We are convinced that if we minister to hearts and do that well, the outside will surely become clean too (Matt. 23:26). Because it is indeed from our hearts, where God sees us and first connects with us, that our sin originates (Mark 7:21). It is paramount that we engage God and the spiritual in a way that brings the true conversion of our hearts. The popularized concept of the "sinner's prayer" is a construct that tries to get at this, saying we should "accept Jesus as our personal savior and ask him to come into our hearts." Jesus must be personal to us for sure—working in our hearts—in order for us to experience his transforming power. He is not to be distant from us for any reason; we are called rather to draw near to him.

We do not need to *go through* anybody or through any institution to get to Christ (John 1:12–13). We do not require human permission or intervention, but merely assistance—"And how can they believe in the one of whom they have not heard? And how can they hear without someone preaching to them?" (Rom. 10:14).

Others can help us, but none can get us to God *or* keep us from God except Jesus Christ alone. And nothing or no one can forcibly take us from him (John 10:28). Jesus came to be our personal and individualized way to God (John 14:6). But again, do not take that to mean that he will not use others to help us get there or stay there and that he will not use us to help others similarly.

Jesus sees us on the inside; he sees what we are thinking. John observed of Jesus, "Jesus knew in his spirit that this was what they were thinking in their hearts, and he said to them, 'Why are you thinking these things?'" (Mark 2:5). Jesus sees our affections, as he said to the Pharisees, "Isaiah was right when he prophesied about you hypocrites; as it is written: 'These people honor me with their lips, but their hearts are far from me'" (Mark 6:6). Jesus sees the source of the flow of our lives, not just the outcome—"For out of the overflow of his heart his mouth speaks" (Luke 6:45). Jesus sees what is valuable as well as what is worthless in our hearts. He said, "You are the ones who justify yourselves in the eyes of men, but God knows your hearts. What is highly valued among men is detestable in God's sight" (John 16:15). Jesus sees inside our hearts' storerooms—the closets, attics, cellars, and sheds. "The good man brings good things out of the good stored up in his heart, and the evil man brings evil things out of the evil stored up in his heart" (Luke 6:45). Jesus taught us that God not only sees our thoughts; he also sees the motives of our thoughts. David said to Solomon when charging him to build the temple, "The Lord searches every heart and understands every motive behind the thoughts" (1 Chron. 28:9).

God has spiritual X-ray vision.

That is why, I am sure, that salvation must begin in the heart. "If you confess with your mouth, 'Jesus is Lord,' and *believe in your heart* that God raised him from the dead, you will be saved" (Rom. 10:9, italics added). When it comes to God, we must not just *say* that Jesus is Lord though. Jesus must *be* Lord! With Jesus there can be no dissonance between what is said and what is really in our heart. He knows! He said, "Why do you call me, 'Lord, Lord,' and do not do what I say?" (Luke 6:46). Jesus knows the reality of things—our reality. We cannot fool him, even though we can sometimes fool even ourselves! He sees us when we cannot seem to even see within ourselves.

When the Lord comes, he will reveal what he has seen in each of us. "He will bring to light what is hidden in darkness and will expose the motives of men's hearts" (1 Cor. 4:5). "The Lord knows those who are his" (2 Tim. 2:19). Our ultimate salvation—our forgiven relationship with God—is not about our "knowing the Lord," so to speak; it is about his knowing us. During my lifetime, I have known each of our country's sitting presidents. I have known about their families and all sorts of details about them. It is all highly publicized. However, none of them would have taken a telephone call from me. Not a single one of them knew my name. They had no compelling reason to. They had no knowledge of my existence.

It is similar with God and us. All of us know things about him. He has made himself known through creation and through scripture. Thousands upon thousands of books have been written by his people. Most know things about God; apparently only a few are actually known by him (Matt. 7:13–14). At judgment, Jesus says there will be many even among Christians who obviously knew lots *about* him but who were unknown *by* him (Matt. 7:22)! Thus inferring that they had never even been saved. Apparently, they will never have realized it. Satan's deception is alive and well, and we all best beware!

God sees us internally as we see each other externally. Our thoughts and attitudes are to him actions—deeds. "I the Lord search the heart and examine the mind, to reward a man according to his conduct, according to what his deeds deserve" (Jer. 17:10). You catch that? God is looking at our hearts and minds and judging our inner "deeds." To the church at Thyatira, Jesus said,

"Then all the churches will know that I am he who searches hearts and minds, and I will repay each of you according to your deeds" (Rev. 2:23). The deeds of the heart and mind that God sees, but that we cannot, are what determine the outcome of one's life that we can see. So many of Christ's core commands are commands concerning the behavior our minds and the hearts—"Love the Lord your God with all your heart and with all your soul and with all your mind" (Matt. 22:37).

Although we cannot accurately see the motives behind our actions and deeds, but only the outward part, God sees both. Very clearly. Our looks and identity to him are of our whole person and not just the outward, physical behaviors.

God is watching our hearts—seeing their "actions"—just as we would observe another's behavior. We best then be looking at ours and others' hearts through his eyes rather than trying to justify ourselves through our foolish arguments. It is what it is, and our ruses change nothing. We must see God seeing us to understand if our relationship to him is truly right. What any of us "thinks" about any of it apart from God's word is useless in this regard— "I care very little if I am judged by you or by any human court; indeed, I do not even judge myself" (1 Cor. 4:3).

We cannot impose our will or our opinions on God. He cares what we think and feel about things, but we don't get a vote concerning his judgment about others or even ourselves.

Questions and Thoughts for Reflection and Discussion

1. What are the implications to us that God sees the thoughts of our hearts and minds as behaviors?
2. What is a motive, and why do motives matter so much to God?
3. Why might it be true that our motives are ultimately what define us?

4. With what kind of "eyes" is Jesus looking at our hearts with, and what should that mean to each of us?
5. How does God enable us to clean ourselves from the inside out?
6. What is our role in that, and what is God's role?
7. How should the reality that God searches our hearts and minds affect the way we think and live?

CHAPTER 6

SEEING THE VISTA OF GOD: THE SPIRITUAL WORLD AROUND US

When I was born and first saw my surroundings,
My blurred world was simple, small, and secure.
When I lay in my crib warm and snugly,
All I saw was that all seemed sure.

When born again all changed in a moment,
My visual acuity in an instant was heightened.
There was a much bigger world all around me.
I saw the creation anew through eyes enlightened.

One of my sons and I visited another country a few years back, and while there, our host graciously took us to a crocodile/alligator farm—a zoo of sorts. This was far from America, deep in a developing country. Let me just say that the safety measures were quite limited compared to what we spoiled Americans have become accustomed to. We could have easily reached over and touched crocodiles and alligators in some exhibits! We could have with little effort stepped or crawled over the barriers right into most of them! My son and I were at one exhibit and were looking over an approximately three- or four-feet-high rock barrier down the throat of a gator lying right by the wall! I am not exaggerating; it was right there! It was definitely up close and personal!

On top of all that, and sadly so, this exhibit was just packed full of gators. They were literally spread all around within two or three feet of each other surrounding this tiny, seemingly useless, putrid, little pond in a fenced compound that was, as best I remember, probably one hundred feet long and fifty feet across. Many were lying with their mouths wide open. As I said, the stone fence around the viewing side was only a few feet high. Children could have easily climbed right in! It was a very memorable, frightening, and appalling experience.

Just imagine being at such a zoo and turning around to see your child standing solitary in the middle of a pen of gators or crocs like we saw, seemingly completely unaware of the peril faced in trying to get back out without becoming gator food. Parent panic time, huh? But think about it, God watches us living daily in the middle of a spiritual situation much more frightening, as spiritual forces of evil are all around us with their teeth bared, so to speak.

There's a story in the Old Testament in 2 Kings about the prophet Elisha and his servant. Israel was in a war with Aram, and the king of Aram kept setting traps for Israel's army. However, the prophet Elisha, with his direct link to God, was telling the king of Israel where the Aram army was setting the most recent trap. Hence, Israel was able to avoid the enemy's ruses.

In frustration, the king of Aram investigated to see if there was a spy in his own ranks. One of the officers had apparently found out about Elisha's supernatural reconnaissance radar ability and informed the king of IT. The officer answered the king's query as to who the informant might be, saying, "None of us, my lord the king, but Elisha, the prophet who is in Israel, tells the king of Israel the very words you speak in your bedroom" (2 Kings 6:12). Scary adversary, I believe.

The king ordered his army to go surround the city where Elisha was. An army stood against one solitary man of God and his lowly servant—a preacher and prophet. It reminds me of a story my oldest son told me about Mahatma Gandhi facing a hostile crowd alone. Using his nonviolent, Jesus-imitating methods, as I was told the story, and I failed in verifying it, Gandhi ultimately did on one side of India what the army could not do on the other side of the country without fighting—quell an angry mob. Gandhi was a great man doing what great people do—face down evil for the sake of good. He was like a lone child standing in a pen of alligators, mouths wide open!

Elisha was obviously quite aware of what was going on around him, as he had been given the ability to see at least some of what God sees beyond our normal human abilities. Knowing his terrified servant did not have that ability, Elisha told his servant to not be afraid because "those who are with us are more than those who are with them" (1 Kings 6:16). I'm sure it didn't feel that way at that point for the servant. Elisha then prayed, "O Lord, open his eyes so he may see" (1 Kings 6:17). What did the servant see when he was given spiritual vision to see into the spirit realm? The Bible tells us, "Then the Lord opened the servant's eyes, and he looked and saw the hills full of horses and chariots of fire all around Elisha" (1 Kings 6:17). He saw *the vista of God*—a much larger picture than we are able to see with our naked eyes and our limited scope.

There is clearly a whole lot more to see going on from God's vantage point than what human eyes can see. In his eye-opening, insightful book *Seeing the Unseen,* Joe Beam explores biblically the unsettling revelation of this unseen world.[1] Through a careful con-

---

1 Beam, Joe. *Seeing the Unseen: Preparing Yourself for Spiritual Warfare.* West Monroe, LA: Howard, 2000.

sideration of scriptures, he challenges us to see in our mind's eye some of what God sees in the spiritual realm. In the Elisha story, what the servant saw was the spiritual angelic army of God poised to protect God's servant. Comforting for sure. Angels are said to be ministering spirits sent to help us (Heb. 1:14), and in fact, we may meet up with them and not even be aware of it (Heb. 13:1). But they, as God, care greatly for us and rejoice in our safety and wellbeing (Luke 15:10). God's realm is infinitely larger than this present one.

However, in addition to the angelic army of God, there is also a powerful evil army fighting in the spiritual realms as well. Frank Peretti wrote a series of similarly provocative books. Among others were *This Present Darkness*[2] and *Piercing the Darkness*.[3] These are fictitious stories based on biblical concepts that present descriptive visualizations of the angelic and demonic forces operating in human contexts. The imagery draws from numerous biblical references in bringing to light the evil forces' unsettling reality. Discomforting for sure!

Paul says it this way, "For our struggle is not against flesh and blood, but against the rulers, against the authorities, against the powers of this dark world and against the spiritual forces of evil in the heavenly realms" (Eph. 6:12). The spiritual, heavenly realm is every bit as real as the physical realm, the one that we can see with our earthly eyes. Arguably it is more real, as the physical realm emanates from the spiritual one and not the other way around. Satan is a ruler of the dark world as it intersects this present age, and Paul calls his domain "the kingdom of the air" (Eph. 2:1–2). It is in this same spiritual realm that God gives Christians new life (Eph. 2:6), giving us power and purpose to operate in it. And

---

2 Peretti, Frank. *This Present Darkness*. Wheaton, IL: Crossway Books, 2003.

3 Peretti, Frank. *Piercing the Darkness*. Wheaton, IL: Crossway Books, 2003.

Christ gives us as his servants some measure of authority *over* the evil spirits by the power of his name (Matt. 10:1; Eph. 6:13).

Just as Elisha prayed for his servant's eyes to be opened to the spiritual, Paul prays as well that we will have the eyes of our hearts opened, saying, "I pray also that the eyes of your hearts may be enlightened in order that you may know the hope to which he has called you, the riches of his glorious inheritance in the saints, and his incomparably great power for us who believe" (Eph. 1:18). God wants us to be able to see the blessings that surround us as Christians in this heavenly realm in which we have been raised again to live and operate (Eph. 1:3, 2:6).

When God looks at us in our daily lives, he sees so much more going on in and around us than we have been given the ability to see. Just as a parent sees a child in the much larger context of this world, which the child cannot possibly yet see, God sees us in a much larger context of both the physical and the spiritual realms, a context we are incapable of fully grasping. This inability on our part gives us faith challenges of course, which is why growing our faith in God is so vital. It is as with a small child who must trust his or her parents' awareness and perception, as they see much more than he or she is capable of seeing and understanding.

Things that may seem to be serious issues to God may seem so innocuous and small to us. Teenagers often struggle to understand why their parents make such big deals about avoiding certain activities and such that to the teen seem so normal, okay, and enticing. Teens have not lived long enough to see and understand the bigger picture, even though in their emerging psyches, they usually think themselves to be much more aware than their "fuddy-duddy" parents! Well, it is the same with God and us. We sometimes sadly surmise that we are the ones in the know and that God is somewhere else. We are like the child I mentioned in my first story, standing alone in an alligator pen. We too are often a bit oblivious to the clear and present danger about us and perhaps having "fun" in the curiosity of a moment of such unrecognized peril!

You see, God sees not only our present situations but also where the roads we travel lead. Through his spiritual X-ray vision of our hearts, he has a "satellite view" of our inner paths as well. He has a tracker on each of us. He also sees our pasts from this same "fifty-thousand-feet view" of our world. We only see the present—what we can see from a few hundred feet above the ground. And at times, we can't seem to see beyond our own noses, even though we obviously have been given some ability to project a bit and make predictions about the future of our courses. However, unfortunately, we too often fail to even take advantage of our strategic thinking capability. Thus, we end up failing to think realistically about the real destinations or results of our life choices. We can also remember our pasts, although our memories are often distorted and skewed. And sadly, we often ignore and perhaps even scoff at those who might warn us of the impending challenges, threats, and even doom that might lie ahead on the various courses we might choose. We often seem to throw caution to the wind and crawl over the sometimes too-short life barriers that protect us and enter spiritual alligator pits that seem so interesting and alluring. We frequently seem to simply "not get it." But God always gets it!

God not only see us—heart, mind, body, soul, and spirit—but he also sees what is going on around us in the spiritual realm. He sees the ever-lurking forces of evil—the "alligators" lying near us with hungry mouths wide open. (By the way, in actuality alligators open their mouths while sunning to maintain their body temperatures. Nonetheless, they can still crunch down with the same force!) These ancient beasts are ancient hunting and killing machines with little thought, wired with pure instinct to satisfy their own hunger.

Satan, although not in any way an ignorant beast, is as well an ancient serpent and is also bent on satisfying his own thirst for blood—our blood! He is set on our destruction. Thus, Peter compares Satan to a lion and warns us: "Be self-controlled and alert. Your enemy the devil prowls around like a roaring lion looking for someone to devour" (1 Pet. 5:8). John refers to the devil similarly as, "The great dragon . . . that ancient serpent called the devil, or Satan, who leads the whole world astray" (Rev. 12:9). He is as an alligator lurking nearby with his mouth wide open. Although no specific text tries to thoroughly describe the inner workings of the spiritual realm that God sees, the Bible does reveal plenty about it.

Small children will surely at times get a bit tired of their parents constantly warning about how dangerous certain things are. And teenagers will often even take parents' constant care and warnings as distrust of the teens themselves. The reality is, however, as I've already mentioned, that parents are able to see a much clearer and bigger picture of all that is going on around their children and have a much deeper understanding of the spiritual realities that are unseen by inexperienced youth. The parents may in fact completely trust the child, but are simply being wary of the traps and perils that surround their children who they know to be inexperienced and unaware. A little trust in their parents is in order from those youngsters who are much more limited in their viewpoints. With children, a little faith in the parents will go a long way in self-preservation. And in regard to God, it is always that way! It will always be with us the same as it was with Israel, "If only you had paid attention to my commands, your peace would have been like a river, your well-being like the waves of the sea" (Isa. 48:18). Just as God does, good parents are constantly looking out for the children they love, even when the children can be so oblivious, unaware, and unappreciative.

In the same vein, all of us would also be well advised to listen to our spiritual and church leaders, teachers, and mentors, as well as the spiritual parents and peers we acquire along the way, who may have lived considerably longer than we or who may have more experience and knowledge than we. We need not follow blindly or ignorantly though, as Jesus made clear that we could recognize the bad ones by their fruit (Matt. 7:15–20). Also, "remember your leaders, who spoke the word of God to you. Consider the outcome of their way of life and imitate their faith . . . Have confidence in your leaders and submit to their authority, because they keep watch over you as those who must give an account" (Heb. 13:7, 17). Consider the outcome of their way of life. Talk is cheap. In discerning whom to follow, remember, "Wisdom is proved right by her deeds," as Jesus said (Matt. 11:19). Although different in many ways from the parent-child relationship, spiritual leaders—pastors, elders, ministers, teachers, and so forth—too have seen and heard a lot more than most ever have opportunity to. And contrary to what is often portrayed, the vast majority of spiritual leaders are sincere, spiritual, and loving leaders who have the best interests of their charges in mind and who in no way want to subjugate, control, or spiritually abuse anyone, but only help!

As with the concern of parents and spiritual leaders, it is even much more that way with God. He is always looking out for us, even when we are oblivious and unaware. Perhaps more so when we are oblivious and unaware. And in those moments when we *are* actually aware, and it may seem so bleak for us that we cry out in fear and despair, we need to remember that God has a spiritual army in the heavenly realm that he dispatches to take care of us. It all will work out for our good if we will trust him (Rom. 8:28). God will work everything out to conform to his divine will (Eph. 1:11–12). Those who are for us will always outnumber and have greater firepower than those against us (1 John 4:4). Thus, we must trust and let them protect us.

Too many of us just wander ignorantly onto the evil side however. I heard a preacher once say something to the effect of, "If it's just God and me, we got 'em outnumbered." The reality is that God truly is much more powerful than Satan—no real comparison in fact—and his forces are more numerous as well. His angels are dispatched at his command to help us, as we read, "Are not all angels ministering spirits sent to serve those who will inherit salvation?" (Heb. 1:14). Just as Elisha prayed for his servant's eyes to be opened to see the powerful forces of God, so we too must have our eyes of faith opened to see what God is doing in around us. As Jesus said, "Very truly I tell you, the Son can do nothing by himself; he can do only what he sees his Father doing, because whatever the Father does the Son also does" (John 5:19). We must learn to see what God is doing in and around us and join him, both in our own personal lives and in the lives of those we encounter.

We must also remember that even in those moments when things may seem so safe and serene, the powerful forces of evil are still lurking and waiting for their opportunity. They are set on our destruction. They scheme against us and lay out traps to ensnare us. They will spring these traps when we least expect it. Sometimes they will do it by force even when we have become aware of their efforts, as Paul wrote, "We are not unaware of his [Satan's] schemes" (2 Cor. 2:11, brackets added). We must be ever vigilant and trusting of God and his word and not caught dull or unaware by evil spirits! As Elisha warned the king of Israel about Aram's traps, so God warns us to be attentive to the traps before us. And as Elisha opened the servant's eyes to see God's protective forces, we too need our eyes opened to the innumerable spiritual blessings for us in the heavenly realm! Learn to listen to God because he is looking out for you. Only he can best the evil forces bent on our sad demise!

Pretty much all Americans, at least those who were old enough at the time to be fully aware, remember all too well the fateful day of September 11, 2001. It has simply come to be known as 9/11 in the United States. It was a day that changed much about how our whole country and world operate. That day, terrorists carried out a concerted and well-laid-out attack on our country. Vivid memories play out often in all our minds, as well as in the replays of the actual videos on anniversary newscasts, of passenger planes flying into the sides of two of the world's most well-known buildings—the twin towers of the World Trade Center. They were veritable symbols of America and its free enterprise system. Back in 1980, my wife and I had dinner in a restaurant on the 114th floor of one of those buildings! So seeing them fall on television was simply surreal and seemed more a Hollywood film trick than a terroristic act.

Nineteen terrorists from Al-Qaeda, an Islamic terrorist group, hijacked four passenger planes that evil morning. Two were crashed into the twin towers of the World Trade Center in New York City. Another was crashed into the Pentagon. The fourth ultimately crashed in a field in Pennsylvania when, it is believed, brave passengers attempted to take control from the terrorists before it could apparently be crashed into the Capitol or the White House. It was the worst attack ever carried out on American soil from outside the country. Nearly three thousand people died. Incredible damage was done, not only to lives and property but also to the collective psyche of our country and most of the world. It was unforgettable. Fateful. Frightful. Unbelievable! It was an "evil day" (Eph. 6:13). And evil days are ultimately generated in the spiritual realm. The destruction was seen here; however, the real plans were laid out in the spiritual realm by the principalities and powers that operate there! The people who perpetrated it were merely their pawns. They were "played."

However, it started out as a normal early twenty-first-century day, when schools and colleges around the country were in start-up mode. Football teams practiced, bands marched, citizens worked, and grassroots Americans prepared for one of their favorite times and seasons. It was autumn, and the air was finally cooling again as the fall fun and festivities heated up. The signs were in the air. I was waiting to start a ministry staff meeting, listening to what had happened as staff members filed in stunned, giving accounts of what they had seen on television and heard on the radio. It was bizarre and unthinkable. It would be a several hours before I could be in a position to watch any of the reports on television. But watch I did. As a country and world, we were collectively in shock for weeks and months, trying to get our minds wrapped around what had really happened. And how our world had been completely altered.

But the "day of evil" had come upon us. Satan had had his way for the day. Obviously, the trap was being set years before it was ready. Paul warned us to prepare for evil days. They ultimately will come in all of our lives, individually sometimes, collectively others. Paul said, "Finally, be strong in the Lord and in his mighty power. Put on the full armor of God so that you can take your stand against the devil's schemes . . . put on the full armor of God, so that when *the day of evil* comes, you may be able to stand your ground . . ." (Eph. 6:10, 11, 13). A day of evil came so unexpectedly and astoundingly on our country. It was a devastating day we were quite unprepared for, even though national intelligence agencies knew well that Al Qaeda and other terrorist organizations were bent on such an attack! In the same way, days of evil will come on each of us. Traps will be sprung and surprises will come. We can all be assured of it. We *have been* assured of it. In a short parable concerning two houses, Jesus expressed our need for a strong foundation against what was to come. One house was built on shifting sand; the other on bedrock. He pointed out that storms would come upon each house, saying, "The rain came down, the streams rose, and the winds blew and beat against that house . . ." (Matt. 7:25, 27). He warned us all that really bad storms would come. He did not say *if* the storm comes; he said *when* it came. As Jesus illustrated, the storm—the evil day—came upon each structure. One crashed. The other remained standing. Each house represents one of two potential fates for each of us. The wise person builds their house upon the rock!

Jesus is the bedrock on which we are to build our houses—our lives. He is to be our bedrock. We must build on him, not on sands of the times of this present world, so that when the evil day comes we will remain standing. We should not be surprised when an evil day comes, as though something unexpected is happening (1 Pet. 4:12).

We thus should listen well to God before those days come. Ancient Israel should be a constant reminder to us. We have the historical records of the Old Testament to remind us that when they listened to and obeyed God, things went well with them—victories were won and the nation lived well. On the other hand, when they failed to listen and obey, defeats mounted and suffering ensued. In one of the sadder writings by God's prophet, Isaiah, God laments Israel's undoing, saying, "This is what the LORD says—your Redeemer, the Holy One of Israel: 'I am the LORD your God, who teaches you what is best for you, who directs you in the way you should go. If only you had paid attention to my commands, your peace would have been like a river, your righteousness like the waves of the sea. Your descendants would have been like the sand, your children like its numberless grains; their name would never be cut off nor destroyed from before me'" (Isa. 48:17–19).

So we need to listen carefully to God. We are indeed standing in the middle of a spiritual alligator pit. We are not actually alone; however, we face great danger. We must not try to do it on our own. Apart from God, we are merely naïve bait for the ancient serpent, Satan. We must look and listen to God because he alone sees the entire picture. Only he can protect us. He is the ultimate "gator-fighter," and he commands the heavenly army! If only we will listen to his commands, our peace will be like a river. We will be safe, and we will be forever saved.

Although we rarely anticipate it ahead of time, the evil day is coming. We must make sure we have on God's full armor so that we will not be caught off guard and suffer devastating defeat at the hands of the forces of evil—the forces that only God can actually see at the moment, the forces that only God can defeat.

We need to trust him because God sees us, and the world around us, most clearly and completely! It is his vista, his creation, and his battleground!

Questions for Reflection and Discussion

1. How should a constant awareness of the spiritual world around us, and especially the evil army lurking there, change the way we live out our lives on a daily basis?
2. What kinds of traps can you think of in your own life, or in the lives of those you know, that God has clearly warned us about but that we still careless step into?
3. Why do we, as humans, find believing in an ever-present spiritual realm difficult?
4. What part of God's spiritual armor, described in Ephesians 6:13–17, might you not have on or might not have on well?
5. Describe our vulnerabilities when any part of the armor is not in place for us?

CHAPTER 7

THE EYES OF THE LORD

An Intelligence is behind our universe,
Ever-watching and completely all-knowing,
Not flesh and blood such as we are,
His nature not yet fully showing.

But he sees all; all can surely sense it.
There's a "knowing" in us that He is,
He's not contrived by our imagination,
But we were derived by His.

We know not now all about how He sees us,
We know not now how it is He feels,
We know not how as Spirit He senses,
His full nature he still conceals.

One of the more baffling challenges for a deep-thinking child of God is trying to grasp any real sense of how God actually "sees." We are pretty stuck in our present physical world experiences, and perceiving things is defined by how our own physical bodies perceive them. Our vision is probably generally the most important of our senses. And no doubt, our ability to see physically in some way reflects God's ability to see spiritually. If we are to be better able to see God seeing us, we probably should develop some idea of how God actually sees in the first place.

The Bible speaks regularly of "the eyes of the Lord." So how do we define vision in a spiritual world? Likely there is no way we can at present understand what the eyes of the Lord "look" like or much about how they work. But on the other hand, I do believe we need to at least reconcile what we can glean from nature and scripture to what is revealed about God's vision. To God, "seeing" refers to his way of perceiving and knowing. We of course generally use "see" to refer to our actual vision. But we also speak about it similarly to God in a broader sense as well, as if to say someone "sees" the problem, meaning to perceive or understand it. Although our vision emanates from God's, his sense of vision may have little to do with our own vision, which depends on the physics of light and our own human physiology. Or maybe it does. We are made in the image of God, and while we often think of this as in spirit only, there is an argument to be made that our physical nature is possibly, in some way, also in God's image as well. While God's nature and existence are certainly impossible to interpret and understand from our present vantage point, we can indeed still understand him to the extent necessary.

Suffice it to say, seemingly countless books on theology have been written about God's being and nature, speculating and drawing conclusions from all sorts of biblical texts, as well as from orthodoxy, tradition, human logic, and elsewhere. Many of the views presented can to me seem grossly simplistic, considering God's magnificent nature. Still others seem painfully overanalyzed, highly speculative, narrow-minded, or just plain confusing. In reality, the best we can probably do is to simply have an image of him that reconciles to most of the biblical texts, as well as to the creation itself, without doing severe injustice at any point. We need to try to do this while also maintaining a sense of awe and worship of his all-surpassing presence, knowledge, and power. Too much speculating can, in fact, lead us to some pretty dangerous places faith-wise, I believe. Of course, ultimately, we see God best and mostly through Jesus himself, who lived for a while in our form (Heb. 1:3; John 14:9)! We can behold Christ in our mental imagery from the descriptions of the first-century witnesses who beheld him literally (John 1:14).

Beware, however, of those who want you to think they have God all "figured out." Be careful of those who would have you believe they have all the "right" answers to everything dealing with God. In my way of thinking, arrogance and closed-mindedness are sure signs someone does *not* have much figured out about God at all! Humble confidence, on the other hand, bespeaks of one who has studied and thought out faith, remains in an open-minded growth mode, and is not threatened by the chance of being shown to be wrong or of being able to learn something new.

With all that said, what are "the eyes of the Lord"? There are lots of scriptures that mention God's eyes. Arguably, most can easily be interpreted to mean "from God's perspective." To have a perspective though, God must perceive or see in a particular way or multiple ways. One of the first references to God's eyes and his seeing simply says, "Noah found favor in the eyes of the Lord" (Gen. 6:8). The eyes of the Lord, huh? Another instance, and an important lesson for all of us concerning the eyes of the Lord, is found in a story in an Old Testament story (2 Chron. 15 and 16). Asa was a king of Judah, who generally tried to do what was right. In fact, the scripture says, "Asa's heart was fully committed to the Lord all his life" (2 Chron. 15:17). This however did not keep him from making mistakes, even serious ones. During his reign, Baasha, king of Israel, threatened Judah (Israel was the northern half of the divided Jewish nation and Judah was the southern half). Instead of turning to God, Asa made an alliance with the foreign king of Aram for help. God was definitely not happy with his reliance on a foreign king rather than turning to God himself, and God sent the prophet Hanani to deliver a message to admonish Asa. Hanani's rebuke concludes with, "For the eyes of the Lord range throughout the earth to strengthen those whose hearts are fully committed to him" (2 Chron. 16:9).

God has his eyes open, looking for individuals with hearts ablaze for him. As previously described, God looks at and identifies us mainly by our hearts. In fact, as the prophet said, God's eyes range the whole earth, looking into the hearts and at the lives of those committed to him. Much like he had done when Noah found favor in the Lord's eyes.

Jesus once told a Samaritan woman he spoke with that God was actually seeking "true worshipers" who would worship him sincerely and honestly, in spirit and truth (John 4:23–24). God is watching us, and he is seeking to strengthen those whose hearts are truly devoted to him in worship and awe. God devotes himself to those who are most devoted to him—"Anyone who loves me will obey my teaching. My Father will love them, and we will come to them and make our home with them" (John 14:23). Jesus promised, "Blessed are the pure in heart, for they will see God" (Matt. 5:8).

Further, in the New Testament, in the book of Hebrews, it is written, "Nothing in all creation is hidden from God's sight. Everything is uncovered and laid bare before the eyes of him to whom we must give account" (Heb. 4:13). God's eyes see all, from the inside out. Omniscience. Peter says, "The eyes of the Lord are on the righteous and his ears are attentive to their prayer, but the face of the Lord is against those who do evil" (1 Pet. 3:12). So God is attentive to those he deems as "righteous," but he closes his eyes to, and turns his head away from, what "grosses him out," so to speak, in those who live evil lives. Isaiah said the problem was not that God was weak or limited, but simply the way God, in his own nature, responds to bad hearts. He says, "Surely the arm of the Lord is not too short to save, nor his ear too dull to hear. But your iniquities have separated you from your God; your sins have hidden his face from you, so that he will not hear" (Isa. 59:1–2). God's arms are not too short to "reach" us nor are his ears too dull to "hear" us. God will reach out to us when we reach out to him in humility, ready to be done with sin—"For you have spent enough time in the past doing what pagans choose to do—living in debauchery, lust, drunkenness, orgies, carousing and detestable idolatry" (1 Pet. 4:3).

How are we then to think about Isaiah's references to God's *arms, hands, ears, eyes,* and so forth? Such attributes are noted both in the Old and New Testaments. Are these just examples of anthropomorphism (attributing human characteristics to nonhuman things or beings)? Or are our human faculties, such as our eyes, in some way in the image of God too?

Many scholars consider these expressions to be purely metaphorical. Others take them much more literally. A smaller group interprets them literally. But however we may interpret and visualize these attributes of him, God wants us to know that he has a presence in this world and a way to "see," "hear," and "face us" (or not face us). Through his faculties, he "reaches" out to us. Moses boldly asked God to let him see him! Here was the response from God: "And the Lord said, 'I will cause all my goodness to pass in front of you, and I will proclaim my name, the LORD, in your presence. I will have mercy on whom I will have mercy, and I will have compassion on whom I will have compassion.' 'But,' he said, 'you cannot see my face, for no one may see me and live.' Then the Lord said, 'There is a place near me where you may stand on a rock. When my glory passes by, I will put you in a cleft in the rock and cover you with my hand until I have passed by. Then I will remove my hand and you will see my back; but my face must not be seen'" (Exod. 33:19–23). Hmm. Moses got to see God's presence, but just not his face.

This is an amazing and bewildering account. God had a physical presence that he manifested to Moses, albeit only his back. Moses was to stand in a place that was "near God." What does that even mean with an omnipresent God? But whatever the case, Moses got to see God in some way! God has a presence that can be manifested in our world.

And it is this God who is always seeing us. It reminds me of being a parent. My wife's and my eyes have always been and still are constantly on our four children. When they were very young, one of our sets of eyes were pretty much and literally always on them, in that we wanted to be watching and looking out for them constantly. And if we couldn't at that time be watching, we made sure some dependable adult's eyes were on them. It seems that when kids are in their twos they are bent on their own destruction as well as the destruction of many other things and even other people. As parents, we, of course, are bent on defeating them in their quest, lest we live with lifelong guilt! I'm only kidding, but even now that our kids are adults, our eyes are still on them, although in a much more general and metaphorical way.

One of my favorite kid stories is one my wife relates. Our lone daughter is the youngest. When she was still quite young, my wife was with our daughter and our youngest son at the grocery store. At some point, our little tomboy daughter punched her older brother in the stomach for some unknown reason. It obviously did not feel good, and when he complained about it, my wife asked her what in the world she was doing. She simply pleaded ignorance, saying, "I didn't recognize him." She pled not guilty by reason of lack of recognition." Might just work in our present-day court system, but it did not with their mom that day! But I digress. It is a funny story, and I think it perhaps illustrates that while we as parents have our eyes on the kids, they certainly do not always keep their eyes on us. Or on their siblings. I wonder if she would have still punched him if she *had* recognized him? When was the last time you punched another of God's children in the stomach, so to speak, because you did not "recognize" them as such? Or failed to recognize God as God?

When I attended my kids' events and activities, I would certainly watch the other children some, but my eyes were mostly on my own children. I have no doubt it was the same way with the other parents and their own children. After games and activities, I would often go up, hug them, and whisper in their ears, "You're the only one I came to watch." I wanted them to know that there was one set of eyes that was squarely on them and that their every move was most important to me. I was and am always their number-one fan, along with their mom, of course! As I said, there was, and still is, a constant awareness in us of our own children, watching to celebrate their successes, to console their failures, and rescue them lest they be injured or threatened. We definitely have their backs!

Well, it is that way with our Heavenly Father with us. He is always looking out for us. He sees us in some way constantly—"he is not far from any one of us" (Acts 17:27). Somehow each of us is the one he watches. He celebrates our successes, such as when we turn away from sin—"I tell you that in the same way there will be more rejoicing in heaven over one sinner who repents . . ." (Luke 15:7). He is a fan of each of us. When *only* one person out of the 7.2 billion people on earth repents, he sees it and makes a big deal out of it! God also comes to rescue us when our hearts are broken—"The Lord is close to the brokenhearted and saves those who are crushed in spirit" (Ps. 34:18). And "He heals the brokenhearted and binds up their wounds" (Ps. 147:3). By whatever means he sees us, rest assured that he sees us. He is serious about looking out for us. Our very salvation is dependent on our faith in this, and our refusal to trust and depend on him will lead to our being separated from him. Why then do we still keep running from him in our sin, shame, and failure—hiding in the bushes behind our fig leaves, as Adam and Eve did?

So with all that said, what is to be made of God's "eyes"? How are we to think of them? I would like to consider a few more ideas before addressing it further. The Bible affirms that God is indeed an omniscient God. *Omniscience* and also *omnipotence* and *omnipresence* are words used mostly by theologians to describe God's awesome nature. As I have mentioned already, they mean all-knowing, all-powerful, and ever-present, respectively. However, the use of such words, I believe, can create some unhelpful views of God, much as I discussed earlier as when our church would sing about the "all-seeing eye watching you." S-c-a-r-y. While as a minister and pastor, I must affirm that I firmly believe in God's all-surpassing, divine nature, I must also argue against what I believe are views that present unnecessary and perhaps even questionable views of him that can constrain our relationship with him and prevent us from seeing him as he is. We can create such intellectual and even "plastic" views of God that we completely depersonalize him into a sort of universal ether, devoid of life and personality!

While God is all-powerful, he has definition and a nature. There are even things that he cannot do. For instance, he cannot lie (Heb. 5:18), nor can he sin or tempt others to sin (James 1:13). Also, while God is present throughout the universe, he has a very real presence at specific places and at specific times, such as in the story above of Moses who was allowed to stand at a certain place "near" God and then see him from the back side. Adam and Eve apparently had direct encounters with God. Genesis records that, as Adam and Eve hid from God in their shame and embarrassment after their original sin, they "heard the sound of God as he was walking in the garden in the cool of the day . . ." (Gen. 3:8). Think about the visual that is being presented that God was walking at a certain time of the day? Hmm. God "saw" Israel's suffering in Egypt and was "coming down" to rescue them. God said, "I have indeed seen the misery of my people in Egypt. I have heard them crying out because of their slave drivers, and I am concerned about their suffering. So I have come down to rescue them" (Exod. 3:7–8). Interesting, huh?

So an omniscient, omnipresent God "sees" his people's suffering from somewhere else and then "comes down" to rescue them. In some sense, God knows everything; in another sense, he apparently, at times, becomes more aware or cognizant of some things, and in still other things, he seems to choose not to hear or know. Somehow he "moves" closer to and farther from us at various times. The question is: Is the Bible just communicating the infinite God into our finite, present-day terminology and experience or is there an experiential reality for him in these words? If it is not the latter, it seems a bit misleading to me. Either way, because I trust God, I know there is indeed a plausible explanation.

In some way, God is communicated as ever-present, but in another way, he is described as bringing a special presence of himself to specific times and places. Further, in other situations, he seems to choose to absent himself. Isaiah admonished Israel to "seek the Lord while he may be found; call on him while he is near" (Isa. 55:6). So God is apparently "nearer" at certain times, and there are also more opportune as well as inopportune times to find him. It is so easy to develop a view that God is far away and removed or, on the other hand, to so personalize him that we trivialize him as if he were our personal lapdog trailing us around no matter how we behave toward him. Or worse, "God is my copilot!" Oh my! Do not even get me started on that. Neither extreme, I believe, is fair or accurate. As mentioned previously, Paul said to the polytheistic Athenians, in affirming the observation of one of their own poets, "[God] is not far from each one of us. For in him we live and move and have our being" (Acts 17:27–28). So he is never far away, but he is not always so "near" either.

There are many other such passages from which we can draw inferences, but all these suggest that while God is omnipresent, he does in some here and now present way have an image and a defined nature, and he does manifest himself in our world at specific places and times. It is simply unreasonable for us to expect to clearly understand all of this, given our own time and place limitations—our finiteness. We do not know how an infinite God sees, hears, knows, feels, and retains knowledge. He is however not simply ethereal. Nor is he human or a humanly concocted notion. Humanity has believed in God from our beginning. Because God is our beginning!

Suffice it to say, "God is spirit" (John 4:24). After Jesus's physical body was resurrected, he took on some immortal but still visible and touchable form, and he was taken up into heaven before eyewitnesses who died for testifying to what they saw! They simply could not renounce what they had witnessed and knew to be the truth, even in the face of torture and death. What had previously been unbelievable had become to them quite believable.

To understand the eyes of God though, we must understand there are moral and spiritual laws, truths of existence, and certain realities of the dimensions God exists in outside of our own, just as there are certain laws that govern our three dimensions of space—length, width, and depth—plus the fourth dimension of time. However, even modern physicists are not satisfied that there are in fact only these dimensions. To reconcile what is presently understood with those things that are not understood, leading scientists have proposed a "string theory" that suggests there are nine or ten spatial dimensions plus the time dimension. To even begin a discussion of this topic would do it an injustice; thus, I only mention it briefly for our purposes here. It is in fact from out of one of these other dimensions that some modern physicists believe gravity emanates. Many of us assume that these other dimensions are simply the "heavenlies" or spiritual realms.

Let me make it clear that even though I did study science in college and have at least more than an average knowledge of the subject, I not only do not claim to be an expert on this subject I also not even purport to understand much of this. But I do love science and follow it from a reasonable distance. However, I think most have come intuitively and experientially to believe that what we see in the world around is not always what we get, so to speak. In a 2014 Pew Research Center survey of 35,000 Americans adults eighteen and older, only 3.1 percent and 4.0 percent of respondents reported themselves to be atheists and agnostics, respectively. Meaning *some 93 percent of American adults believe in divine and the spiritual.*

In the atomic and subatomic world, there is just a whole lot going on that we cannot see and still do not clearly understand. However, we all experience it daily, living it out in our own personal atomic, molecular, and cellular structures—our bodies. Dark matter? Anti-matter? The Higgs Boson—the "God particle?" Ours is an incredibly complicated and intricate universe! But through our experience, and by the scientific process and our ongoing research, we believe in things we cannot see.

It is by the same kind of scientific, evidential "faith" that we have in the unseen physical world that we believe in the unseen spiritual world of God. The Bible in fact says, "Now faith is assurance of things hoped for, a conviction of things not seen" (Heb. 11:1, American Standard Version). *Assurance. Conviction.* These are reality words, not merely "want to believe" words. True biblical faith is not at all blind faith but rather is based on observation, evidence, experience, and reason. Just like the science of the unseen physical world. Just as gravity seemingly emanates from unseen and unseen dimensions, so it is with the dimensions of God. I believe there are indeed these other dimensions—dimensions in which God exists and functions—that interact with our own. Through these, God experiences us in ways that we do not fully experience him. Our human faculties comprehend length, width, depth, and time, and we are often blown away in our perceptions of them. This is especially true as we work to understand and interpret our world. Also, our minds and spirits can sense beyond the physical realm to at least some degree, hence, the presence of human faith from our beginnings. God can do so much more than we can imagine (Eph. 3:20).

For instance, God, when we come to have faith in him, gives us a much greater ability to see and perceive the spiritual. Jesus said unless one was born again he would not "see"—perceive—the kingdom of heaven (John 3:3). He said this would be a spiritual rebirth (John 3:5). Concerning this rebirth, Paul said that by it God "seated us with him [God] in the 'heavenly' realms" (Eph. 2:6, brackets added). Also, it should be noted that Paul speaks of these realms in the plural, not just a singular "heavenly" realm but the heavenly realms, or heavenlies (plural), according to some translations. Whatever word or expression is used, Paul is speaking of other dimensions—additional dimensions, perhaps the ones science suggests, and further maybe dimensions in which only God and the spirits can exist and operate. These constitute a realm outside of our own physical, visible existence that we can sense only by scientific inferences as well as the work of the Holy Spirit in believers.

Likely, physical science cannot really probe many of these realms or dimensions because of physical science's inherent limitations to the here and now material world. Paul says that when we are given the Spirit we are able to intuitively or spiritually probe this unseen realm. "No eye has seen, no ear has heard, no mind has conceived what God has prepared for those who love him—but *God has revealed it to us by his Spirit*" (1 Cor. 2:9–10, italics added). Paul asserts that it is God's Holy Spirit that brings a harmonious interaction between God, in his infinite nature, and us, in our finite one—intellectually and experientially. He goes on to explain that without the Spirit in us the realities of the God-realm will seem foolish (1 Cor. 2:10–14). He said that the Christian belief in the Cross of Christ for our redemption was also foolish to those who do not believe it (1 Cor. 1:18–25). Well, of course, it seems foolish. It is through his Spirit that God gives believers spiritual life and thus a vision of and an experience in the spiritual dimensions, be they the other ones science suggests as existing or perhaps ones science is unaware of.

I believe that it is in these dimensions that God sees and experiences us in our present world, using his perceptual faculties we cannot comprehend. These places are where his dimensions or realms intersect ours. These dimensions allow him to be present everywhere and at all times, as well as to be specifically present at a particular time and in a specific place. I believe it is in these dimensions that truth and spirit abide. As gravity influences our present dimensions, and yet science cannot fully explain it, we are indeed influenced by these other dimensions from outside our four dimensions. Although we cannot fully experience them, we can however sense them. We simply cannot explain them.

There are existent things outside our direct experience that are inexpressible in our context (Cor. 12:1–4), likely I believe because we do not have any words or constructs by which to understand or comprehend them, let alone express them. It is through the Spirit of God that we can know (experience) what we cannot know intellectually. For instance, concerning the love of God, Paul uses a dimensional model to express this, writing, "I pray that out of his glorious riches he may strengthen you with power through his Spirit in your inner being, so that Christ may dwell in your hearts through faith. And I pray that you, being rooted and established in love, may have power, together with all the saints, to grasp how wide and long and high and deep is the love of Christ, and *to know this love that surpasses knowledge*—that you may be filled to the measure of all the fullness of God" (Eph. 3:16–19, italics added).

Note his use of our dimensions—width, length, height, and depth—to pray for our knowledge and perception of the love of Christ. But notice further how he prays that we would be able to actually "know" (experience) this love that in fact surpasses, or is beyond, our knowledge (human intellect). This is why Paul prays that God's Spirit would strengthen us in our inner beings so that through our faith in him we could reach out and experience the real and powerful force—God himself—coming from another dimension or other dimensions (realms), dimensions in which God and the spirit realm function.

We have been given the ability to experience what physical science cannot explain. To understand the spiritual realm, one must rely on the "spiritual sciences" instead of only the physical sciences. Our spirituality helps explains our ability to existentially experience art and music and awe—the spiritual realm. This explains our ability to know beyond intellect and to exist beyond ourselves. Modern existentialism teaches that existence determines essence. That is to say that we exist, and through our consciousness of it, we determine our identity and purpose. I believe it is clearly the other way around—our essence defines our existence. And our essence emanates directly from the Creator God in the spiritual realms.

It is thus in this spiritual vein that we begin to "see" beyond our present dimensions, while still only dimly and partially. God however sees keenly and completely (omniscience)—"Now we see but a poor reflection as in a mirror; then we shall see face to face. Now I know in part; then I shall know fully, even as I am fully known" (1 Cor. 13:12). As previously mentioned, it was in this other realm (or these other realms) that Paul was given the experience of things that were inexpressible in the here and now (2 Cor. 12:1–4). We simply do not have the words, nor can we grasp the concepts. I think this is why when the Bible speaks of what is going on in heaven it often seems strange to the point of being just bizarre. For just one example, read the first chapter of Ezekiel.

Still, as already noted multiple times, our present restricted domain is a reflection of the infinite domain of God—"For since the creation of the world God's invisible qualities—his eternal power and divine nature—have been clearly seen, being understood from what has been made, so that men are without excuse" (Rom. 1:20). God's nature, the unseen, is seen through the created—that which we are able to see. Yet through faith it is the unseen that we are to focus our eyes on—"So we fix our eyes not on what is seen, but on what is unseen, since what is seen is temporary, but what is unseen is eternal" (2 Cor. 4:18). What we see now is what is created and temporary. What is eternal is yet unseen with our physical eyes. Even the temple in Jerusalem was said to be merely a physical expression of what is in the heavenly realm. Speaking of the service of Israel's priests in their temple, it is said, "They serve at a sanctuary that is a copy and shadow of what is in heaven" (Heb. 8:5). What is unseen is best understood for now from what can be seen even though much remains unexplainable, and likely will remain so until the next age.

I believe it is foolish for science to set itself up in such a way as the all-powerful tool for understanding all, as some try do, when it is by its very definition limited to what it can measure. The modern seeming "religion" of science—I call "scientism"—is, I believe, often acting foolhardily and arrogantly, as religion is admittedly often so prone to do as well. Science is incapable of explaining or experiencing the dimensions of God, because science is limited to using tools that exist only in our four dimensions! Would it be able to extrapolate and suggest there are things outside of this natural world? I suppose so. Deny it or probe it? I don't think so.

Robert Jastrow, a well-respected scientist with a PhD from Columbia University, once said in an interview: "Astronomers now find they have painted themselves into a corner because they have proven, by their own methods, that the world began abruptly in an act of creation to which you can trace the seeds of every star, every planet, every living thing in this cosmos and on the earth. And they have found that all this happened as a product of forces they cannot hope to discover. *That there are what I or anyone would call supernatural forces at work is now, I think, a scientifically proven fact"* ("A Scientist Caught Between Two Faiths: Interview With Robert Jastrow," *Christianity Today*, August 6, 1982, italics added).

A scientifically proven fact, huh? A respected scientist said it. And he is certainly not alone among many other scientists who conclude similarly. Sadly in the often emotional, closed-minded world of science, any who believe in intelligent design and the divine are considered scientific heretics and thus castigated, disrespected, and marginalized. In my experience, I believe many atheists and agnostics disbelieve not because of intellect but because of emotion. But it is a well-documented fact that many scientists honestly disagree with the Christian position on the world, and that is their prerogative. I personally have great respect for science and good, fair-minded scientists. There are scientists, highly respected in the scientific community, who believe that science leads us to a belief in God and others that believe that it clearly does not. When science attempts to speak to the nonmaterial or nonphysical, it operates outside its arena of expertise—the physical sciences— and becomes a religion—a faith, and in my opinion a terrible one at that. It is clearly driven by modern humanism. However in my opinion, a lack of faith is by definition an expression of faith and therefore an acknowledgment of it.

Just as science cannot as yet explain such forces as gravity, properly using our own dimensions, and thus need to suggest the existence of others, we also cannot properly explain the spiritual—the things of God—using only our present dimensions. Both involve beliefs—hypotheses—that, while concerning what is not seen, are drawn from what is seen and experienced. This is far from blind faith or wishful thinking that scientists, philosophers, and especially humanists often like to accuse believers of possessing. This is far from fantasy. The edges of science are always probing the speculative in order to determine what should be considered and researched. Speculation is the seed of discovery. And hypotheses and theories are the substance of its faith—the faith of materialists who believe only in the physical, thus denying the existence of the spiritual.

So how does God see? I believe that our eyes are indeed a copy and shadow of God's eyes, and they give us insight into his qualities that are as yet invisible to us. Unlimited by the physical, the scope of his vision is absolute—he sees all. His is the omniscience of the ultimate supernatural. Supra natural really. He is himself the designer and the pattern for everything that is. And as we experience with our own eyes what we have the capacity to experience in our present dimensions, God, in his omniscience, experiences with his eyes (his infinite experience) something much more profound and absolute. Through dimensions (realms) that we cannot in this present time probe, God experiences and interacts with the world, as we presently know it.

When we project outside our present seemingly fixed dimensions, we discover the relativity of time and space and the equivalency of matter and energy. We see the "unknown." Just because something is unknown to us does not mean it is unknowable, or even unknown to everyone else. Again, in Paul's description of his own experience, he said that in the realm of God he "heard" things that were, in his own words, *inexpressible*, meaning most likely, I believe, not that it was unlawful for him to tell about, but they were too unique and sublime to describe. He also wrote that in our continued growth and progression into the next age that we presently see the spiritual realities only dimly; however, eventually we will see it all quite clearly (1 Cor. 13:12). But for the time being, in Christ we have been given a supernatural "knowing" from the Spirit. It is a taste of God's own omniscience, a taste of the divine. It is a knowing that comes from the spiritual, not from the physical.

It is indeed seeing (although still dimly) as God sees (clearly). It is hearing, if only to a very small extent, as God hears. It is feeling, if only to a very small extent, as God feels.

The word for the "life" that God gives us when we are born again is the Greek word *zoe*. It means spiritual life—life as God experiences it. It is the life in us that died and was lost immediately at humanity's fall into sin, and it is the life that is restored through the redemptive work of Christ through his death on the cross. It is the life that grows in us as we grow in Christ. It is the life that we are given in the heavenly realms. In a previously mentioned text, Paul explains this, saying, "But because of his great love for us, God, who is rich in mercy, made us alive with Christ even when we were dead in transgressions—it is by grace you have been saved. And God raised us up with Christ and seated us with him in the heavenly realms in Christ Jesus, in order that in the coming ages he might show the incomparable riches of his grace, expressed in his kindness to us in Christ Jesus" (Eph. 2:4–7).

In our rebirth, God "made us alive with Christ." In Christ, we are "seated" in the heavenly or spiritual realms. We are given life in the spiritual realm. And through it, we are given the ability to experience beyond these present dimensions. Hence, concerning such dimensions as God's, we can then "know this love that surpasses knowledge" (Eph. 3:19). This is a knowing that means to experience it. It is not first physical and intellectual; it is of the spiritual and from outside these present dimensions. The Spirit reveals things to us, which no human eyes have seen, no human ears have heard, and no human mind has conceived (1 Cor. 2:9–10). From the Holy Spirit, we are given an ability to know beyond what can be learned intellectually, because we receive knowledge from outside of this present realm (1 John 2:20, 27).

We are given a taste of seeing as God sees. Not merely with the eyes of the mortal, but with eyes of the immortal. Not with finite eyes, but with infinite ones. Not with limited vision, but with vision unlimited. We come to experience life as God experiences it.

So rest assured, the eyes of the Lord are watching. He is experiencing us in ways we are incapable of fully experiencing him. However, we experience him in the spiritual realms by his Spirit when we are born again, and we can hone this ability as we grow. And he gives us his Spirit to guarantee what we are to experience with him in the age to come—"Having believed, you were marked in him with a seal, the promised Holy Spirit, who is a deposit guaranteeing our inheritance until the redemption of those who are God's possession—to the praise of his glory" (Eph. 1:13–14).

God works and functions in other dimensions to draw near to you, to draw you near to him, to love you, to teach you, to renew you, to transform and grow you, to empower you, to rescue you, and to console you. He invites us, and he promises, "Come near to God and he will come near to you" (James 4:8)!

God has revealed himself to us through the ages first through creation and then through the scriptures he inspired to be written down to help us know and understand his purposes and work in and through his creation. This is our God who is more beautiful than we can imagine, more creative than we can grasp, more intelligent than we could ever comprehend, more powerful than can be measured, and more graceful than we could ever dream. He is the ultimate engineer. He is the ultimate architect. He is the ultimate designer and inventor. He is the ultimate decorator. He is the ultimate artist. He is the ultimate pattern for us as image-bearing males—he apparently loves fires and explosions and power and battles of strength, as well as being smart, kind, and protecting. He is the ultimate of image-bearing females—loving beauty and sensitivity and kindness and wit and ingenuity, as well as being lovely and intelligent. Please pardon my gender stereotyping, as I know the overlaps are extensive, but I hope you get my point. He made male and female together in his image, and only together do we fully bear his image.

The eyes of the Lord are watching us all. From places and in ways we have yet to understand. His world intersects our world at various times and in various ways and places still unknown to us. God's eyes are most loving eyes. We are invited through faith to begin our relationship journey with him here. The Bible tells us this journey ends in a very, very special place! We shall then see clearly, even as we are now clearly seen.

That is very good news.

Questions and Thoughts for Reflection and Discussion

1. How have you previously thought of what the eyes of the Lord might imply?
2. Why do you suppose some think these expressions to be simply manners of speech and not descriptions of anything the Lord actually does?
3. How does it or will it affect you if you believe and have a constant awareness of God actually watching us?
4. How do you think it can be that we can know (experience) something we cannot know (intellectualize)?
5. What are the implications to each of us of knowing and believing that God sees everything, inside and outside, hidden and unhidden, seen and unseen—that nothing in all creation is hidden from his sight?

CHAPTER 8

PONDERING GOD'S FEELINGS

Most times I know what I'm feeling,
Other times I don't have a clue,
But for sure I can't see in another's heart;
It's just something one can't do.

I don't understand feelings anyway.
They often make little sense to me.
We just somehow feel as God feels,
The way he made us to be.

But feelings are made known by actions,
Behaviors come from the heart,
Knowing others and God is part science,
And the rest of it is pure art.

And to truly know one better,
You best know how they feel,
Otherwise you'll miss them completely,
And with them you'll have no good deal.

I am a pretty melancholic guy, and after serving in the ministry for over forty years, I think that I am pretty much "in touch with my feelings," as we sometimes like to put it. In fact, I have written a book about emotions, or at least one kind of emotion called, "Fighting and Beating Depression: My Practical Thoughts and Spiritual Journey." However, even though I have a lot of experience in the area of human emotions and behavior, I regularly face the reality that I often do not understand my emotions all that well. In fact, I believe all of us can relate to this, just as the apostle Paul must have when he said concerning his inability to do what is right instead of wrong, "I do not understand what I do" (Rom. 7:15).

To understand someone at the deepest levels, we have to understand not just their outward identity and what they *think* about things; we have to get to know how they *feel* about things. It is the heart that controls our behaviors (Luke 6:45; Prov. 4:23). So in the same way, if we want to know God better—to see him seeing us, we must understand his feelings better. And not only that, we must understand our own feelings better.

I remember a popular line a lot of people used back in the 1970s in joking about their various "misbehaviors." It was a catch phrase from a popular television comedian, Flip Wilson, who was the lead actor in his own show, *The Flip Wilson Show*, that ran on NBC from 1970 to 1974. The catch phrase, which I believe came from one of his stage characters, Geraldine Jones, was simply, "The devil made me do it!" A dangerous thing to joke about, however, sometimes it seems to be the best explanation for our otherwise inexplicable undesirable feelings and behaviors!

Not only do I often not understand my own feelings very well, after all these years, I also do not understand my wife's feelings very well, as I am sure she would attest. And quite frankly, she does not understand mine very well either. The reality is that to understand someone a lot like us, it takes effort, time, careful listening and learning, and a lot of unmitigated determination! And it takes even more effort to understand someone who is quite different, such as a member of the opposite sex! Understanding human emotions and behaviors is just a difficult thing.

So it should surprise none of us that trying to understand God's feelings is an infinitely more daunting challenge. Impossible, I believe, to any great degree. But in spite of this difficulty, the Bible does mention God's emotions quite often.

Stephen Covey, in his book *Seven Habits of Highly Effective People*,[1] lists his fifth habit as "seek first to understand; then to be understood." This is the habit concerning effective communication. This principle is certainly true in our interpersonal relationships with others, and it is even truer, I believe, in our relationships with God. I think too often our spiritual lives can consist of our regularly gabbing away to God, perhaps thinking, "I pray a lot so that makes me close to God." Or "I know the Lord" because I pray! Good for you. Perhaps. But only if God knows you, is listening, and accepts what you say. A key question is: does he "hear" you at all? And equally importantly, do you ever really "hear" him?

Jesus confronted the harsh reality that there are many "lost" Christians. In his conclusion of the Sermon on the Mount, he said, "Many will say to me on that day, 'Lord, Lord, did we not prophesy in your name and in your name drive out demons and in your name perform many miracles?' Then I will tell them plainly, *'I never knew you.* Away from me, you evildoers!'" (Matt. 7:22–23, italics added). "I never knew you." Words no one wants to hear spoken regarding themselves on Judgment Day. But here Jesus forewarned that there are many "Christians" among us who claim to know Jesus, but *whom Jesus does not know*—"I never knew you." They call themselves Christians, and according to their own accounts, they will have in their lifetimes done Christian things that would indicate

---

1 Covey, Stephen R. *The 7 Habits of Highly Effective People: Restoring the Character Ethic* [Rev. ed.]. New York: Free Press, 2004.

the power of the Holy Spirit in their lives—prophesying, driving out demons, and performing miracles.

But as it turns out, they will have never been saved in the first place! These individuals most assuredly incorrectly assumed that when they came to "know Jesus" and "got saved," to use common Christian vernacular, he automatically came to know them. However, this assumption was patently wrong, according to Jesus's own words. Perhaps the core problem is that many among us seek more to be understood by God than to first understand God. We make him out to be what we want him to be or think he ought to be, and thus we miss *him* altogether. Thus I suppose, Christ's prophesied lack of recognition of them on Judgment Day. We should safely assume that until we take the time to truly know God, independent of our own personal desires concerning who he ought to be, we will miss out on being assured that he knows us!

The apostle Paul also has inferences concerning this same harsh reality. In his rebuke to the legalistic leanings of the Galatians Christians, he modifies, or even corrects, his own statement when he says, "But now that you know God—or rather are known by God—how is it that you are turning back to those weak and miserable forces?" (Gal. 4:9). The truth is that it is more important that God first knows you than that you think you know God. And it follows, I believe, that if God knows, you surely know him. And his knowing us is what ultimately determines our salvation—that he "sees" us as "holy and blameless in *his* sight" (Eph. 1:4), not that *we* see ourselves as holy and blameless in his sight. Paul remarked to the Corinthian church, "But whoever loves God is known by God" (1 Cor. 8:3). Again, notice the emphasis on being known by God, not on our knowing him. We must get the order correct, or we will in the end receive an order we will regret eternally—"I never knew you. Away from me, you evildoers!" (Matt. 7:23).

I have already briefly used the illustration of my "knowing" the president of our country, but the reality was that he does not know me. In fact, I have lived through—"known"—quite a few different presidents, all the way back to Eisenhower. However, in all of the years of my knowing these presidents, and even feeling a bit "close" to some of them, not a single one ever knew me. Even a little bit. Imagine they made no effort to get to know me! It is in fact a very difficult thing to even get in close proximity to or communicate with a president. Each of these presidents was said to be "the most powerful man in the world" during his tenure. And a president is infinitely more limited than the infinite God. They are finite and neither omnipresent nor omnipotent. But in spite of all his powers—omniscience, omnipotence, and omnipresence—God does not listen to everybody or "know" everybody in a "saved," relational sense (John 9:31; Ps. 66:18; Deut. 1:45). And just because one can talk the "God-talk" and claims to know and be empowered by God, it does not mean God "knows" us and feels similarly toward us. Got your attention on this yet? The point being made here is not to try to invoke fear in insecure Christians or try to "scare [the] hell" out of anybody, but to support a clearer vision of reality—to help us better see how God sees. And to grasp the utter essentiality of our seeing how *God* sees us and not just how *we* see us! Or him!

So what is it that strums God's heart-chords, so to speak? Does he actually "feel" emotions, and if so, how does he even "feel" or experience them? The Bible speaks fairly often of the emotions of God, such as anger (Deut. 1:37), joy (Zeph. 3:17), regret (Gen. 6:6), and so forth. Generally, there are two main branches of thought or theology seeking to explain and understand God's "emotions." One is classic theology, which asserts that God is immutable (unchangeable) and thus impassive (without common human emotional mood changes). This position posits that the Bible, in speaking about God's sudden anger and such, is using a figure of speech called anthropopathy, which as previously mentioned, is assigning human emotions to nonhuman beings or things.

The other view is open theology, which is arguably the more prevalent branch. It is seen in many fundamentalist, conservative, and evangelical churches today. I am thankful that with the growth of nondenominationalism and more openness within denominations, it is much more difficult to "pigeonhole" whole churches or people groups into certain narrow views, which by the way produces division within the body of Christ. In the open theology way of thinking, God, even in his infinite, immutable nature, is indeed seen as having real emotions and feelings, although emotions that are obviously different from our own physiologically and biochemically generation ones. In this view, the scriptures are generally taken more literally, and although explaining such a thing as God's emotions is difficult, it is believed in faith by many to be literally so in God's own nature and experience. And materialists and humanists do not believe in the truly spiritual at all, so they surely cannot grapple with emotions associated with anything nonmaterial. Even many Christians are amazingly humanistic and hold to materialistic views of the creation.

As with many things about God, starting out it may seem pretty simple and straightforward, like the ocean surface seen from above a reef. On top, it may look vast and nondescript like any other part of the surface of the ocean. However, when we take a look at the reef below the water's surface through a pair of goggles we see a very complex system teeming with life of all kinds, colors, and shapes. God is that way and so much more. He may seem simple and easy to define on the surface, but to those who bother to look more deeply with open minds, he reveals himself as the gloriously divine—an infinite personality who is wonderful beyond measure and complex beyond our comprehension! His wonder is utterly inexpressible. Thus as with all things about God, after further deliberation, things can get very complicated very quickly.

However in the end, all roads that lead us to truth, in fact, lead us to Jesus. That is as they are intended to do, I believe, as Jesus said, "In fact, the reason I was born and came into the world is to testify to the truth. *Everyone on the side of truth listens to me*" (John 18:37, italics added). But when Christ came into the picture, God made a relationship with him seem simpler again, as Jesus said, "No one comes to the Father except through me" (John 14:6) and "Everyone who believes in me *is really believing in the one who sent me*" (John 12:44, Easy-to-Read Version, italics added). The Bible clearly asserts that those who seek the truth ultimately end up on the side of Jesus, who it says *is* the truth.

Paul wrote of this simple, single focus on Christ, saying, "I am afraid that just as Eve was deceived by the serpent's cunning, your minds may somehow be led astray from your sincere and pure devotion to Christ" (1 Cor. 11:3). In my own desire for simplifying matters, seeing the big picture before overanalyzing, and understanding things from the inside out, this verse resonated with me early on in my Christian walk. I was trying to sort my faith out during a very introspective, troubling period in my later college years and was bogged down in the denominational and sectarian squabbling about most things to do with God and the Bible. How was I to have any sense of the truth or what was right? Why could Christians, and even those in the same denomination, seemingly agree on so little? I was at that time using the King James Version (KJV) of the Bible, which was generally thought to be the only accurate translation in my church and in my part of the country at the time. Here is how the verse reads in the KJV: "I fear, lest by any means, as the serpent beguiled Eve through his subtlety, so your minds should be corrupted from *the simplicity that is in Christ*" (italics added). While the underlying meaning in our modern-day terms seems most assuredly to me to be how the NIV renders it, the ultimate implication is still how the KJV reads, because a pure, sincere devotion to Christ leads to a kind of "simplicity" in Christ. This is the kind of simplicity that is good, I believe.

Simplicity in Christ was appealing to me then and still is because it brings me back to a simple trust in Jesus rather than to a trust in some complicated and controversial view of God, the God too magnificent for us to fully comprehend anyway. On the other hand, many, and perhaps most, of the theological approaches seemingly end up in a roiled, deep quarry of controversy, confusion, and doubt. Confusing us. Dividing us. Puffing us up in our presumed intelligence and doctrinal and theological "rightness." One can just drown in it. I was a troubled young soul pondering God and seeking meaning and purpose at a critical life juncture. Getting bogged down in religious complexity and disagreement was most counterproductive and the last thing I needed.

I took quite a lot of psychology in undergraduate and graduate school. In one of my graduate counseling classes, I was required to do a battery of psychological tests on myself as if I were a third person counselor evaluating me as a client or student. I was then to write a paper as the counselor evaluating myself as the counselee, based on the results of the tests along with few "pretend" counseling sessions that had been conducted. This assignment required significant self-analysis that few twenty-two-year-old young men have not done. Although I was a very introspective child, adolescent, and young adult, I had not had any such tools as these tests to see myself objectively in a psychologically normative way. But with my background, I had been somewhat forced to do more self-evaluation than most. Still I did not know myself well at all, as I learned.

I realized one thing about myself—perhaps not unlike many others, I needed to take complexity and simplify it. In my leisure time during those times, I just needed to try to slow down and unwind—to "decompress." I wanted things to be simple, probably because to me the world I had grown up in was painfully complex and unsure. I longed for things to be simple. As I pondered myself during this testing and self-evaluation exercise, one of the things I remembered was that for as far back as I could remember, while I was at home, on Sundays I usually read the Sunday comics. One of the them, among a few others, that always caught my eye, and thus that I often read (confession time now), was one called *Nancy*. It was really odd because the characters, the plots, and so forth were not anything like what usually drew me. It was about a goofy little girl, for goodness sakes! I surely would not have wanted anyone to know I liked it, and don't you be judging me now either! But the drawings and the dialog were short and simple. It was odd that I even remembered it, but it nonetheless became iconic in my mind for what I was drawn to. And "the simplicity that is in Christ Jesus" was for me just that!

I longed for simplicity. My studies in the physical and behavioral sciences were complex. But my strength in the sciences was always taking the complex and simplifying it to its basics. Thus "the simplicity which is in Christ Jesus" or "A pure and sincere devotion to Christ"—became a defining principle for me. Jesus is Lord, and that is that. I got it. If one comes to realize that as true, then it is by definition to be the defining truth of all the others, because the Lord leads, guides, and decides all. Those who know me know that I still cling to the principle of simplicity. I use simple axioms and adages to summarize more complex constructs, both for my own applications and for teaching and leading others. And I am quite repetitive about them believing that repetition is the friend of the adult learner!

In reading the gospels, it seems to me Jesus had a way of simplifying deep realities. Although Jesus said certain of his parables and stories were designed to befuddle his self-righteous antagonists (Mark 4:9–12), others were clearly designed to simplify and apply spiritual truths to daily life. Still others were designed to provoke deeper, introspective thought. I think that's why those living in the smog of complexity and subjectivity missed and resisted much of what he said. I think it is why so many still do. Jesus however pulls us back to the surface of the water where we can breathe and live, rather than drown underwater trying to figure out the complexity of the spiritual reefs below. But he gives us the goggles—the lens—to safely look beneath the surface and see the beauty and divine complexity from which we derive our being and life. Jesus had a way of focusing people and discussions on the issues that were important and critical, without trying to explain everything he clearly knew about God.

When it comes to God and religion, I have long felt that so much of it involves an *overanalysis of the ambiguous to the neglect of the obvious.* Churches and Christians can be so fixated on the rightness of each of their doctrines and be downright cold, dogmatic, ideologically fixated, and unloving in overanalyzing fairly ambiguous doctrines while neglecting the obvious love commands of Jesus. Jesus said of the Pharisees, "Woe to you, teachers of the law and Pharisees, you hypocrites! You give a tenth of your spices— mint, dill and cumin. But you have neglected the more important matters of the law—justice, mercy and faithfulness" (Matt. 23:23). I believe we humans, in our desire to control and prove ourselves right, can all act this way! But Jesus was not that way.

After answering his question and telling him the truth about rebirth, Christ challenged Nicodemus, a leader of the Israel nation, "I have spoken to you of earthly things and you do not believe; how then will you believe if I speak of heavenly things?" (John 3:12). Nicodemus, being a religious leader, was, as most Israelites were, obsessed with the Torah with all its rules and teaching and thus bogged down in the ensuing complexity of their interpretations. He too "strained out gnats while swallowing camels" (Matt. 23:24). But Jesus challenged him to see the obvious—to see the big picture first!

We all have enough trouble simply believing all the things about God that we have actually already been allowed to hear, see, and experience. Trying to go beyond that can be in fact fairly daunting. And there are things about God that apparently cannot be told in this present world. As mentioned previously, Paul said, after visiting the "third heaven," that "He heard *inexpressible* things, things that man is not permitted to tell" (2 Cor. 12:4, italics added). We simply must learn to focus on the obvious.

Job's story is of a man who is allowed by God to suffer greatly, while consistently being accused of sin or given misguided counsel first by three, and then by a fourth, of his friends (Job 1–37). However, God still soundly rebuked Job for daring to ask questions about things beyond humankind's comprehension. This seems to be because the kind of "why" questions Job was asking ultimately brought the righteous and just nature of God into question (Job 38–41). Job went from asking questions of God to questioning God! The reality is that when men try to explain things about God that we clearly are not positioned well to answer or understand, bad assumptions and inferences are drawn. Thus bad things tend to happen in respect to our relationship to him and our subsequent effects on others! Heresy often flows, I believe, from overspeculation due to scant information.

In fact, I conclude that all actual heresy has at its roots some misconception, misapplication, or misunderstanding of God. John said it this way, "This is how you can recognize the Spirit of God: Every spirit that acknowledges that Jesus Christ has come in the flesh is from God, but every spirit that does not acknowledge Jesus is not from God. This is the spirit of the antichrist, which you have heard is coming and even now is already in the world" (1 John 4:2–3). As if to say, if you get Jesus wrong, you've got God wrong. Human speculation concerning the "unanswerable whys" usually does not improve our understanding of God or our lots with him. Since Jesus is the exact representation of God, any incorrect view of him will lead to an incorrect view of God, and vice versa, thus justifying Christianity's strong defense of Jesus as the only way to God (John 8:24, 14:6).

Paul warned those who were drifting away from the simple truth of Christ, and thus of God, and were getting bogged down in human thinking, traditions, and doctrines, saying, "See to it that no one takes you captive through hollow and deceptive philosophy, which depends on human tradition and the basic principles of this world *rather than on Christ.* For in Christ all the fullness of the Deity lives in bodily form, and you have been given fullness in Christ, who is the head over every power and authority" (Col. 2:8–10, italics added). Jesus is to be the ultimate interpretive benchmark of everything to do with God!

Surmising from these verses, Paul seems to make it clear that it is our responsibility as Christians to look to Jesus to develop a correct view of God. And with that challenge in mind, I believe I can summarize for practical-minded Christians a simple, overall approach to scripture that is logical and consistent: The Old Testament is designed to get us to "Jesus *is* Lord." The gospels then build on that foundation to convincingly demonstrate "Jesus *as* Lord." The rest of the New Testament illustrates what happens when those two realities converge in the lives of God's people. Jesus chastised the Pharisaical Jews concerning their rejection of him, saying, "You diligently study the Scriptures because you think that by them you possess eternal life. These are the Scriptures that testify about me, yet you refuse to come to me to have life" (John 5:39–40). One can certainly read and even memorize scripture and miss God completely! Conversely, people can actually find God at a basic level without having scripture at all (Matt. 7:7–8; Rom. 2:14–16).

The fact is that anyone of us can get God wrong. Anyone of us can accept a false-Jesus—a view of Jesus that is not really Jesus at all. Paul said, "For if someone comes to you and preaches a Jesus other than the Jesus we preached, or if you receive a different spirit from the one you received, or a different gospel from the one you accepted, you put up with it easily enough" (2 Cor. 11:4). You get that? There are those who preach and believe in a "different Jesus" that comes from a "different spirit," which thus creates a different and *false gospel*. Unfortunately, too often we are eager to hear and believe false gospels probably because they are generally designed by Satan to pander to our fallen, prideful human spirits! These are evil-inspired, human-fashioned "gospels" that tell us as sinners what we *want* to hear rather than the truth we *need* to hear. We end up just like Adam and Eve when they believed Satan's "pseudo-good-news" lie in the Garden of Eden—"you will be like God, knowing good and evil" (Gen. 3:4). They were not satisfied to just be with God or to be like God in character and nature, as they were designed to be; they wanted to be gods! Paul warned early on about the false preaching that would come, saying, "The time will come when men will not put up with sound doctrine. Instead, to suit their own desires, they will gather around them a great number of teachers to say what their itching ears want to hear. They will turn their ears away from the truth and turn aside to myths" (2 Tim. 4:3–4).

In the end, the true gospel elevates Jesus and thus elevates God. In the end, false gospels denigrate Jesus and thus denigrate God, rather than magnify them, all the while ultimately elevating sinful humanity. As with the original false doctrine swallowed by Adam and Eve in the Garden, false doctrine ultimately always seek to elevate *us*! In reality, if we get Jesus wrong, we get God wrong. If we get God wrong, we get *us* wrong. If we get us wrong, we have everything wrong!

Further, Paul said of fallen humanity's efforts at trying to assume the god-position, "They said they were wise, but they became fools. Instead of honoring the divine greatness of God, who lives forever, they traded it for the worship of idols—*things made to look like humans*, who get sick and die, or like birds, animals, and snakes" (Rom. 1:22–23, Easy-to-Read Version, italics added). If we mentally exchange the truth about who God is and what his truly divine nature is like for things patently untrue, idolatry inevitably engulfs our lives. Whether we realize it or not! The very essence of humanity is that we will serve something. The way we define ourselves and thus the way we live ultimately determine what life purpose that we serve. Anything we serve, other than God himself, is to us an idol.

Idolatry is the great human tragedy. The priceless is traded for the worthless, "They exchanged the truth about God for a lie, and worshiped and served created things rather than the Creator— who is forever praised" (Rom. 1:25). Be it a stone, a statue, an idea, a purpose, money, or ourselves, if we place them before God as our life priority, they become our idols. Christ said, *"No one can serve two masters.* Either you will hate the one and love the other, or you will be devoted to the one and despise the other. You cannot serve both God and money" (Matt 6:24, italics added). Paul said that greed itself is idolatry (Eph. 5:5). Serving Christ and serving *any other* thing are mutually exclusive purposes. Even though from arm's length the behaviors and lifestyles involved may not necessarily look that differently when observing one who is "Christian" outwardly but who is in actuality, on the inside, "serving" money or other self-serving interests—idols rather than God.

When we are able to see God for who he is, we can see ourselves for who we are. When we fail at this, we fail at everything else that matters, because we have exchanged life-giving truth for damning lies. In effect, in the world apart from God, we believe and live out a sham—a lie. In fact, whether we like it or not, realize it or not, or admit it or not, our whole life becomes nothing but a worthless scam. The world is a human Ponzi scheme—a giant con game, in which everyone tries to get something for nothing, or at best exchange things of equal value. We repay others with what we have wrested from others caught up in the same selfish, self-serving system! Satan's version of the world is a barter system world—nothing is ever truly given "expecting nothing in return," as in Jesus's kingdom. And living in this desperate way may get us what we *want* in the short run, but it will never get us what we *need*! And it will not get us where we will want to be in the age to come—in the eternal kingdom of God. In fact, it will get us exactly the opposite.

Sadly, even many Christians, and perhaps most, come to God in a kind of blind and ignorant acceptance. Because by the nature of the world itself, we are taught what our families, churches, countries, or other institutions and social orders believe to be the truth. Schools and universities become pawns of humanism—the religion where man is the center and is to be worshiped. Graduates think they are thinking, but they are infected, and they merely spew out what they have been filled with. But inadvertently or purposely, ultimately only Satan is worshiped in humanism. And humanism *is* the curse. It is the original sin, and it is still the core sin. It inevitably invades everything that is human, religions, governments, social institutions, families, business enterprises, friendships, and even the church of Christ—we worship and serve created things rather than the creator, who is to be forever praised!

We are not taught *how* to think. We are in effect taught *not* to think. We are taught to repeat. We are taught to parrot. We are controlled by systems and ideologies that keep us within our tribes. Even through churches, we are too often "led to God" with preselected scriptures and the personal views of people who lead us to them, not Him. Unfortunately, churches across a broad spectrum tend to give us the "right answers" and make us followers of their self-proclaimed "right" ideology, rather than teaching us how to seek out God, how to think, and how to ask the right questions, thus making us followers of Jesus Christ, the Truth himself! It is just so much easier and simpler though to do it the easy church way. At least in the short run.

We can seemingly be programmed in a point of view and a doctrinal belief system, and then consciously or unconsciously, we are taught to resist anything or anybody who would even suggest anything we were taught could possibly in any way be wrong! As if to say we are *right* (with God), because we *are right* (about everything to do with God). Often our personal decisions to commit ourselves to God were made in moments of emotion and passion with little thought about who God is, what he wants, or what he expects. Or proxy parents, guardians, or religious leaders making us committed to God. But rarely does anyone ever take the time and care to disciple us to simply follow Jesus (2 Tim. 4:2–4). Or we just grew up assuming our way was the right way, not ever really deciding on it.

Often Christian "conversion" comes in childhood or early adolescence out of childlike thoughts and emotions. Our decision for God becomes raw and emotional like human sexuality and its passion. And this is especially true with teens. Rallies and camps are great times to stoke emotions and provoke shallow commitments to God all in the name of saving their souls! But things said and done out of raw passion, emotional moments, and gut instinct, rather than careful thought, good reasoning, and valid logic, cannot lead to depth of true commitment. Such are many Las Vegas marriages. I once knew a guy who was on his fifth marriage, and struggling with that one. One of the marriages, I think number three, he didn't even remember the ceremony. Yes, it was in Las Vegas. According to him, he simply woke up from a drunken stupor one morning in a bathtub with a wedding ring on! During moments of excitement, inebriation, or passion, it becomes all about our emotions in the moment—what I or others want, what I fear, what I feel, how to find relief for my desire, or how to maximize my own pleasure. What "feels" right at the time however may not at all *be* right. Very often, it is clearly not right.

Youthful sexual intimacy starts that way—we simply do not even understand our own feelings, and if we turn loose, we just sort of "go with it." It is always a train wreck. Yet the world programs children through media and even education that having sex is a human need, as much as the need to eat. People are made to believe it is an entitlement and a right, not a privilege and a gift. It is taught to be central to our identity as human, when our real image—our God image—predates gender differentiation (Gen. 1:26–27). It chooses us we are told; we don't choose it. We must identify with how we feel and what we want or desire. And it is normal and okay, the lie goes, to meet these supposed sexual "needs" however and whenever we want as long as we are both (or all of us in some cases) "consenting adults" and no one is "harmed." Who makes this stuff up? It takes really educated, high-minded people, narcissistic, and out-of-control people to sell this to society, but Satan is much more powerful than any of us can imagine!

How, in moments of intense passion, could we possibly expect to understand the feelings of a partner so opposite from us as a member of the opposite sex or even the same sex? It takes time, experience, and learning to understand the sexuality and intimate desires and feelings of our own selves, let alone learn about others. Emotional religious experiences in "choosing God," devoid of true open-minded learning and evaluation, are like determining whether a person would be a good mate and then marrying that person, vows and all, during the middle of having passionate pre-marital intercourse very early in the relationship! To express in an understatement, we would be just a little naïve and ignorant, just a bit distracted, just a little too emotional, and just a little irrational, do you not think? But for too many, especially born out of "being raised in the church" or even revivalism, that is how it happened. Then we feel forced to spend our lives justifying and validating what we decided emotionally—to "accept Christ" as our Savior and Lord, regardless of the reality that it was from the start based simply on what we were told. We accepted Christ by the informal fallacy called *Argumentum Ad Traditio*, accepting something as right because it is according to the tradition we know, not what was learned through sound rational and biblical reasoning of our own.

Many others of us simply had Christ selected *for* us in infancy. We "became Christians" by the faith of others. Then later, we were "taught" the truth by those who decided what those truths were.

They decided it for us. That is the way it has to be for us growing up. No doubt these traditions and points of view have reasons for their practices, but as with much of Christian tradition, generations have accepted it without much question for centuries, as Paul told us *not* to do. Most of us are taught to not question, but to accept and repeat what our church or tradition says to be the truth. However, in this scenario, our parents or other guardians arrange our marriage to Christ before our personalities even emerge. We may have been taught intentionally or unintentionally to be wary of anyone who disagrees with our tradition's teaching or challenges us to simply learn, to examine it, and to take responsibility and to think for ourselves!

That simply is not what making disciples is all about. Discipleship is all about teaching people to be followers and learners of Jesus, not teaching them to be blind followers of men, even parents—"Anyone who loves his father or mother more than me is not worthy of me" (Matt. 10:37). This kind of programming teaches us to be followers of men and un-open to other messages, unfortunately including Jesus's own core message! That form of faith proves pretty lame for those who sense within themselves the necessity of doing their own thinking and making their own decisions about their life purpose.

I do indeed believe parents and churches should raise their children to know and worship God. But shaping children's minds should be done with the most gravity and respect, not carelessly by simply dropping them off at Sunday school and sending them to summer camp. If they are to be fully devoted followers of Christ, they must not be relegated to obligatory church attendance, rote acceptance of Christ, and cursory commitments to certain doctrines. The failure of the Christian church in this regard is a large part of the reason that various surveys indicate that around 75 percent of "Christian" teens leave the church, that is stop attending, when they leave home. And further, less than half of those who leave ever return to the church.

Thus it becomes clear that their purpose and aim in conversion, if they even have experienced one prior to leaving home, has clearly not been to resolutely die to themselves and live out their lives for Christ. They have pleased their parents. They have pleased their church. They have gone along for the ride with their youth groups or Christian friends. And when those things are gone, so are they! And the church generally feels powerless to do anything about it even though the masses of our young people are leaving! The reality is that the church at large is not willing to change what needs to be changed in order to stop the bleeding.

The fact is that God gives each of us the responsibility and the ability to seek out and know God for ourselves. This is a huge responsibility though and certainly not one to be made carelessly, flippantly, or out of following the crowd. Parents must not become their children's intermediaries with God; only Christ can be that. Parents and teachers must zealously lead child *to* God and not allow them to make shallow flippant commitments to him in the name of "getting them saved," as we do when we buy life insurance for them! Instead we try to help them acquire an eternal fire insurance policy!

I think the spirit of Jeremiah's prophecy was getting at this principle and that Hebrews then echoes that promise in discussing Christ's new covenant, saying, "No longer will a man teach his neighbor, or a man his brother saying, 'Know the Lord,' because they will all know me, from the least of them to the greatest" (Jer. 31:34; Heb. 8:11). John writes a similar spiritual sentiment concerning our ability to learn from God for ourselves: "But you have an anointing from the Holy One, and all of you know the truth . . . the anointing you received from him remains in you, and you do not need anyone to teach you. But as his anointing teaches you about all things and as that anointing is real, not counterfeit—just as it has taught you, remain in him" (1 John 2:20, 27).

I have waded off into some deep theological and doctrinal waters here in order to challenge Christian sectarian conventions that I believe tend to seemingly "brainwash" us rather than make us disciples of Christ—fully devoted followers of Christ and honest learners ever seeking the simple, unadulterated truth of God. Such entrenched tradition leads us to believe that we have to go through someone else to have Jesus and that we have to believe what those who came before us believed in order to have Jesus. And arguably much of orthodoxy was in its own origins not so "orthodox" itself! It becomes as if to give the impressions that if we do not agree with those who taught us, we are not only rejecting them, but we are also rejecting God and the truth itself! Wow! How do we get to such places? Oh yeah, remember the original sin was to make *us* like God, knowing good and evil. So it seems we just keep playing like we are God—possessing, owning, and controlling. In doing so, all we actually control and own is as God explained to Adam and Eve, the toxic "knowledge of good and evil." It is clearly deadly. We are not qualified to deduce from it alone the "truth." Never were, never will be! Jesus is our truth and thus to be our only bond of peace.

Jesus said, "If you hold to my teaching, you are really my disciples. Then you will know the truth, and the truth will set you free" (John 8:31). We must be devoted to a pure and sincere devotion to Christ alone. And we must be devoted to leading all we influence to the same singleness of purpose. We must eschew any desire to program our children or anyone else to our own ways of thinking in order to inadvertently validate ourselves or feed our own egos. False prophets lead others to them. True prophets lead others to Him (Christ)! We must get out of the way and let our young and our seekers come to Jesus unhindered by our own layers of human teachings and requirements.

Our task is not first to discover the truths of spirituality; our task is to discover Jesus and to live out his teaching. "Everyone on the side of truth listens to me [Jesus]" (John 18:37). The ultimate truth of God is not finally found in academic pursuit; it is found in living as Jesus did. John said, "We know that we have come to know him if we obey his commands. The man who says, 'I know him,' but does not do what he commands is a liar, and the truth is not in him. But if anyone obeys his word, God's love is truly made complete in him" (1 John 2:3–5). Truth is learned most in the obeying from the heart, not in the speculating of the mind alone. Truth does not enslave us to terminal, closed-minded thinking. Truth does not lead us to mental, spiritual, or academic bondage; fear; and slavery. Truth leads us to freedom. "Now the Lord is the Spirit, and where the Spirit of the Lord is, there is freedom" (2 Cor. 3:17). We need not fear truth. "The Spirit you received does not make you slaves, so that you live in fear again; rather, the Spirit you received brought about your adoption to sonship" (Rom. 8:15). Where God's Spirit is, there is freedom. Where there is no freedom, it can probably safely be said there is little or no Spirit.

In reality, what we need to be wary of are those institutions and individuals that claim monopolies on truth and thus, as Paul put it, "take you captive through hollow and deceptive philosophy, which depends on human tradition" (Col. 2:8). Rather we need to get our faith in Jesus right (John 6:29). If we get Jesus right, we will get God right. Only when we get God right can we be "right" ourselves. If we do not see and get God right, we can never see and get ourselves right.

God is infinite and awesome. We can never fully understand the depth of him, and those from the past can have had no better grasp on him than we. We must free ourselves from any sense of obligation to defend the beliefs or voices of the past, or we risk being bound to humanly inaccurate, shortsighted, or otherwise patently wrong views of our God. We must hear them. We must respect them. We must respect tradition and orthodoxy. We must carefully listen to their proponents and take their views into careful consideration. But we must never be bound to them or by them—held captive. Each generation must again reform the church, paring out unnecessary traditions, skewed interpretations, and cumbersome constructs. In fact each one of us of must reform in our own life what has been handed to us, exacting our faith only in Jesus and conforming our pattern of belief and life to him alone.

It is never then dangerous to move ever forward in pursuit of the truth of God—"Ask and it will be given to you; seek and you will find; knock and the door will be opened to you" (Matt. 7:7). However, it is infinitely dangerous not to vigorously pursue truth. It is in fact much more respectful to our traditions to pursue that which they originally pursued—the truth God—than to make the traditions themselves the objects of our pursuit. We do not have to condone what has been believed, done, and what we might disagree with to simply not condemn it. God have mercy on us all.

To rightly begin to wrap our minds around God's feelings, we must first rightly wrap our minds around what God has revealed to us about himself. Our traditions and "faiths" tend to turn God into a thing instead of revealing his infinite personality. Instead of relationship, we get religion. But before the Bible reveals a way to believe and live, it reveals God. And the God of the Bible sees, hears, and feels, but not with a brain and physiologically induced processes, but with a being much more marvelous that we currently experience and comprehend. But feel he does! When we finally get that God feels, then we can finally feel him.

In other words, to see ourselves, we must first see God. We must approach him and worship him with supreme reverence— "Therefore, since we are receiving a kingdom that cannot be shaken, let us be thankful, and so worship God acceptably with reverence and awe, for our 'God is a consuming fire.'" Perhaps

Paul's words conclude it all best: "Yes, God's riches are very great! His wisdom and knowledge have no end! *No one can explain what God decides. No one can understand his ways* (Rom. 11:33, Easy-to-Read Version, italics added).

Questions and Thoughts for Reflection and Discussion

1. Why is it important to understand another's feelings (especially God's) in order to relate well to them?
2. Why is it important to seek to first understand another in order to make yourself understood?
3. How can our claim to "know God" not necessarily mean God knows us?
4. Compare the illustration of the experience of looking at the ocean surface above a reef and then looking under the surface through goggles with that of looking only at the surface of God, his creation, and the Bible as compared to looking deeply into them.
5. Why might it rightly be said that false "prophets" lead you to them and true prophets lead you to Him (Christ), by prophet meaning someone who claims to be speaking on behalf of God, formally or informally?
6. Why is it important to get God "right" in order to get yourself "right"?

CHAPTER 9

ISSUES OF KNOWING GOD

Flesh and blood knit together,
Atoms, molecules, and cells,
Matter and energy in harmonious interaction,
Of God's being and design it tells.

Pure energy became pure matter.
Matter was made to feel and think,
Now reflecting and pondering its Creator,
Body, soul, and spirit in existential link.

I have spent my lifetime interacting with and working directly with people, first as the youngest of a large family and then as a minister and pastor. Ultimately, I believe that working with people "one on one is how it's best done." By that I mean that the ministry of helping others find God and a relationship to him is best done face-to-face in personal relationships. Jesus was a shepherd, not a herder, and thus we should be that as well. Jesus mainly avoided the crowds and chose to work with the twelve apostles or with two of three of the apostles separately. He is also depicted interacting variously with other individuals along the way.

In each of my ministries, I have dedicated my life to spending the time to build close, personal relationships with a few men, and women as appropriate, to help develop their spiritual lives and "raise them up" in Christ. We lead people to Christ through sharing the faith of the gospel (sowing the kingdom seed), and then in the same way, we help them develop and mature in their walks with God (watering, discipling) (1 Cor. 3:5–9). Our mission is at its core singular and simple, making us mature disciples of Christ through the strength God gives us—"So, naturally, we proclaim Christ! We warn everyone we meet, and we teach everyone we can, all that we know about him, so that, if possible, we may bring every man up to his full maturity in Christ. This is what I am working at all the time, with all the strength that God gives me" (Col. 1:28–29, J. B. Phillips New Testament).

I think church assemblies, with their worship practices, their sermons, and other lessons, were originally intended to strengthen what goes on in personal lives from Sunday to Sunday, rather than church itself being the main event that defines one as a Christian. Rather than just preaching and leading classes and groups, I have worked very closely and individually with many for some four decades now, first as a Christian leader in college and then in vocational ministry. I began small group ministry back in 1974 before the small groups approach came into vogue. I guess it was because of me and others like me, with relational discipling and small groups ministry, as said in the country song, "I was country before country was cool" ("I Was Country When Country Wasn't Cool" by Barbara Mandrell, 1981). I in fact was country when the dream of so many was to move from the country to the city, not as it is today when so many want to move from the city out into the country! In the last four decades, many churches have found their way back to the personalization of ministry the way Jesus did it, while still others have moved in the opposite direction in building mammoth churches, struggling in vain to somehow personalize ministry to everyone within them.

Suffice it to say, doing ministry directly and personally, I have built many, many very close personal relationships. I counsel, but unlike many pastoral and clinical counselors, I have close ongoing relationships with many of those I counsel. I get to see their daily lives and know the others involved in their lives. As I also preach and teach in many types of situations, I get to see Christians in all their various settings. In our church communities, we have very active and vital ministries for all ages, and we are an age-integrated community. We are structured into moderate-size churches that work in smaller, specialized ministries and home groups. We seek to help each member have at least a few close personal relationships as well. Each group no matter the size is designed to support and be interdependent with the others. It's the body of Christ, and each is a part of it. We seek in the wisdom of Christ to, in ministry and church, get the "best of big and the best of little."

One of the ministries that we are actively involved in that many churches are not is campus ministry. We support a now independent ministry that operates on multiple campuses in our metropolis, which has hundreds of students involved annually. Thus as the pastor of a church where a number of the college students and campus pastors attend, I regularly counsel with college students and help mentor their leaders.

I still relate to college students at several levels, I guess because it was in college that I searched out God and came to know him. I remember becoming a Christian and then quickly encountering the intense controversies between various churches. As I have previously mentioned, far too many of these views also ended with the assumption that those who disagreed were just clearly "not right" with God. And further those who disagreed with us, and thus were by definition patently incorrect, were also likely going to hell. I was there myself early on because of the fellowship I was in and what I was being taught and tried hard, I think, to get there completely, although the harder I tried to believe it all, the less I was able to believe it at all. Inside I never really did.

Sadly, sometimes it seems churches are not at all troubled by our discord, dissonance, and confusion. Some doctrinal positions are surely essential and even right in some instances, but the underlying sectarian, divisive, and factious spirit involved is just, in my opinion, a shameful Christian reality. Fundamentalism in America was born out of a narrow view of the Bible, as divinely dictated and thus inerrant and infallible, and of the essential doctrinal beliefs contained in it. It followed stressing the need for churches and Christians to vociferously and in some cases violently defend these views. This DNA seems bred into many churches, especially those who might now be called Evangelical.

But as a college student, how was I, who hardly knew Jesus at all, supposed to, with any level of confidence, come to definitive conclusions on Christian doctrines such as the trinity, gifts of the Holy Spirit, predestination, biblical inspiration, premillennialism, communion, church assembly and worship, and baptisms? I had neither the scope nor depth of understanding to be adopting narrow views and making them fundamental to my faith. This was before I had even read the Bible through, thought out my faith, and was even grounded in Christ himself. Sadly, in hindsight, although I was sincerely hungry for Jesus, for my first four or five years, I think church and ministry inadvertently distracted me from a pure and sincere devotion to Christ. I spent more time discussing and mostly arguing with my other immature, naïve Christian friends about baptism and the possible millennial reign of Christ and such! Or about the hot button issue of my church as to whether it was "biblical" to use instruments of music in Christian worship. Or if Christians could speak in tongues and "heal" one another. And so forth *ad nauseam*.

I had a young college student in my office some years back. She was and still is one of the sweetest, most conscientious Christian girls you could ever meet—a beautiful girl inside and out. Yes, of course, she struggles with all the things young ladies deal with, but she loves God and is intent on knowing and loving him. She has been baptized multiple times, and in churches that do not even believe baptism has a place in a saving experience. However unbelievably, she was wondering if she should be baptized a fourth time! She was laden with guilt not only over her own life struggle, but also over "getting it all right in order to please God!" Most specifically, she was struggling with the doctrine of predestination and the differing views on salvation. It just breaks my heart to see someone so young and vulnerable trying to come to a conclusion about something that great Christian minds have been divided over through the centuries ever since Christ walked on the earth! And she was, in my estimation, unnecessarily fixated on making "getting it right" an issue in her very salvation!

When are we going to get it that we mostly do not have a clue about how God does anything? How does the infinite interact with the finite? But we take great delight in our theologies and philosophies and act like we have got something figured out that no one else has figured out and would in reality never have figured out. Yes, I believe these important subjects about God are worthwhile to think about and reconcile in our own minds. But I do not think it is all right to overanalyze, split hairs, and make people believe we know more than we know—that we have things figured out that we could not possibly ever figure out to any significant degree. I do not think it is okay to be factious and arrogant and divide over this stuff. I do not think it is okay to torture otherwise godly people by trying to make them choose between warring factions—defending one and condemning the other. Christ is in fact defamed by much of this, in my opinion!

Christ wants us to strive for unity (John 17:20–22; Eph. 4:3). Certainly not at all costs, but Paul says there will inevitably be differences and dissensions among us as Christians as some can be right and others wrong on critical issues (1 Cor. 11:19). But Christ wants us to seek to be agreeable with each other rather than disagreeable (1 Cor. 1:10). We are called to be peacemakers (Matt. 5:9) and to be at peace with all men if it is possible (Rom. 12:18).

This young Christian lady I am speaking about has a pure and sincere devotion to Christ and has had it all along. But here she was trying to struggle with the opposing "proof-texts" in the ongoing battle over just exactly who does God predestine for what and how does God do it! She was an emotional mess that morning. It broke my heart. And further, she had been to a counselor at another church who was trying to get her to sign up for their "sin-addiction" recovery group, as she was told by the counselor that she was addicted to sin. No, I don't make this stuff up!

This young lady is not alone; rather she is representative of an all-too-common segment in the church at large. I have watched too many young people over the years leave our campus fellowships and churches because we did not take a definitive stand on their tradition's pet view. Usually their parents and home churches were feeding these fires of division. Some of those who left most assuredly fell off a cliff into the typical college lifestyles and associated sins, rather than associate with such "unscriptural" people. They likely became part of the 75 percent of young Christians who leave church membership when they leave home. Sometimes I feel like some churches would rather have their young leave God than simply to leave that tradition. I do not think this situation makes our Lord very happy. Not happy at all!

We have an anointing given to us when we are saved that teaches us at the most fundamental and critical level to "remain" in Jesus (1 John 2:20, 27). We do not need anyone else to teach us about that because no one else is qualified to teach us about that. God reserved that teaching point for himself only—"no one can come to me unless the Father has enabled them" (John 6:65). This I believe to be the most simple and profound Christian reality of all, "you do not need anyone to teach you." Because they cannot teach you what God has reserved for the Spirit to teach you. "For those who are led by the Spirit of God are the children of God" (Rom. 8:14). Others can lead you *to* Christ, but only God can draw you *into* him, add you to his own body, and help you to remain in him. It is by the Spirit of God that we are baptized into Christ (1 Cor. 12:13). It is God's work and domain. It is not of man. Yes, man baptizes us on the outside, because God commanded it. It is by Jesus's authority, in the name of the Father, the Son, and the Holy Spirit. But God does all the inner work (Rom. 6:3–10; Rom. 2:28–29). We are given by God the right to be reborn without seeking the consent of any human "authorities" (John 1:12–13). And the rebirth of the Spirit gives us an anointing that teaches us at the basic level to live in Jesus, the true life-sustaining vine, just as he intends (John 15:1–6; 1 John 2:27). God has "got it all covered." He really does not need our personal assistance or even our clear understanding to do what he has reserved to be done only by him (1 Cor. 3:7). We need rather to focus clearly on what he *has* in fact given us to focus on, and we need to have faith that God can handle the details he has reserved for himself.

But we taint even salvation itself with human control and squabbling, arguing over baptisms versus a prayer of acceptance versus other forms of "Orthodoxy." I have lived it all out! We argue over the various views of predestination and just exactly how Jesus is going to handle the second coming. We seemingly tend to "knock each other's heads off" with "beams sticking out of our own eyes"—our own "self-rightness." And even if we don't argue, we privately look down on all the errors and shortcomings of the other Christians. We make certain doctrinal views fundamental to our faith that are perhaps not actually ever directly mentioned in scripture and argue and bicker over the inane while a watching world discounts us as ridiculous. And maybe deservedly so. Then we wonder why our young people leave in droves, disregarding what they have previously been taught. There are some of us with special vantage points to watch young, vulnerable Christians in despair over not being able to have it all figured out themselves—figured out of course just as they were told to have it figured out! Of course too, by the time they are sixteen or twenty-one! And we dare wonder why the world scoffs at us!

I do not believe this ongoing Christian milieu to be an accident. I believe it is the direct work and ploy of the evil one himself. We are playing into his hands by "majoring in the minors and minoring in the majors." But, of course we have our rightness to maintain. Right? Lots of us make our livings off our right view though. We have got our seminaries and colleges to maintain. Defending well the correct views merits lots of choice positions. There are lots of books to be sold and read and lots of attention and prestige to be doled out. Of course, all the while we all assume we are the faithful ones and our leaders the truly "right" ones, all defending the truth of God. I got caught in it myself. I have lived it. Sadly I have done it. But I will not do it anymore.

Jesus came to reveal God to us. He showed us God as best as can be done—the way God planned it. "The Son is the radiance of God's glory and the exact representation of his being, sustaining all things by his powerful word" (Heb. 1:3). However still, in actuality, he revealed so little of God's infinite, spiritual nature. He could not reveal very much of it because it was not possible in God's divine creation and plan. It is likely that much of who and what God is, and where he exists, is just not "translate-able" into our humankind "language" and our finite dimensions. Remember again Paul's own experience when God allowed him to visit heaven, hearing things that were "inexpressible" and that man was not allowed to "tell" (2 Cor. 12:1–4). Again Paul concluded, "Oh, the depth of the riches of the wisdom and knowledge of God! How unsearchable his judgments, and his paths beyond tracing out!" (Rom. 11:33). Rather, why can we not simply boast in knowing God, not in knowing everything about God? "This is what the Lord says: 'Let not the wise man boast of his wisdom or the strong man boast of his strength or the rich man boast of his riches, but let him who boasts boast about this: that he understands and knows me, that I am the Lord, who exercises kindness, justice and righteousness on earth, for in these I delight,' declares the Lord" (Jer. 9:23–24).

So the goal should be to know God, not to control the very concept of God. No church, organization, or individual can possibly have a monopoly on God, although we sure can often act like it. Knowing God will produce humility, not arrogance. Knowing God will produce mercy, not harsh judgments. Knowing God will produce confidence in his grace and goodness, not constant fear of not being right about everything. The way God has given for us to know him is through Jesus (John 14:6). But how much then of Jesus's own humanity—those traits of him that are clearly human—should we in fact attribute to the infinite, eternal, spiritual God? How can he be, as we like to say, "fully God and fully man"? What of Jesus was fully human and what of Jesus was clearly divine? How can these mutually exclusive claims both be true!

Jesus told the apostles that in seeing him, they had already seen the Father (John 14:9). Physically? Spiritually? Behaviorally? Attitudinally? What part of Jesus shows us the actual "God-part" and what part of him demonstrates the man-part? In Jesus, we see all the manifestations of mankind, emotions and all. Through his life here, we get our clearest glimpse of God in the flesh, in all of his glory—"The Word became flesh and made his dwelling among us. We have seen his glory, the glory of the One and Only, who came from the Father, full of grace and truth" (John 1:14). I believe Jesus reveals God, that he is the crux of the scripture, and thus he should be the "interpretive benchmark" by whom we interpret whole Bible.

Sadly, though, I believe since the Reformation first began, many have tended to make Paul's letter to the Roman church, as well as other parts of letters and verses, the core of theology, rather than making Jesus the core. Therefore, to me, the gospels and their revelation of the life and person of Christ often seem to be minimized and are interpreted through an a priori ("from what comes before" or "before the fact") lens. Thus according to this way of reading the Bible and seeing Christ, Jesus is interpreted by, and to be understood first through, a reading of Paul, rather than the other way around, as I believe it should be. On the contrary, I think we should first see God (Jesus) as he really is (John 14:9)—not how we want him to be or how others want us to see him. Nor merely by how we were taught to see him in a moment of youthful, immature excitement or emotion or through a one-dimensional, conclusive presentation of a particular position. For it is only when we see Jesus clearly, as the gospels are designed to do for us, that we will we be able to understand the writings of the apostles and prophets in the rest of the New Testament. Only when we see Jesus clearly will we be able to see "us" clearly! As if to say, if you have seen Jesus—really seen him as he is—then you have seen the Father. And if you have seen the Father—really seen him—then you can finally truly and rightly see *you* by seeing through the ultimate eyes of truth.

But for too many of us, theology, like the rest of our pursuits, is sort of like medicine. We take it to make ourselves feel better. And in fact, as we often have to take medicine because we have somehow hurt ourselves or mistreated our bodies, we are often pursuing God because we have harmed ourselves with sinful living. We humans generally pursue things to either relieve a pain or discomfort or to give ourselves pleasure. The vast majority of us mostly just want to feel good and enjoy life. We want to live as healthy and comfortably as we can, and as long as possible, and to be able to do it as easily, conveniently, and cheaply as possible. To do that, we have developed whole branches of science and philosophy to study about the physical, psychological, and spiritual health and well-being of humankind. These are very deep and complex subjects. We should certainly all be glad there are those smart enough and willing enough to put in the time and do the research necessary in such pursuits. However, most of us really do not put much of our own effort into the pursuits. We want an easy way—a quick fix. We want someone else to do the hard work. We just try to find the doctor and the approach that seems best (usually easiest, I think) for us and go with it. We want a pill and a simple, easy solution. Our lives are not spent studying medicine; we just want to live our lives and let someone else do the heavy lifting. The masses tend to be shallow and just want to be happy, enjoying life more. Preferably a lot more, for most of us! We do the same with theology. In the end, we want a great relationship with God and to be able to live out our lives as best we can accordingly. We want to know him so that he can bless us, help us out in our problems, and otherwise just make life easy and pleasurable. Right?

Unfortunately, theology and all its trappings can form a seemingly impenetrable barrier around God for true seekers who are otherwise "unschooled, ordinary" people (Acts 4:13). The religious can certainly be guilty more of blocking people from God than of leading others to him (Matt. 23:13). We are taught more to accept and parrot than to think and learn. Salvation and a walk with God are usually said to be by faith in Christ, but then seemingly inferred to be by our "rightness" on the "important" doctrines and faith in our leaders. Faith itself appears to me to have become a seemingly meritorious work for too many!

But relationships are never easy, especially with the divine. We have to know others to be truly known, so we have to get to know

God in order for him to know us. But when a relationship with God is made unnecessarily cumbersome and complicated, the tired and beaten down, the ones Jesus invited (Matt. 11:28–30), walk away, feeling it impossible for them. Remember what Jesus will say to the deceived Christians at the end: "I never knew you" (Matt. 7:23), lest we begin to think our knowing about him assures his knowing us. But they only thought they knew him. Thus they wrongly assumed he knew them. They did not know him in reality. He did not know them in reality. He never had. Sad. Eternally sad! God wants hearts that are wholly devoted to him and not so reliant on everyone else (2 Chron. 16:9). God wants hearts that are not even reliant on themselves!

There is this statement I read some time back by Christian theologian John Shelby Spong. I looked it up again. If you know of him and are wondering, I am not advocating his general theological views, but I agreed with this challenge and thought it insightful. He said, "Christians don't need to be born again. They need to grow up."[1] Clearly, I believe one does in fact need to be born again to be a Christian (John 3:3–5). But once you are, you do not need to be born again a second or third time by running down the aisle to the altar at every revival. You need to mature at home on your knees. But as with infatuation, youthful passion, and in the marital "honeymoon" stage, many want to keep the magic of those early days of dating and marriage. We can go to some ridiculous lengths to do so. We can develop some unrealistic and really undesirable expectations. In doing so however, we fail to take our marriages, relationships, and other endeavors to the even better places they can go—to an even more mature way of loving and living. Rather, too often it all stays in a frustrating state of limbo, with us trying to go where we in reality are not capable of going

---

1 Spong, John Shelby. Why Christianity Must Change or Die: A Bishop Speaks to Believers in Exile. San Francisco, CA: Harper Collins, 1999.

and stay where we are incapable of staying. Thus we fail to take it to the place it is supposed to be and where we actually could take it if we weren't so misdirected. Far too often, I think we do exactly the same sort of thing in our relationships with God.

As I regularly reference because of its defining effect on me, my mother died five days before my twelfth birthday. As most people, I loved my mom dearly. I was the youngest of eight children—I was the "baby"—and she loved me dearly. I was a preadolescent when she died. I went through puberty later than most. In the fifty years since her death, which I have lived my life without her, I have obviously reflected back on her innumerable times. She lives inside of me. But my memories of her are all memories of a less than twelve-year-old boy. I never knew her from an adult perspective. I have had to over the years get an adult perspective of my mom from my older siblings and other relatives who knew her as an adult.

I was worshiping with our church on a Sunday morning some twenty years ago, and between songs, I was handed a folded-up piece of paper. I couldn't remember getting a note passed in church since I was a kid, I suppose. Perhaps never. But I had been passed a note. I unfolded it, expecting a request for prayer or for an announcement I needed to make at the start of my sermon. Instead the note read, "The Spirit just told me to tell you that you mother is very proud of you." It was from one of my dearest friends in the world and sons in the faith, who knows me about as well as anybody. I believed it when I read it. But, oh my! I think I had to leave for a few minutes to regain my composure. Yes, my mother and her view of me still packs the same punch as it did as I watched her get sicker and sicker and die.

A few years back, I got to visit with one of my older cousins, my mom's niece, who was just a few years younger than my mom. She had grown up around my mother and knew her from a peer and adult perspective. I was taken aback by the different perspectives she had of my own mother! Her perspective was not bad, even though I am sure she knew many of the youthful sins and such. In fact, she loved and admired my mom greatly. Her views were just different. She had known my mom over a much longer time span than I had. My view was and is most special—a child remembering his mom. There's nothing else like it. My cousin could not have known her in that way, of course. But mine was a perspective that ended abruptly at nearly twelve years of age. This older cousin was close to ninety years old at the time we visited.

None of us can easily change the perspectives we have of our deceased loved ones, but we still can nonetheless at least right-size them. We can visit with others that knew them differently, better, or longer than we. And we can similarly change our perspectives of God as long as we continue to live here, because God is alive and ever-present. Jesus died, but God did not. And Jesus rose from the dead, but God didn't need to. Eyewitnesses testified to Christ's resurrection, and they laid their lives down in defense of that testimony. No selfish motivation could have led any of them to do that. They clearly knew what they had witnessed and were convinced of it. Peter wrote, "We did not follow cleverly invented stories when we told you about the power and coming of our Lord Jesus Christ, but we were eyewitnesses of his majesty" (2 Pet. 1:16). John testified to it similarly, referring to Jesus as, "That which was from the beginning, which we have heard, which we have seen with our eyes, which we have looked at and our hands have touched—this we proclaim concerning the world of life" (1 John 1:1). They knew. You can trust it more than most all other historical narratives because these gave their lives in its defense. With God you can keep learning your whole life. In fact, the more you learn, the more you are able to learn.

God is a clear, bottomless quarry of pure beauty, full of wonder and magnificence! "Oh, the depth of the riches of the wisdom and knowledge of God! How unsearchable his judgments, and his paths beyond tracing out!" (Rom. 11:33). Don't let others' limitations be your own.

With all that said, how do we know about God's feelings and emotions? The fact is that we cannot understand them very well in this life, just as I as a young boy could not understand my mother at the time. God is too infinite and awesome. He is the great divine mystery—"[God] . . . who alone is immortal and who lives in unapproachable light, whom no one has seen or can see" (1 Tim. 6:15–16). The Bible writers surmise that if we, in our human forms, saw him as he is, we would die. In a baffling exchange between Moses and God, God said to Moses, "You cannot see my face, for no one may see me and live" (Exod. 33:20). If one so esteemed by God, as was Moses, could not see God, I know it is just not possible for humankind at large. Other scriptures affirm this reality.

But I do know that Jesus said if we could just see him, we would really see God (John 14:9). For now I suppose that is truly the only way, and by far the best way, we can see the Father—through Jesus. First, by our knowledge of who and what he is, found especially in the gospels and then through the rest of the New Testament. Then experientially through the creation, the Holy Spirit, and the church. Jesus said, "I am the way and the truth and the life. No one comes to the Father except through me" (John 14:6).

I think our problem in this is the same as the original sin. We do not want to just *see* God. We want to *play* God or be gods to ourselves and to those around us. But it is still just as disastrous a mistake today as it was the first time it happened. We want to eat from the Tree of the Knowledge of Good and Evil and be like God. But it is just as deadly today as it was in the beginning. Sadly, I think most of our churches lovingly, but unwittingly, plant seedlings from this hopeless tree in our sanctuaries and classrooms. We feast on it regularly, thinking *we are right* because we are "right." We have bowls of "rightness fruit" in our statements of faith and in our messages. We have the monopolies on the truths of God in all our "rightness," or at least we are at the true center of the church, and everyone else is included by God's great mercy and his forgiveness of all their "wrongness"! Sadly, in doing so, we sate ourselves, feeding our egos with our pride-feeding knowledge, and then have no room in us for the fruit of the Tree of Life, which is Jesus himself!

With that said, I believe that we do indeed need to try to grasp the things that have been revealed to us, for it is God himself that revealed them—"The secret things belong to the LORD our God, but the things revealed belong to us and to our children forever . . ." (Deut. 29:29). But trying to overreach and overanalyze paralyzes us individually and divides us collectively. I believe that it conflicts us internally and weakens rather than strengthens our faith. Jesus came to simplify and unite, not to puff us up, divide us, and exalt us.

But finally on the point of this chapter along with those just before it, the reality is that in some divine invisible (to us at least) way God sees and hears and touches and feels. The created emanates from the spiritual—from the Creator himself, rather than the other way around. Apparently, *our* emotions are primarily physically generated. Clearly though, they are intertwined with our spiritual natures. God made the physical elements that comprise our living, breathing bodies. Then surely our physically generated emotions are reflective of God's spiritually generated ones. God gets angry and pleased and joyful and disappointed. How? We do not know. Heck, although neuroscience has come a long way, we're still trying to figure out how and why we humans experience emotions. And to quote Jesus again as he spoke to Nicodemus, "You are Israel's teacher and do you not understand these things? . . . I have spoken to you of earthly things and you do not believe; how then will you believe if I speak of heavenly things?" (John 3:10–12). God's feelings obviously originate from a different set of experiential dimensions, ones that are infinite and inexpressible. How are we then, as finite, changing, and emotional beings, to understand the emotions of the infinite, unchanging God? We are much, much more limited in this effort than a twelve-year-old boy would be in trying to understand the feelings of his then forty-eight-year-old mother!

As I proceed from these chapters on the nature of God—this profoundly and impossibly deep topic—I share Paul's lofty praise of God found at the end of his first letter to Timothy: "God, the blessed and only Ruler, the King of kings and Lord of Lords, who alone is immortal and *who lives in unapproachable light*, whom no one has seen or can see. To him be honor and might forever. Amen" (1 Tim. 6:15–16).

I must second that, adding my own adamant "amen" as well! Just simply looking at what has been created, we can see that our God is more beautiful than is humanly conceivable. Our God is more giving (graceful) than humanity can imagine. Our God is more powerful than can be measured. To quote the lyrics of a beautiful song by Mark Altrogge ("I Stand in Awe of You," 1987):

> *You are beautiful beyond description,*
> *Too marvelous for words,*
> *Too wonderful of comprehension,*
> *Like nothing ever seen or heard.*
>
> *Who can grasp your infinite wisdom?*
> *Who can fathom the depth of your love?*
> *You are beautiful beyond description,*
> *Majesty enthroned above,*
>
> *And I stand, I stand in awe of You!*
> *I stand, I stand in awe of You!*
> *Holy God to whom all praise is due,*
> *I stand in awe of You!*

Take it for what it is and eat of Jesus, the Tree of Life, and let others, if they must, suffer the theological dysentery caused by eating too much fruit from that "other" tree, trying to know the unknowable. Trying not just to know God but trying to play like God!

God has got it handled! Salvation is by grace through faith. Faith in God alone through Jesus Christ!

Questions and Thoughts for Reflection and Discussion

1. Compare and contrast developing and maintaining a close, intimate relationship with another person to that of doing so with God.
2. Why is it essential that churches and parents make it a priority to pass down a tradition of open-mindedly seeking to know and understand God rather than handing down to the next generation a slavish adherence to its own past beliefs and traditions?
3. How can church theology and doctrine possibly form a barrier around God rather than offering easier access to him?
4. How might studying in order to simply be "right" be counterproductive in building a right relationship with God?
5. How does acceptable worship (acceptable to God, that is) flow from the wonder and awe in the heart of a worshiper, and how can minimizing God to a set of doctrinal beliefs inhibit it?

CHAPTER 10

HOW GOD CHOOSES TO SEE US

The groom's face shone as the sunlight,
Smiling brightly to greet his bride.
The guests were breathless in anticipation;
But when the doors opened, in shock they cried!

The bride looked as a sad, battered prostitute,
Or perhaps more like a movie witch.
The viewers all gasped in disbelief;
There must have somehow been a switch.

The groom's face said he saw her differently,
Something hidden he seemed singly to behold,
Gazing at her through lens of bestowed virtue,
Placing on her finger his ring of pure gold.

The crowd saw only an ugly woman,
Looking old and withered and worn.
Her face bore marks of hard living;
Her dress was dingy, dirty, torn.

But the groom who'd chosen her as his bride,
Saw her with a heart of mercy and grace.
As the vows ended and he kissed her,
She was utterly transformed by his embrace.

The book of Ephesians concerns itself with what it means to be "in Christ." As Paul reveals, God sees us through the grace-filled eyes of Christ! Such magnitude of grace is unparalleled and hard to believe, such that the apostle prays to God that the eyes of their hearts would be opened—or enlightened—so they could see the incredible blessings that were theirs in Christ. He writes, "For this reason, ever since I heard about your faith in the Lord Jesus and your love for all God's people, I have not stopped giving thanks for you, remembering you in my prayers. I keep asking that the God of our Lord Jesus Christ, the glorious Father, may give you the Spirit of wisdom and revelation, so that you may know him better. I pray that the eyes of your heart may be enlightened in order that you may know the hope to which he has called you, the riches of his glorious inheritance in his holy people, and his incomparably great power for us who believe" (Eph. 1:15–19).

It is as if Paul was praying, "God open their eyes so that they can finally truly 'get it'!" Many have witnessed the same kind challenge with teenagers who lived in wonderful homes with godly, loving, hardworking, and generous parents. These teens have it all, but too many of them resent their parents, fail to appreciate the hard-earned, comfortable lifestyles afforded to them, reject many of the opportunities being given to them that so few in the world have ever had, and rather than be thankful and glad, choose to live as unhappy, directionless, deprived outcasts. Some of them act, live, and dress like they come from squalor and poverty! Many behave as if they have no one at home who loves them! For sure, all parents are imperfect, and sadly many have failed to teach their children self-respect and the respect of others, as well as to carefully instill such basic virtues as thankfulness. But many are seemingly great parents who are getting hit in the face with the teen years syndrome of defiance and resentment. Unfortunately, teens soon pick up this surly ungratefulness from their peers, the media, and sometimes from those same loving, hard-working parents, who ultimately behave the same way toward God!

Paul clearly recognized that just because they had been saved and were in the body of Christ, it did not mean that they were seeing themselves clearly through the eyes of God. It was "for this reason" that he was praying for them to have more of the Holy Spirit who could give them a deeper understanding of what it truly means to be a child of God. He specifically mentions, (1) the *hope* God has called us to, (2) the enormity of *our inheritance* as heirs of God's kingdom, and (3) his *incredible power* available to believers. I think all of us who have been Christians for some time can remember certain things of and about God that we early on perhaps "knew" intellectually but that we still had not yet internalized. Thus our experience of the gospel was being limited and the Spirit within us inhibited. This is at the core of the principle of learning to see God seeing you—to see yourself through the eyes of God and thus see yourself rightly. But that will never happen for us if we continue to see ourselves through the eyes of the world. Until I get *God* right, I can never get *me* right.

It is odd how those of us who have come to believe the amazing gospel of Christ can sometimes perceive ourselves as so hopeless, worthless, poor, or powerless. We are beaten down by the accuser, Satan, and believe his lie about us in spite of knowing, even if only intellectually, that God loves us so much, that his mercy toward us is great, and that he clearly demonstrated his immeasurable love and mercy for us by sacrificing his life. Instead, God wants us to be people of hope, to experience just how eternally wealthy we are, and to be fully tapped into his power. We are to be living, human messages to the world of God's incredible mercy as seen in his kindness to us as Christians (Eph. 2:6–7).

It is a belief issue of course, but it is not only a belief issue. It is a deeper, spiritual issue. Paul has much to say about this subject elsewhere as well. In another of his letters, he explains that God's Spirit is now revealing the things he was and is doing in Christ that were previously kept a mystery. Paul writes, "We do, however, speak a message of wisdom among the mature, but not the wisdom of this age or of the rulers of this age, who are coming to nothing. No, we speak of God's secret wisdom, a wisdom that has been hidden and that God destined for our glory before time began. None of the rulers of this age understood it, for if they had, they would not have crucified the Lord of glory. However, as it is written: 'No eye has seen, no ear has heard, no mind has conceived what God has prepared for those who love him'—but *God has revealed it to us by his Spirit*" (1 Cor. 2:6–10, italics added).

God was revealing through the Holy Spirit what had been kept secret before the revelation of Christ into the world. Paul wrote that God was revealing to us through the Spirit what prior to Christ's death on the cross no eye had seen, no ear had heard, and no mind had conceived—what it is that God has prepared for those who love him!

But how does God do this? In talking about the work of the Holy Spirit in each of our personal regeneration, Jesus said in response to the question of Nicodemus concerning the rebirth of the Spirit, "The wind blows wherever it pleases. You hear its sound, but you cannot tell where it comes from or where it is going. So it is with everyone born of the Spirit" (John 3:8). Curiously, and likely not accidentally since the physical creation is said to reveal God's divine nature (Rom. 1:20), the words for Spirit and wind come from a common Greek word *pneuma*. The Spirit apparently works in the spiritual realm in ways the wind behaves in the physical world—moving things, refreshing things, bringing fresh "air," providing power, and so forth. Thus when Jesus cites the wind as an example for how the Spirit moves and works, it should come as no surprise.

So while we may see *some* of the effects of the Spirit's work with our human eyes, we can only see the full extent of his plans and his work in us with the eyes of our hearts, when they are enlightened by God's power. Only the Holy Spirit can fully open the eyes of our hearts to see the work of God.

Ultimately then, it is only by the Holy Spirit that we can finally and fully see how God sees us. It is in seeing God as he reveals himself in Christ that we come to be transformed to be like him—"And we, who with unveiled faces all reflect the Lord's glory, are being transformed into his likeness with ever-increasing glory, which comes from the Lord, who is the Spirit" (2 Cor. 3:18). Paul is using in this scripture the example of Moses going up on Mt. Sinai to spend time alone with God and returning down the mountain aglow from God's effect upon him. It scared the people such that Moses covered his face to conceal the still fading glow. Paul says the same thing happens to us in our spending time with Jesus—that as we spend time with him, striving to see him as he is, to know him, and to experience his holy and divine presence, his Spirit transforms us to be like him. It transforms our countenance. However, unlike Moses, we are *not* to cover our faces but are to leave them unveiled to show Christ's effect on us to the world—"Never flag in zeal, *be aglow with the Spirit,* serve the Lord"(Rom. 12:11, Revised Standard Version, italics added). As was Moses in his interaction with God, so should we be in our interaction with Christ. But contrary to Moses, we must let its effects clearly show.

We are intended to be living testimonies of God's love for mankind. Paul states that it was God's intent to demonstrate his grace to the world through us saying, "And God raised us up with Christ and seated us with him in the heavenly realms in Christ Jesus, in order that in the coming ages he might show the incomparable riches of his grace, expressed in his kindness to us in Christ Jesus" (Eph. 2:6–7). But if we do not perceive his gracefulness to us, we will fail to reflect this incredible kindness to the world around us! And thus we will fail to be living examples to the world of God's work in us!

Paul says we as Christians are a divine message from Christ to the world, "You show that you are a letter from Christ, the result of our ministry, written not with ink but with the Spirit of the living God, not on tablets of stone but on tablets of human hearts" (2 Cor. 3:3). If we fail to internalize and obey Christ's message ourselves, to repent (literally change our minds about God) and believe the good news (accept that God is good, loves us, and wants us to be saved to be with him forever), how in the world are we to reflect it to others? If we do not live in the good news ourselves, then there is no way it will show on our faces and in our lives.

But God is good, and he has given us very good reasons to believe it!

Although God is lofty, mysterious, and powerful beyond our imaginations, we can still know and experience him in our daily lives, and that should be our overarching goal. He has made himself accessible to us. God said through the prophet Jeremiah: "Let not the wise man boast of his wisdom or the strong man boast of his strength or the rich man boast of his riches, but *let him who boasts boast about this: that he understands and knows me,* that I am the LORD, who exercises kindness, justice and righteousness on earth, for in these I delight" (Jer. 9:23–24, italics added).

Real wisdom is not to know as man knows; it is to know as God knows. The ultimate in wisdom is in fact to *know* God. This is true wisdom and insight. God is kind, just, and righteous. He is perfect and he is sufficient within himself. His essence defines his existence, as it should be with each of us as well. God needs nothing, but he gives endlessly. God is completely trustworthy and reliable.

We can and should trust him, but not to do what we might simply want him to do for us, but rather to do what is best for us all.

Paul praises God for his marvelous blessings, writing, "Praise be to the God and Father of our Lord Jesus Christ, who has blessed us in the heavenly realms with every spiritual blessing in Christ. For he chose us in him before the creation of the world to be holy and blameless in his sight" (Eph. 1:3–4). At the core of all of God's spiritual blessings for us in Christ is that God *chooses* to see us in Christ as completely holy and blameless. God chooses to see us as perfect. Astounding!

The Old Testament prophet, Jeremiah, forecasted God's new covenant in Christ—God's consummate blessing offered to all humankind (Jer. 31:31–34). The New Testament quotes him in discussing how much better the ministry offering of Christ is than that under the Law of Moses, saying, "The ministry Jesus has received is as superior to theirs as the covenant of which he is mediator is superior to the old one, and it is founded on better promises" (Heb. 8:6). Summarizing a few verses later what is at the crux of the promise of God, it is written, "For I will forgive their wickedness and will remember their sins no more" (Heb. 8:12; Jer. 31:34).

I have heard it suggested that this means that God literally forgets our sins, with no future remembrance of it ever having happened. Maybe it is so; however this presents to me an inherent contradiction: how can an all-knowing God just forget or act as though he does not know about something, in this case about my past sin? Is it an act of dishonesty on God's part to act as though something that did happen did not happen? Can God just be in denial about us by choice? I personally do not think that is the point here, and what I think it actually means is even more powerful in its implication. God's forgiveness is about his canceling our debt much as we would cancel a debt owed us by someone else. We forgive it and thus it is no longer owed. We "forget," or forgive, it as a current debt even though we will likely long remember it was once owed. We might even lament at times the loss of the money and the good things we had planned to use it for.

However even though God forgave Israel, he spoke about some of those same sins later. In other words, even though he "forgave" those sins, he still remembered that they had been committed and that he had indeed remitted them. God *chooses to see* us as holy and blameless. God chooses to forgive the debt our sin creates. It is a divine act of unbelievable mercy and grace. But still, even though he is aware in some way of its original accrual, he chooses to ignore it and treats us (sees) us as though we never committed any of it! It seems, in this way of thinking, that it makes this act of mercy even more significant in its eternal implications, while reconciling what God does to his divine nature, in this case, his omniscience.

I think each of us, when we ponder it a while, can just be overwhelmed with the enormity of our sin, especially when we are looking deeply inside ourselves and remembering our evil thoughts and motives, let alone looking just at the things we have done outwardly in the flesh. We can be so self-centered, contemplating and focusing on the things we think, we feel, and we desire to have or do. When sin entered the world, it corrupted everything. Nothing about any of us escapes any of it. It seeps out of our cores. Jesus said it is out of evil in our heart that our evil actions flow—"For out of the heart come evil thoughts, murder, adultery, sexual immorality, theft, false testimony, slander" (Matt. 15:19).

As noted previously, not only does God see our outward behaviors, he also sees our thoughts and feelings deep in our hearts, and he sees them as behaviors as well. And not only does God also see our thoughts and feelings as behaviors, he even sees and judges the motives behind them! King David told his son and successor, Solomon, "The Lord searches every heart and understands every motive behind the thoughts" (1 Chron. 28:9). God said through Jeremiah, "I the Lord search the heart and examine the mind, to reward a man according to his conduct, *according to what his deeds deserve"* (Jer. 17:10, italics added). God commanded us to love him with our hearts, souls, and minds (Matt. 22:36). The love that is commanded here (*agape*, Greek) is a love of the will, not a love of sentiment or feeling. It is an active love. And we are commanded to exercise it with *all* of our hearts, souls, and minds! And we *all* surely fall short of it *all* of the time!

Yes, reckoning with our sin on our own can and should be overwhelming to us because it is in fact impossible for us. We were made to eat from the life-giving Tree of Life, not from the deadly Tree of the Knowledge of Good and Evil. When we try to relate to God as equal to him (be *like* God), based on our own performance, we look into the face of the utterly, ridiculously impossible! However, reckoning with our sin in view of God's mercy immediately and eternally changes our whole life equation from a negative proposition to a gloriously positive one.

When we come to Christ, we realize that God has from creation made provision to see us without sin—completely holy—such that no longer is condemnation to be feared (Rom. 8:1–4). In Christ, God sees us without sin, even though we clearly are not without sin. None of us are (Rom. 3:23). In reality we all know we are patently *not* holy and blameless, even after coming into him (1 John 1:8). But our God calls things that are not as though they are. He is sovereign, and he can do as he divinely chooses, as he has purposed from the beginning of it all.

How can an all-knowing God just pretend he does not see what is in fact actually there? The answer to that question lies in God's divine nature. It resides in the pure, endless waters of his deep abiding love. The best human approximation is the love godly parents have for their children. Nothing they could do would stop us from loving them. We love them through and in spite of their worst offenses and weaknesses. We love them because of who we are—parents—not because of who they are—mere infants. It is infinitely greater for us with our loving Father in Heaven.

He is the Father; we are mere infants. But in Christ we are *his* infants!

And what he has done and still does for us assures us that he is indeed a loving, inviting, forgiving Heavenly Father! And it is he who said, "I will remember their sin no more." God is the one who calls things that are not into being, and in this case, in Christ he declares us, when we are sitting on the verge of annihilation on death row, as not guilty (Rom. 4:17, 5:6–10).

From his Great Commission (Matt. 28:19–20) and his Great Commandment (Matt. 22:36), Christ lovingly and sacrificially extends to each of us his *Great Invitation*, "Come to me, all who labor and are heavy laden, and I will give you rest. Take my yoke upon you, and learn from me; for I am gentle and lowly in heart, and you will find rest for your souls. For my yoke is easy, and my burden is light" (Matt. 11:28–30).

Questions and Thoughts for Reflection and Discussion

1. Like the teens who were mentioned early in the chapter and who behave as thankless outcasts when they are in reality loved and blessed, how can we as Christians behave similarly with God?
2. How have you experienced God opening your eyes to truly "get" something about him and your relationship to him that you had never comprehended or experienced before?
3. How does God directly "reveal" things to us by the Holy Spirit?
4. How can the testimony of our lives be a witness to God's kindness and mercy, and how might it also serve as the opposite when we don't behave accordingly?
5. When we trust that God chooses to see us on an ongoing basis as completely sinless, how should it affect how we live out our lives?

CHAPTER 11

THE VIEW FROM THE CROSS

Viewing ourselves as well as others,
We see us both distorted—askew.
Sadly looking from our own fallen anguish,
From a sinful person's obstructed view.

God sees us not only through eyes in heaven,
Nor through the sad eyes of a human heart at a loss.
He sees us clearly through a lens of suffering,
Peering down on us from the Cross!

One of the most challenging faith feats of all is to see through the eyes of Christ, as he looks down from the Cross. Literally as when he was actually hanging there at the time. Figuratively, as he sees us daily and forever through his infinite perspective gained through it. But suffering for others can indeed help us to see them much differently.

What happened with *God* at the cross? I personally believe some of the philosophical and theological views handed down to us unnecessarily shackle and limit our ways of thinking about him. As I have clearly stated, I do not purport to have God all figured out. But also I do not think others do either. Just because one is a religious scholar, theologian, or pastor or knows much about God doesn't assure they know God much at all. In saying this, I certainly do not intend to denigrate those who are capable in the field; I am only saying that we must not be overly impressed with any human or their title. We must first consider the "*outcome* of their ways of life" (Heb. 13:7) before choosing to believe and imitate them. Does their life reflect the life of a true disciple? And, further, we must be able to clearly see that their joy and their boasting is merely in knowing the Lord, not knowing all about the Lord (Jer. 9:24). At the foot of the cross, we are all equals.

Suffice it to say, any limitations in our knowledge about God's view of us from the cross will limit our knowledge of God. And any shallowness in our knowledge of God will limit our ability to see him seeing us from the cross—his ultimate view of us. So it is paramount that we consider carefully not just our view of God, but how we use the Bible and creation to determine what we think about God and who he is. Scripture and our view of creation can enable us to know God better or inhibit us in knowing him much at all. We must strive to make sure that for us it is the former and not the latter!

It was Jesus himself who said to Jews who were clearly knowledgeable about scripture, "You diligently study the Scriptures because you think that by them you possess eternal life. These are the Scriptures that testify about me, yet you refuse to come to me to have life" (John 5:39–40). "You refuse to come to me," he says. You know *things*, but you don't know *me*! He said this in spite of the fact that those whom he was addressing had likely memorized huge chunks of scripture, and perhaps the whole Torah (Genesis to Deuteronomy). Jesus said to them just before this, "You have never heard his [God's] voice or seen his form, nor does his word dwell in you . . ." (John 5:37–38, brackets added). You do not see God, you do not hear God, and you do not, in reality, even have his word in you! It is as if he was saying, you have memorized his words but in your hearts made them out to be yours. Thus in you his word does not abide. You are clueless about God! You missed it.

We must all be dedicated to not making a mistake of such grave and eternal consequences, for the sake of ourselves and for the sake those we influence—"Pay close attention to yourself [concentrate on your personal development] and to your teaching; persevere in these things [hold to them], for as you do this you will ensure salvation both for yourself and for those who hear you" (1 Tim. 4:16, Amplified Bible, brackets are part of quote).

The Jews were God's chosen people. He chose them for several, and perhaps many, reasons. Chiefly, they were the bearers of all his promises and especially of the ultimate promise to bless the whole world through the universal blessing of a Savior for all nations (Gen. 12:3). He gave them numerous assignments and experiences that foreshadowed all that was to come in Christ. They were a physical nation; we in the church comprise a spiritual nation. They had a physical bondage in Egypt; before we are saved, we have a spiritual bondage to sin. They had a physical deliverer that led them from a physical land of slavery; we have a spiritual bondage and a spiritual deliverer that gives us life and leads us from our slavery to sin and death. They had a physical Passover lamb; we have a spiritual Passover lamb in Jesus. They came to a physical rock from which God gave them water; we have a spiritual Rock (Christ) from which God gives us spiritual water (the Holy Spirit). They had a physical journey to a physical promised land; we have the spiritual versions. The foreshadowing metaphors (*types* and *antitypes* as seen in biblical typology) are rich and numerous.

Paul uses such metaphors, pointing out that the kinds of things that happened to Israel are examples to us and are written down to warn us, on whom the end and culmination of this present age comes (1 Cor. 10:1–13). Israel's experiences were foreshadowing the challenges Christians face and served as examples and even warnings for those who would enter the kingdom of Christ. Paul uses them as metaphors to teach and caution about the danger of disobedient and careless ways. In effect, Paul says, "Israel was baptized; Israel took the Lord's Supper; and Israel still fell and fell hard!" He warns us all about doing exactly the same thing. It was as if he was saying, "You were baptized into Christ; you have participated in the Lord's Supper, partaking of his body and blood; but you too can still fall!" He concludes, "So, if you think you are standing firm, be careful that you don't fall!" (1 Cor. 10:12). What had happened to Israel was real, but it foreshadowed what the church would also do as God's eternal plan unfolded through Christ.

In reiteration, Israel was directly spoken to by God through Moses, had been led by God, had God's law, were his holy nation, were the people of his plan, and had seen and heard of his powerful miracles of leadership and testimony to himself. Yet many of them, especially among their leaders, had missed God completely. They had made God out to be someone he was not. They did not really know God; they knew the skewed version of God they had developed—ultimately the "God" they had made up. So when the real God showed up in Jesus, they did not even recognize or accept him—"He came to that which was his own, but his own did not receive him" (John 1:11). They were looking for someone else made in *their own* image—what they thought God should look like. They had made God out to be who they wanted him to be for their selfish, self-centered reasons and then passed down their mistake to the generations to come. It was as if they had for some unknown reason decided Jesus was a very tall, skinny white guy, and then when he came for a visit, he was a short, stocky black guy, whom they did not recognize. So they did not believe Jesus was the Messiah. And they thus got him killed him for what they saw as his alleged fraud!

But the only fraud involved was their own!

As a nation of God's people, they had "seen it all," so to speak. They had experienced the highs and lows of serving God on this battleground known as earth. Yet in the end, they rejected the very culmination of the whole plan—Jesus Christ! They made it about them, not him, which was ultimately what the original sin was all about—the ultimate sin that humankind has passed down through the ages. This is the underlying sin that is completely contagious and spreads to all men (Rom. 5:12). Adam and Eve ate the fruit, thinking it would make them "like God," knowing good and evil for themselves. They wanted to be self-reliant, which they were not qualified to be. They did not want to trust God; they wanted to trust in themselves. And this leads to all the other sins that follow.

The Jews then bore the burden of it in their hearts, trying to do it for themselves through living by the Law—a system of right and wrong—"the knowledge of good and evil." God gave them their law to protect them and define them as his people. Instead of accepting it as another expression of his grace and goodness toward them, they turned it into a system for achieving and proving their own righteousness. They failed at it as God had said all humankind would fail at it—"all have sinned and fall short of the glory of God" (Rom. 3:23). The reality is, as Paul said, "Clearly no one is justified before God by the law" (Gal. 3:11). But God was not surprised by all of this. He knew what would happen and planned for redemption through Christ from the beginning. "Law" to humankind was and is representative of the Tree of the Knowledge of Good and Evil, a choice they were clearly told to avoid—"you must not eat from the tree . . . when you eat from it you will certainly die" (Gen. 2:17).

So, why did God do it all in the first place, most minds will ultimately ask? Why did he create the world? Why did he plant two choices in the Garden before humankind? I do not know. Nobody does because he does not really tell us. As with most of the deeper things of God, we are not capable of fully understanding it anyway (Job 38:2). But what I do know is that before this creation there was the real and present danger of sin, even in heaven, as evidenced by Satan and the "angels that sinned" (2 Pet. 2:4). And after this finite world is all wrapped up, the possibility of sin will be no more. It seems there is an eternal change in the God-realm that happens through this present age! In speaking of Jesus's final act, Paul says that finally Christ will hand over the kingdom to God the Father, after destroying the dominion of evil ruled by Satan (1 Cor. 15:24–28). The last enemy to be destroyed will be death itself. Christ will finally put everything completely under his own dominion. Then, when that is done, Christ himself will subject himself to God. God will thus subject a part of himself to himself. Hmm. Surely a divine mystery.

The triune nature of God baffles us. Okay, excuse me; some schools of thought hate the use of trinity or triune to describe God, because the wording represents only a construct to try to express God as Father, Son, and Holy Spirit. This is what is sometimes translated as the "Godhead" or the "fullness of God." Translators struggle with words to describe such spiritual things. Views of God's nature, among those who spend their whole lives studying this stuff, vary significantly, and a certain school of thought can be fairly incredulous at the supposed ignorance of the others. Many see, quite arrogantly I believe, any who would dare disagree with them as veritable heretics, and this because of something none of us can really understand! But what we do know is that the best rendering of the Hebrew text into English basically says, "God said, 'Let us make man in our image' . . ." This is "one" God calling himself "us." In English, it is plural possessive. Yes, I indeed have read the lexicons and commentaries, and there's plenty of disagreement, pointing out that God did not explain it all to us.

I do not know Hebrew. I am a pastor and a lifelong student of God though. Some would see me even discussing this as naïve and ludicrous. Perhaps it is, but I see it as essential for each of us in understanding God to at least broach the subject.

The kingdom was initiated, by God's own design, through "unschooled, ordinary men" who had simply been with Jesus (Acts 4:13). I feel somewhat as Luke described those original apostles. I also take a similar stance as Paul did in his situation—though I may not be a Hebrew or Old Testament scholar, "I do have knowledge" (2 Cor. 11:6). All believers do to a God-given degree (1 John 2:20, 27; 1 Cor. 2:13–16). Perhaps knowledge of an equally important kind too—divine *knowledge* learned from the Holy Spirit and further honed on the anvil of real, daily Christian life. Knowledge gained from a study of the Bible and from ministering God's word at the most basic human levels, fighting the street-level battle with the "little" people. This is to say that I think I have learned a few things about God beyond the scope of the classrooms and out in God's world itself—God's classroom of creation and life.

Hebrew scholars rendered God's statement about himself to say that a singular God referred to himself as "us" and "our." The same thing happens three other times in scripture, in Genesis 3:22 and 11:7 and Isaiah 6:8. Some believe he was referring to himself along with all the angels and other heavenly beings. Maybe so. But we get a peek through a crack in the door to infinity into something about God himself and his heavenly realms. I believe he is referring to the "trinity"—the Father, the Son, and the Holy Spirit. Some get even more complicated. Personally, I do not know for certain but just how I think about it. Unfortunately, God does not explain it with footnotes or margin commentary, even though others might have written their own margin notes of explanation.

But all of the theological arguments passed down through the ages through all sorts of Judeo-Christian traditions can shackle us as we can then mistakenly think all truth has been discovered and finalized. Further, we unwittingly can be led to feel we must be defenders of tradition's answers rather than seekers of the pure truth of God. Yes, we must learn and even build on what others have explored. But we must also not be hindered by it from honesty and continued truth seeking. While I believe God's basic nature is unchanging, that does not mean he cannot change things in his realm at all. God creates. He calls things that aren't into being. He can do as he purposes. We are made in his image, and we change and grow and the realm he made for us changes (2 Cor. 3:18). Is that not true? It is true, and this present world reveals and reflects God's invisible qualities. So what does the reality of change here say about God's "invisible qualities—his eternal power and divine nature"—and his heavenly realm (Rom. 1:20)? Yes, I am aware of the scriptures about the immutability of God and have considered them carefully.

So, how it is communicated is that something happens within the God-realm, perhaps even within God himself. Jesus made an eternal choice coming here, a choice he did not have to make. Jesus is said to have been "slain from the foundation of the world" (Rev. 13:8), so the entry of sin into the picture was certainly not unanticipated. It is portrayed as having started basically at humanity's inception. Jesus said, "The reason my Father loves me is that I lay down my life—only to take it up again. No one takes it from me, but I lay it down of my own accord. I have authority to lay it down and authority to take it up again. This command I received from my Father" (John 10:17–18). The Bible makes it clear that Jesus did what he did of his own accord.

Paul wrote, "Your attitude should be the same as that of Christ Jesus: *Who, being in very nature God, did not consider equality with God something to be grasped,* but made himself nothing, taking the very nature of a servant, being made in human likeness. And being found in appearance as a man, he humbled himself and became obedient to death—even death on a cross! Therefore God exalted him to the highest place and gave him the name that is above every name, that at the name of Jesus every knee should bow, in heaven and on earth and under the earth, and every tongue confess that Jesus Christ is Lord, to the glory of God the Father" (Phil. 2:5–11). Jesus was in the form of God before he took on the form of man. He was God; then he became man. John tells us Jesus was God before he came here, "In the beginning was the Word, and *the Word was with God*, and the Word was God . . . And *the Word became flesh* and dwelt among us, and we have seen his glory, glory as of the only Son from the Father, full of grace and truth" (John 1:1, 14, italics added).

Jesus apparently carefully considered coming to live and die as he did while still in the infinite domain of God. He then decided not to retain his "equality" with God—his God form, which he obviously still had during his deliberation. God the Son humbled himself to God the Father, and then God the Father exalted God the Son to the highest level. And then Paul points out that in the end Jesus, God the Son, will eternally subject himself to God the Father (1 Cor. 15: 28). With all of that said, any thorough understanding of the spiritual reality and implication of all of this is beyond human comprehension, I believe. I only delve into it to stretch our minds to be able to see more clearly through the eyes of Christ.

God seemingly did all that within himself. Further, through the spiritual war fought out through humankind, he determined to destroy even the possibility of sin in the God-realm. He actually condemned sin itself by what he accomplished through the work of Christ (Rom. 8:3–4). In a statement debating about its meaning, Paul says, "God made him who had no sin to be sin for us, so that in him we might become the righteousness of God" (2 Cor. 5:21). Some translations insert the word "offering," but others do not. God made Jesus to be "sin" for us. Perhaps it gives deeper meaning to Jesus's haunting words spoken from the cross, in some of the few New Testament words rendered in Aramaic, the common language of the Jews. Matthew records it this way, "Jesus cried out in a loud voice, '*Eli, Eli, lema sabachthani?*' (which means 'My God, my God, why have you forsaken me?')" (Matt. 27:46, parentheses part of quote). Could such passionate words be considered only rhetorical, or was there a tearing in the very soul of God that occurred at the cross? Consider this: "He who was seated on the throne said, 'I am making everything new!' Then he said, 'Write this down, for these words are trustworthy and true'" (Rev. 21:5). Write this down; it is the truth. I am making everything new! Even making something about himself new, perhaps.

Or perhaps something was to change in the heavenly realm itself—"But in keeping with his promise we are looking forward to a new heaven and a new earth, where righteousness dwells" (2 Pet. 3:13). In John's vision in Revelation, John records, "He who was seated on the throne said, 'I am making everything new!' (Rev. 21:5). John describes, as the fulfillment of new heaven and new earth promise, a seeming merger of heaven and earth in a glorified redemption of creation. Some might argue that the heaven that is being made new is the universe we see from this world—the heavens we speak of looking into the sky. However, the heaven that is coming down to earth in John's vision is the dwelling of God. Nonetheless, it is impossible for us to know or understand what all of this means. There are various plausible interpretations to the meaning of all of this, but there are still challenges with each one of them.

Whatever is being implied, God is clearly making everything new. Everything.

Through the cross, God at least took, and perhaps even gained, a different point of view—on humankind, and maybe even on himself and his own realm in some way. Seemingly, the cross experience gives the God-realm a different perspective on the human realm, and perhaps even a different perspective on the heavenly realm. Consider this passage: "Therefore, *it was essential that* He had to be made like His brothers (mankind) in every respect, so that He might [by experience] become a merciful and faithful High Priest in things related to God, to make atonement (propitiation) for the people's sins [thereby wiping away the sin, satisfying divine justice, and providing a way of reconciliation between God and mankind]. Because He Himself [in His humanity] has suffered in being tempted, He is able to help *and* provide immediate assistance to those who are being tempted *and* exposed to suffering" (Heb. 2:17–18, Amplified Bible, brackets, parentheses, and italics included in quote). He became something so that he might apparently be able to do something that he apparently in some way was not previously able to do.

Some suggest he did this only for our benefit so that we could see that he experientially understood our plight. It sure does not look to me like it was only for our benefit though! Jesus was and is the eternal Word and God (John 1:1). The Son was and is God. Jesus, the man, is the Son in the flesh, the incarnate God. Jesus said, "Anyone who has seen me has seen the Father" (John 14:9). You see me; you see the Father. Again, "The Son is . . . the exact representation of his [God's] being" (Heb. 1:3, brackets added). Yet the scripture also says, "Jesus was the Son of God, but he still suffered, and through his sufferings he learned to obey whatever God says. This made him the perfect high priest, who provides the way for everyone who obeys him to be saved forever" (Heb. 5:8–9, Easy-to-Read Version). At least in human form, he learned some things, and he was made something.

However, it is not to be doubted that God's character is unchanging. Consider the following scriptures: "I the Lord do not change . . ." (Mal. 3:6), "Every good and perfect gift is from above, coming down from the Father of the heavenly lights, who does not change like shifting shadows" (James 1:17), and "Jesus Christ is the same yesterday and today and forever" (Heb. 13:8). So let me reiterate that I am in no way inferring that God had to remove sin or the possibility of sin from himself, but only that something was changing eternally from before this present age to after it, both on earth and in heaven. The issue then becomes what "unchanging" mean in these scriptures and how and if adjustments occur with Yahweh, who is of unchanging being and character.

So, since Christ's death on the cross, God sees us through the eyes or perspective he apparently gained through it. I believe that when one open-mindedly looks at the traditional scriptural and logical construct that is built up concerning immutability, the scriptures it is built on, and conclusions drawn from it, some of the conclusions drawn are just not quite as compelling as the emotion behind it would imply. Again, I believe that so many arguments in Christianity, and religion in general, are shored up and protected as much by emotion, sentiment, and tradition as they are by compelling, logical arguments that account for all that is revealed. Sure, many varying points of view are arguable, but it is not fair or wise to close-mindedly protect our own doctrinal interpretations and conclusions by saying or implying that those who might question their exactness are heretics, deny scripture, blaspheme God, and so forth. In my experience, it seems the more emotional and defensive we are in the defense of our points of view, the less reasonable and sure is our position.

The reality is that God is not to simply be a subject or a doctrine to us any more than my wife is to me. He is to be a person to be related to. I do not have to understand everything about him to relate to him, just as I do not have to with my wife. But I do have to trust them both.

Remember, the Jews accused Jesus of blasphemy as he tried to demonstrate to them who God really was and is! God forbid that we not do the same to those who might honestly disagree with our cherished positions.

I am okay if I am wrong, but I believe that to really see God seeing us from the cross needs careful consideration. I believe we are saved through our faith in the grace of God offered through the redemptive work of Christ, not by being right about all the details of God. Trying to be right by being right is of the wrong tree. Jesus is the Tree of Life, and he reopened the Garden of God so that we again can eat freely of the Tree of Life. He is the gate.

To summarize this thought, we know that simply put, God is God. He is completely sovereign, and he is unchanging. How can he be unchanging and still be changing things, even in the heavenly realm, and perhaps even in some way himself? I do not know. Nor does anybody else.

To see God how God really sees us, we have to try to really see God. To see God, we may have to look around or beyond some long-held views that might actually be obscuring him from us by keeping us closed-minded. But we must not let anyone or anything get between God and us. God can handle our honest, sincere questions, just as a loving parent understands and even appreciates the honest questions their children ask them. He knows well that he and his essence baffle us and that we are really fairly incapable of truly understanding much of it. I think that if there is laughter in heaven, God must laugh at our theological discussions, much as we would laugh at a six-year-old's explanation of sex after a brief conversation with her parents about it. What is a youngster capable of understanding about human sexuality? In the same way, what are finite humans capable of understanding about the inner workings of God?

Whatever you do though, do not come to your own conclusions and then assume you have cornered the market on the truths of God. Let's not keep repeating that sad old tale.

What we do know is that the New Testament gives us a view of God looking down on us through the lens he made for himself, and for us as well—the cross. It is a lens of incredible love, mercy, and yes, justice. It is a lens of reality and suffering. It is a very human lens. And it is very much a lens of God. It is a lens of a perfect Christ being falsely convicted of and then executed for the worst sin of all—blasphemy. It is a lens of injustice. It is a lens of unfairness. The cross is raw and it is real. It is where we live though—beneath it. It is a lens that, because of God's own blood component, allows God to forgive us and see us as completely holy and blameless. Really. It is a lens that removes for God the barrier of sin that compels him as a holy God to withdraw from us as unholy, sinful beings (Isa. 59:1–2).

Jesus's statements while he was on the cross give insight to his view from it. Consider the seven statements the gospels record:

1. "Father, forgive them, for they do not know what they are doing" (Luke 23:34). This statement clearly demonstrates the mercy of God manifested in this painful, gruesome moment. His concern was for humanity, even those who directly perpetrated his unjust crucifixion. The cross represents where the best of God meets the worst in humanity, where the glorious of God meets the inglorious of humans, and where the light of heaven meets the darkness of earth. And all that is of God wins out over all that is not of him. God chose from creation to see us as holy and blameless in Christ, and at the cross he made it happen.

2. To the thief who asks Jesus to remember him in his kingdom—"Truly I tell you, today you will be with me in paradise" (Luke 23:43). As Jesus had done in his life—bring healing to those who needed a physician—he did in his death. We are all thieves. We all deserve to die on the cross. But Jesus did it in our place so that we would not have it. As Jesus had reached out to the ostracized and marginalized in life, he did in his death. As Jesus had given his best for the worst in his life, he did in his death. As he had shown the power to forgive sins in his life, he showed the power to destroy sin in his death. God is a God of mercy, and he looked down in his pain through his lens of mercy.

3. To his mother, Mary, concerning the apostle John and to the apostle John concerning Mary: "When Jesus saw his mother there, and the disciple whom he loved standing nearby, he said to her, 'Woman, here is your son,' and to the disciple, 'Here is your mother'" (John 29:26–27). Jesus is said to have been fully God and fully man. He was God in the flesh, Emmanuel, God with us. Concerning the very human exchange he'd had with his mother at the Cana wedding, when she had volunteered him to solve the hosts' problem of running out of wine, he said, "Woman, why do you involve me? . . . My hour has not yet come." To which she simply responded to the servants, "Do whatever he tells you" (John 2:4–5). Does that sound typical of a mother with a son or what? In Jesus we experience both his utter humanness and his utter Godhood.

4. *"Eli, Eli, lema sabachthani?"* (which means "My God, my God, why have you forsaken me?") (Matt. 27:46). As already mentioned, this is one of the few phrases in the New Testament in Aramaic, the common language of the Jews during Jesus's time. Using this language is perhaps a more telling statement that Matthew wrote it that way, but also possibly reflective of Jesus's personal, informal language he had used with his Father and his early family all along. The statement by Jesus clearly is to hearken us back to the amazingly precise Messianic prophecy of Psalm 22, quoting the first line of it, voicing not only his own agony in having the sins of the world laid on him as the ultimate atoning sacrifice but also giving voice to the horror of those souls who witnessed what evil humanity was capable of doing. Jesus was looking down on us as he looked up toward God, feeling in himself the painful tearing between God and him that we had caused and that we ourselves deserved. He, however, did not deserve it, yet he took it on himself out of his love and mercy for us.

5. "I am thirsty" (John 19:28). To the dumbfounded Samaritan woman he had met at the well, he'd asked, "Will you give me a drink?" There is no indication that she ever did give him that drink. What she did do was engage him in a conversation about living water, about her personal life, about the controversy between Israel and Judah over the proper place to worship, and about true worship. And she went and told the people of Samaria about the prophet that she had encountered (story found in John 4:1–28). From the cross, he had said, "I am thirsty." Again, rather than receiving from humanity a simple drink of water, he was offered vinegar made more bitter with gall. Likely, this was also given as a painkiller of sorts intended to render him insensible to the pain he was enduring. Jesus, however, rejected their substitutionary offer they made him in place of plain water. Perhaps he was reflecting back to humanity what he saw in its stubborn resistance to give him the lowliest offering when he was in that very moment giving us the ultimate one. Perhaps too he was in this statement reflecting the prophetic sentiment of Psalm 42, which begins, "As the deer pants for streams of water, so my soul pants for you, my God. My soul thirsts for God, for the living God. When can I go and meet with God?" (Ps. 42:1–2).

6. "Father, into your hands I commit my spirit" (Luke 23:46). Quoting verse 5 of the Messianic Psalm 31, in this one statement Jesus gives summary to a psalm likely well known among the Jews. In it, Jesus gives us the visual of what he was praying looking up at God, as he raised his head from looking down at us from the cross.

7. "It is finished" (John 19:30). Jesus had told them he had come to seek and save the lost. Jesus told them he had come to serve and not to be served. He had said he was sent to the lost sheep of Israel. His was a mission to preach the gospel of God and to be the gospel of God. He was Emmanuel,

God with us. He came to save the world. He had said a number of times, as recorded by the apostle John in his gospel that his "hour" had not yet come. Finally however, John writes Jesus as saying, "The hour has come for the Son of Man to be glorified" (John 12:23). That he said "it is finished" was in no way a statement of defeat or of any finality of eternal purpose, but just that he had accomplished what he had come here for. His hour had come. All that was left was to conquer death itself, return to his Father, pour out his Spirit on all flesh, and advance his kingdom on into the next age.

These seven statements, I am sure, were carefully chosen by Christ. I believe they were also carefully woven into the cross narrative by the four gospel writers in order to tell a story—the narrative of Christ. They collectively speak reams, as each statement references whole texts and deep concepts. Jesus prays for mercy for his executors acting by proxy for all of humanity. Jesus extends mercy and hope to a repentant criminal. He extends care to his mother and honors "the disciple he loved" by bestowing on him this honorable task. Jesus then shouts out the anguish all humanity suffers with our alienation from God, as well as the seemingly unbearable pain of dying for the sins of the world and the separation from God he felt in doing so. He looks down at us and asks us for the simplest of things—a drink of water. The creator of water asks us for a drink of it. He commits his spirit back to God's justice and mercy and then pronounces that his ministry here to be finished.

Imagine for a moment what God saw in the face of humanity as he spoke these final words. Imagine how God felt seeing us see him. It is in seeing us see him that we can best understand seeing him see us.

The cross is a lens that allows us to look through it and see God in our own very human language and experience. It allows us to see God seeing us through our experience. He wants to be our loving Father. He loves us more than we can imagine. He cares. He knows that we are weak and fallible. He knows we mess up, and sometimes very badly. He sees the pain we suffer because of sin, and often because of our own sin. He sees us when we don't believe in him or trust him. He loves us anyway and continues to beckon us through the generations—"Come to me, all you who are weary and burdened, and I will give you rest. Take my yoke upon you and learn from me, for I am gentle and humble in heart, and you will find rest for your souls. For my yoke is easy and my burden is light" (Matt. 11:28–30).

It reminds me of a song I learned back in college, in my early days as a new Christian. Written and published by Ellis J. Crum in 1977, the lyrics of the first verse are,

> *He paid a debt He did not owe;*
> *I owed a debt I could not pay;*
> *I needed someone to wash my sins away.*
> *And, now, I sing a brand new song,*
> *"Amazing Grace."*
> *Christ Jesus paid a debt that I could never pay.*

The message from the cross is that we can approach God freely and confidently (Eph. 3:12). We thus sing a brand-new song. Through what happened at the cross, we can become God's dearly loved children. We don't have to live as slaves anymore (Rom. 8:15–16; Eph. 5:1–2). To quote Martin Luther King's gripping statement from his famous "I Have a Dream" speech, "Free at last, Free at last, Thank God almighty we are free at last." In Christ, we can finally be free at last!

From the cross, God can see the dead be raised, the lame walk, the blind see, the lost be found, and humanity saved. Looking up at the cross, we see the only eternal hope for humanity. God have mercy on us all.

It is through God's most compelling love shown through the corrective lens of the cross that we can look at God and everyone and everything else from a new point of view (2 Cor. 5:16). It is through this new point of view that we become new creations (2 Cor. 5:17).

God said, "I am making everything new!" He is doing it through what he accomplished by the cross, the lens of God. Through that lens, he already sees us as new—new creations in Christ! He sees us as "holy and blameless in his sight." He planned it that way from creation.

Repent (change your mind), if you need to, and believe the good news! It's the truth.

Questions and Thoughts for Reflection and Discussion

1. How do you think Israel could have been so mistaken about the identity of the Messiah when he came, given they had waited expectantly so long?
2. Why do we rely so heavily on scholars and theologians when the gospel message and subsequently the Christian life itself are at their core quite simple?
3. Why might it matter that God is not only recreating the earth, but he is also recreating heaven?
4. How do you explain Jesus becoming eternally subject to the Father, when he is a part of the Godhead or Trinity?
5. Discuss what the statements Jesus made on the cross and their message to you personally.
6. How would you summarize how you think God sees us through the lens of the cross?

CHAPTER 12

ALL GOD SEES

Nothing in all creation is hidden from God's sight. Every-
thing is uncovered and laid bare before the eye of him to
whom we must give account.

—Hebrews 4:13

I wandered through a cave into darkness,
Could not see even the faintest glow,
Nothing of what lay above me,
Nothing of what lay below.

Walked out, climbed a nearby tower,
In brightest sun scanned the vista wide.
The view was bright and stunning,
In such light nothing there could hide.

Although I finally canceled all my subscriptions and started reading news on phone apps, I have been a newspaper reader since I was a kid. I originally started checking the local paper out to read the Sunday comics. Then I started reading the sports page. I progressed to reading through the whole thing. One of the things I liked about newspapers is that they satisfied my constant curiosity about all things human, and without my having to listen to the gory details about every story to get to the next via radio and television. I can pick what part I want to read—the headlines themselves, the basic details of the stories, or the whole articles. I can choose to look at accompanying pictures or not look at them. Television and radio news is not that way. Unless you record the broadcast so you can control the feed later, they choose what you will hear and see, and you have to listen and watch every detail of one story to get to the next. Then there are those commercials that specifically target one of the primary broadcast news audiences— older white men. You can guess what a lot of those are, I suppose. Because I do not want to hear or see most of any particular story, and because I sure don't like the commercials, I don't watch broadcast news. There's just too much I don't want to see.

Media news mostly tends to be bad news. Seemingly the more tragic, startling, or menacing it is, the better. Terrorist, anarchist groups, and politicians, in no particular order, have learned the power of bad news and the fear it produces in societies and now, with the proliferation of advanced communication and media, the whole world. There have been some attempts over the years to launch good news reports; however, oddly, they have not really succeeded. Paul Harvey, a popular radio personality of the twentieth century, had a radio news broadcast that was pretty positive and did fairly well because of his loyal following. But mostly we feed off the bad stuff. The bottom line is that I just do not want to overfill my mind with bad news. So I read the news apps and occasionally read a newspaper so that I can be informed and yet still be somewhat in control of what I consume.

When I think about God's omniscience, I am overwhelmed with the thought of what *he* actually sees and knows about on daily basis. Ultimately, everything that happens becomes a part of the historical truth. What was is and will always have been. Just ponder for a moment remembering every atrocious event in history with all their gory details. Mind boggling and frightening, I think! Since God is truth and he knows all, he somehow registers and remembers it in all its minute detail. It is an unbelievable amount of information to register. Perhaps he has the ability to suppress it, so that he is not presently aware of some things, but the reality is that he knows it's all there and that is happening. It has all been accruing throughout the history of the creation! Additionally, God does not just see and hear what happens outwardly; he sees what happens inwardly—in our hearts and minds—as well. That is not only scary; it is really pretty morbid to even think about. As a finite human, God's omniscience is to me an unbelievably amazing ability. And as a minister, counselor, and a student of science, grasping his ability to manage all the information is simply incomprehensible.

Jesus explained to us that God is spirit, and to relate to him, we must relate to him in spirit and truth (John 4:24). Thus, God and his spiritual realms are outside the scope of the physical sciences, since the sciences are concerned with and equipped only to deal with the physical realm. The physical sciences do not have the tools to work with the idea of the nonphysical. Secular science is only focused on the material. We must develop spiritual eyes—the eyes of our hearts—in order to see and experience God.

When God commissioned Moses to lead the children of Israel out of Egypt, Moses asked God who he was so that he could tell the people that it was God who had sent him. Here's the exchange that occurred:

Moses said to God, "Suppose I go to the Israelites and say to them, 'The God of your fathers has sent me to you,' and they ask me, 'What is his name?' Then what shall I tell them?" God said to Moses,

"I AM WHO I AM. This is what you are to say to the Israelites: 'I am has sent me to you.'" God also said to Moses, "Say to the Israelites, 'The Lord, the God of your fathers—the God of Abraham, the God of Isaac and the God of Jacob—has sent me to you.' This is my name forever, the name you shall call me from generation to generation." (Exod. 3:13–15)

We live in a finite physical realm of cause and effect. Constant change. We can observe the finite. We can measure the finite. We can affect and manipulate the *finite*. But none of our observations and tools can grapple with the *infinite*. But the sciences are forced to acknowledge the infinite. God is infinite. God said that the infinite is his essence and being—" I AM WHO I AM." As humans we identify ourselves by "where we came from"—our parentage, our heritage, our ethnicity, our race, our homes of origin, and so forth. Our names usually signal our cultures of origin and even the generation we come from. God has no origin though, because he is infinite. He just is. He has no cause, but only effects. I think somewhere in each one of us we somehow know there must be a universal or divine constant. That is what God is.

Simply by the fact that he is spirit, he does not face the same barriers and challenges of existence that we as finite beings face, such as time, space, and resistance. And even in the spirit realm, God is claimed to be the supreme spirit above all others. He has enemies, but he has no rivals. He has no evil equals.

As already noted, the Bible asserts that God is omnipresent, omnipotent, and omniscient. The earliest considerations of the essence and being of God I remember having in adulthood came during a science class while discussing Einstein's general theory of relativity. It was a physical chemistry class in the fall semester of my junior year in college in 1972. The realization hit me that science itself demonstrates that space and time are relative, not fixed. It was at the time, as best I can remember, that I began purposely considering the plausibility of the infinite. To me, it meant that the idea of a god and a spiritual realm was not inherently illogical, when previously in my naïveté I didn't even know how to think about it all. I am not trying to express a scientific opinion or even explain any of it, but I am only saying it was in that context that I began purposely pondering God.

As previously defined, "omnipresence" is a term meaning to be present everywhere at the same time. King David, the psalmist, asked a question and then answered it saying, "Where can I go from your Spirit? Where can I flee from your presence? If I go up to the heavens, you are there; if I make my bed in the depths, you are there. If I rise on the wings of the dawn, if I settle on the far side of the sea, even there your hand will guide me, your right hand will hold me fast" (Ps. 139:7–10). The prophet, psalmist, king completely recognized God as infinite and omnipresent.

Through the prophet Jeremiah, God is said to have asked the rhetorical questions, "Who can hide in secret places so that I cannot see them? Do not I fill heaven and earth?" (Jer. 23:24). A proverb says it this way, "The eyes of the LORD are everywhere, keeping watch on the wicked and the good" (Prov. 15:3). So it is somehow true, as I mentioned previously concerning the eerie hymn we used to sing, "there's an all-seeing eye watching you." I love God and am comforted by his omnipresence! Nonetheless, that hymn still creeps me out. But I digress.

As previously considered, although God is omnipresent, he is not some kind of divine ether that the universe seemingly exists in. He is not simply a universal matrix. God is clearly portrayed throughout scripture as a person with an existence, albeit an infinite one. He created the universe and he sustains it, but he is not the universe itself (Gen. 1:1; Heb. 1:3). As with a house, the structure may have been built by loving parents just for their children. Parents then build a *home* that operates within the house. The house and home are sustained and maintained by the parents for their children. But the house and the home are not the same thing. And the home is not the parents, and the parents are not the home. Now to a youngster bent on misbehavior and attempting to be stealthy, mom will often seem omnipresent! Moms know their abodes and they know their kids, and they have a sixth sense about when something is not right. Thus they will soon show up to the scene of the crime. The world was made for God as our house. We make it our home, and if we seek him he will make his home with us (John 14:23). God builds the house and maintains the home.

And God is no more a mere scientific or philosophical subject than a mom or a dad in the house is. Or you or me. He is a person, but unlike us, he is infinite. Our challenge is however even more insurmountable than that of a microbe living on an elephant's back trying to comprehend the elephant. The microbe simply lives on the elephant's back and feeds on dead skin cells or other debris that falls onto it. Likely it has no mental ability or spatial awareness to comprehend the scope of its greater "single-elephant universe" on which it lives. But that in no way excludes the reality of the elephant's existence. The problem is not with the elephant; the problem is with the limitations of the microbe itself. It's the same with us trying to comprehend God, but even infinitely more so. Talk about a proverbial "ten-thousand-pound elephant" in the room when a discussion about God's existence ensues!

Further, the word "omnipotence," as translated from the corresponding Greek words, generally means "all-ruling" or "all-powerful." It is frequently translated "almighty." Jesus described it this way, saying, "With man this is impossible, but not with God; all things are possible with God" (Mk. 10:27). The multitude in the Revelation shouted, "Hallelujah! Our Lord God *rules*. He is the *All-Powerful*" (Rev. 19:6, Easy-to-Read Version, italics added). The all-powerful one rules all. Paul aptly summarizes the implications of omnipotence to us using a rhetorical question, "If God is for us, who can be against us?" (Rom. 8:31). And that is very good news for those who believe.

Additionally, "omniscience" is an even trickier subject to deal with. The Latin origin of the word simply means "all-knowing." Power and presence have a scientific basis that we can start with. But knowledge is philosophical. In philosophy, the study of knowledge is called epistemology. Epistemology deals with what we know and how we come to know it. The philosophical discussions alone about this can easily give one a headache! Science approaches epistemology with the idea of empiricism. Empiricism is a theory of knowledge that emphasizes sensory perception as the basis of learning, and thus it is the basis of the scientific process itself. It stands alongside theories of rationalism, idealism, and historicism as a way to "know" things. But empiricism like the other methods of acquiring knowledge has been clearly demonstrated to be limited, I believe.

The materialist scientists among us see the mind and anything called "spiritual" as constructs generated by the human brain and body. However, the Bible asserts that God has life independent of the created, rather that the universe was created by him and reflects his being (Rom. 1:20), and not the other way around. God's essence and being possess thought, memory, feeling, presence, and the ability to love and be loved. We are made in his image, and we reflect his infinite qualities into the finite world. We can know and be conscience of a lot; God can remember and is conscience of everything all at once.

So the Bible asserts God to be omnipresent, omnipotent, and omniscient. Simply pondering the magnitude of it all is mindboggling. Trying to actually fully grasp its infinitesimal reality is impossible.

With the "magnitude" of his mental capabilities, consider the kinds of things God sees daily. Again, even using the word magnitude to describe God's existence is a misnomer since as an infinite being he cannot be measured. You can surf the web for specific statistics concerning the amount of information produced daily, but ponder these sad and tragic realities:

1. Every day God sees hundreds and perhaps thousands of little children and adults die of hunger, not to mention the ones that are starving but have not yet died. Imagine, from the American perspective, anyone starving at all with all our wasted food. It takes a long time for someone to starve, so this happens over a significant period of time. God watches every one of them, I suppose. To us, those who starve are mostly across the ocean or somewhere in an unreachable country. From God's perspective, they are right across the street from us.

2. Every day hundreds and perhaps thousands of people are murdered or lose their lives in senseless attacks, fights, wars, and other skirmishes. I have personally seen a few people die or seen them right before or after their deaths, at least one from a self-inflicted wound. I cannot imagine witnessing hundreds of such deaths a day.

3. Thousands of children and adults are sexually molested, raped, mutilated, or exploited every day. Women are raped and beaten, and shockingly, often by husbands or boyfriends. Can you imagine seeing all of that? I have counseled a number of sex offenders or potential sex offenders over the years. I remember the chilling account one gave me of his rape fantasies. He would sit in various parking lots, watching women go in and come out. He would fantasize about kidnapping and raping them. It was very stimulating to him! Imagine having to see the thoughts of someone fantasizing of raping your daughter or wife! I have a wife and a daughter that I adore. The thought of someone even

fantasizing about harming them is just awful! In his saner moments, it was awful for him, and he wanted to stop! I had a pedophile once admit to me in counseling that the object of his perverted lust at that moment was one of my own middle school sons, the son who had been alone with him in our church building not a month earlier! I have never really gotten over that scary reality.

4. Thousands are enslaved, held captive, and bought and sold every day. These are real human beings who are treated worse than animals. God watches it happen.

The pain in this world runs deep and is widespread. God sees it all as the present, it seems. It's humanly unbelievable and unbearable. I have studied religion and philosophy my whole adult life, and I cannot even begin to imagine why God lets it all happen. Yeah, I know the platitudes and simplistic answers, but I do not really buy much of any of them, as they seem shallow, naïve, and sometimes dangerously speculative. It is just a mystery to me, and I do not think we are capable of even beginning to understand this mystery. But I also think simply denying the existence of God because I cannot imagine something about him is a big illogical. I do for many reasons believe in Yahweh, the God of the Bible, and as revealed in Christ Jesus. But in all honesty, I daily sense my limitation in comprehending him. Jesus was God "man-sizing" himself so we could comprehend him in our own human experience. Jesus was as an elephant becoming a microbe and living among the elephant's clueless microbe community in order to explain this giant beast they all lived upon and depended on. The elephant was incomprehensible to the microbes, but this new microbe, they could all sense and relate to. Having been both God and human, Jesus similarly communicates God to us in ways that we could understand—our way, even if we are incapable of comprehending it all.

After all the years of study, I only realize more and more how little any of us really know and how much less we are capable of understanding. After a life filled with education, study, ministry, and life experiences, I am just blown away by it all, and my scope of comprehension is miniscule compared to the infinite. Actually it is incomparable to it. However, the infinite is God's reality; it is how and where the omniscient God exists.

Omniscience, as explained, is simply the capacity to know everything there is to know. Imagine having to handle everything ever said, done, or thought! Heck, we have fits dealing with one little negative thing said to us or about us. Think about how "big" and powerful God must be to be able to handle the awful, awful things he sees and knows! Think about the kind of love, mercy, and patience God must have to not just obliterate us all, as he considered doing with Israel in the wilderness journey (Exod. 32:9–14)! A comic once joked that as a dad he had told his son that he had made him and that he could make another one just like him, so the son had better watch out! All parents can likely relate to the sentiment. He was joking. But God really can do that!

The key question, I think, is not first how could a loving God let such evil occur in the world? The deeper question is perhaps how could someone be purposeful and loving enough to exercise such restraint when they could do something else? Or how could one be so loving or self-controlled so as to be able to exercise such restraint and *not* intervene against evildoers, which is to some degree every one of us? Is God any less loving for letting some faraway war continue than he is letting my in-your-face greed continue? Is God to be accused more for giving me a chance to grow out of and be freed from my deceit and selfishness than he is with others who might exercising patience with others for what I might consider greater sins? Is God guilty for letting evil flourish when he knows he will infinitely reward those who endure overcome it? And further, how could someone possess such power and love so as to turn evil into good (Rom. 8:28; Eph. 1:11)? Talk about recycling and sustainability!

How many terrible acts of violence have occurred because of momentary reactions to others' misdeeds or simply undesirable behaviors? Think about how many weak or unstable parents, during moments of lack of self-restraint, have horribly harmed their children for simply childish misbehaviors. Think about how many wives and husbands have been harmed or killed because of common human disagreements often over inane things, not to mention the policemen that have been killed or injured trying to intervene. Think about how many wars have been started because of the anger and vendettas of capricious leaders. Yes, the line between love and hate can be paper thin, and many egregious acts of passion have occurred when the love boundary blurred into hate. But it is not the greatest love to reactively attacking evil out of passion; the greatest love allows restraint to rule, when a greater good is to be attained through it.

I speak above of the acts and behaviors God tolerates that we as humans consider gross and intolerable. But the reality is that God considers all sin as gross and intolerable, even the so-called "little sins"—the dad who is overly angry with his children and lashes out with some angry names or words, the mom who resents her daughter or is even secretly jealous of her, the son who overtly disobeys a parent concerning homework, or the daughter who defies her parents' wishes and continues to text her friend after a parent-set curfew. There are countless behaviors that we might consider wrong, but unlike those acts we consider intolerable, we find these necessarily tolerable for the longer term and greater good. Ours is simply a collective judgment of what we consider intolerable or tolerable in the context. Well, God must do the same thing in a much, much larger scope and context.

That is how loving our God is! The apostle, John, says in fact that *love is what God is*; it is his essence, writing, "Whoever does not love does not know God, because *God is love*" (1 John 4:8, italics added). As already alluded to it, in the Greek language there are several words to describe the different kinds of love. The Greek word used to describe God and his love is *agape*. It is the love of God. *Agape* love is about willing what is right and then following through with it. *Agape* love is not a sentimental love, but rather it is objective, seeking what is right and good. *Agape* love is not a subjective love, based on "what's in it for me." *Agape* love is not self-seeking or selfish. The apostle Paul describes it this way: "Love is patient, love is kind. It does not envy, it does not boast, it is not proud. It does not dishonor others, it is not self-seeking, it is not easily angered, it keeps no record of wrongs. Love does not delight in evil but rejoices with the truth. It always protects, always trusts, always hopes, always perseveres" (1 Cor. 13:4–7).

Agape love is not reactionary but it is "pre-actionary," that is, it determines in advance how to look at things, react to things, or behave in certain situations, even against evil, rather than acting out of emotion or personal interest! It is proactive, taking action to bring about the best even before bad can happen. That is why Jesus taught us, rather than seeking revenge against those who would harm us, to not resist an evil person at all (Matt. 5:39). He gives application to this command, saying that rather than hit back at someone who strikes us, we should turn the other cheek. From the human perspective, the reasoning emanating from God's perspective seems unreasonable or plain foolish. It is the same as a child trying to understand the reasoning of parents, but on an infinite scale.

It is because of our fallen nature that we need to play "God" in our own and others' lives, and which leads us to make decisions in our own self-interests by human wisdom rather than objective, godly wisdom. We attempt to justify our sins and come to believe that to strike back may be to love, when what God says the higher love is to be able to restrain oneself—the love of God. Men and women are simply not qualified to play God, even in our own lives. We as the microbe cannot comprehend the greater picture, given the magnitude of our host. At the micro level, what may seem good may be evil in the macro and what may seem evil in a moment may actually be for the good in the long run. We are not qualified to play god, even in our own life or in the lives of those we love. And certainly not in the lives of those we barely know or have never even met! Nor can they play that role in their or our lives. We too often, however, make those we love into our idols of sorts that we try to shape and control, as one does a crafted religious icon or statue. And we allow these same ones to control us and our behavior. And we end up worshiping and serving these we have so positioned.

Agape love is the kind of love Jesus was demonstrating when he submitted his own life to be butchered and killed by evil men! Not for his sake, but for theirs, for ours. It was and is his very nature! He trusted God, and God ultimately delivered him—"Therefore God exalted him to the highest place and gave him the name that is above every name, that at the name of Jesus every knee should bow, in heaven and on earth and under the earth" (Phil. 2:9–10). Jesus asks us each to trust God similarly that we too will find the right kind of exaltation in our own submission to God and others (Eph. 5:21). But submission is not the fallen, sinful design. Domination, power, and control are the forte of the flesh!

In our limited state as humans, we must make our decisions about what is right and wrong or loving or unloving using limited knowledge. We are mere microbes in the universe. God however is not limited in this regard. He is the elephant, so to speak. God sees and knows everything. His is the divine intelligence. Truth is found in him and is recorded by him. God sees and knows everything about us. We can keep no secrets from him—"Nothing in all creation is hidden from God's sight. Everything is uncovered and laid bare before the eyes of him to whom we must give account"

(Heb. 4:13). We can fool others, we can fool ourselves, but we cannot fool God. We are in fact fools when we try!

So we don't have to be insulated from accepting the love and grace of God, as we often are, with those other humans around us, by the thought that if God really "knew" me on the inside, then he wouldn't love me. He does know us—inside and outside. In fact, he knows us a lot better than we know ourselves. And he does indeed still love us. Jesus lived and died to give us the proof and assurance we need to be assured of his love for us. We have ample communication from God to be able to comprehend at the human level this otherwise incomprehensible love—"to know this love that surpasses knowledge" (Eph. 3:19).

Hence we should not run *from* God with our dark realities; we should run *to* him. We should not hide from God in our sin; we should bare our soul to him. He alone, in fact, can handle our sin; we in fact cannot. No other but God can! And he handled it well in his life, and he finished it off in his death.

It should be with us with God as I taught my kids as they grew up, "If you mess up, call me; if you mess up really bad, call me really fast." Call God really fast. You can trust in his love and power at all times! He loves us all! Paul said, "Everyone who calls on the name of the Lord will be saved" (Rom. 10:13).

In Christ, God is our "home base." On him—in him—we are eternally and completely "safe"—"He is able to save completely those who come to God through him, because he always lives to intercede for them" (Heb. 7:25). So in those moments when we ruefully ponder our human dilemma, realizing again the magnitude of our sin, we must see that although he sees all, he sees us through infinitely loving and purposeful lens. And thus it should be for us as the Christian song, written by Pastor Edward Mote in 1837, says in echoing the words of Jesus, "On Christ the solid rock I stand, all other ground is sinking sand, all other ground is sinking sand."

That is good news!

Questions and Thoughts for Reflection and Discussion

1. Why do you think we have such a curiosity, and sometimes a morbid curiosity, about things close around us and even around the globe?
2. Compare and contrast the microbe/elephant illustration with us and God. Why is it hard for the minute to comprehend the enormous?
3. Consider the implications of God's omnipresence, omnipotence, and omniscience to each of us.
4. Why might it be said that God's present tolerance of evil is for the ultimate long-term good of us all?
5. How does God "recycle" evil, turning it into God?
6. Consider how God's essence (his essence of *agape*) defines his, as well as our own, existence.
7. Why might it be said that agape describes a love that is completely objective, while the other forms of love—*phileo* (friendship), *storge* (family), and *eros* (sexual)—become increasingly subjective? (the italicized words are the other primary Greek words used for love, along with *agape*)
8. Consider the magnitude of the mind required to comprehend and retain all knowledge through human history, not to mention what is to be known in the heavenly realms. How might that affect your relationship with such a God who can do just that?

CHAPTER 13

THE MIND OF CHRIST

We have the mind of Christ.

—1 Corinthians 2:17

I thought with human wisdom,
Nothing made much sense,
Understood so very little,
So much seemed mere pretense.

I heard the truth of Jesus,
Accepted it as right and true.
The heavenly sky of God's world,
Turned crystal clear and blue!

God said long ago through the prophet Isaiah, "'My thoughts are not your thoughts, neither are your ways my ways,' declares the Lord. 'As the heavens are higher than the earth, so are my ways higher than your ways and my thoughts than your thoughts'"

(Isa. 55:8–9). God doesn't think the way we do. As a mature adult's thoughts are higher than those of a small child, God's thoughts are higher than ours because he has a much higher and broader point of view than we are capable of—an infinite perspective in fact. God has an exponentially greater intelligence, comprehension, and retention than we can even begin to grasp. We are foolish when we think we have it all or even most of it figured out, and thus we do not really need God. It is the humanistic deception—the original sin. It is the fruit of the fruit of the Tree of the Knowledge of Good and Evil. Humanity apart from God, trying to simply survive, let alone thrive, in this world is as three-year-olds trying to make it on their own without a parent or guardian. Humanity trying to live without God's infinite knowledge and wisdom is the ultimate in tomfoolery. God is the Tree of Life, and knowledge of him is our food for eternal life. Eve and Adam did not face death because they ate from the Tree of the Knowledge of Good and Evil; rather, they faced death because in choosing the fruit of the wrong tree, they were forbidden from eating the fruit from the Tree of Life!

God has given us as believers direct access to his thinking. In explaining the reason behind God's plan of redemption in Christ being kept a mystery before the crucifixion and resurrection, Paul explains, "We do, however, speak a message of wisdom among the mature, but not the wisdom of this age or of the rulers of this age, who are coming to nothing. No, we speak of God's secret wisdom, a wisdom that has been hidden and that God destined for our glory before time began" (1 Cor. 2:6–7). God was not to tip his hand to his and our arch nemesis, Satan, lest the devil be able to spoil it simply by not leading his pawns to crucify Christ!

Living after the death, burial, and resurrection of Christ, we have the full story of redemption and have been given a more mature or "complete" wisdom about God's purpose and design— more information, better understanding, greater scope. Even Satan does not have this wisdom, because he showed from the beginning that he did not "get" God's ways or his plan! The wisdom we have been given in Christ was previously kept a secret—a divine mystery—and some of it still is to some lesser degree, and those who are not saved are blinded to it—"The god of this age has blinded the minds of unbelievers, so that they cannot see the light of the gospel that displays the glory of Christ, who is the image of God" (2 Cor. 4:4). And it was God's plan all along to do it this way.

The apostle Paul further explains why God kept it a secret for so long. It was so that Satan, his evil spirits, and his wicked followers would not know how to thwart God's plan—"None of the rulers of this age understood it, for if they had, they would not have crucified the Lord of glory. However, as it is written: 'No eye has seen, no ear has heard, no mind has conceived what God has prepared for those who love him'—but God has revealed it to us by his Spirit" (1 Cor. 2:8–10; Isa. 64:4).

The "rulers" of the dark world did not, and still do not, have the thoughts of God. They too are incapable. Even though powerful and operating in the heavenly realms, they, as we, are not capable of thinking as God does—"For the foolishness of God is wiser than human wisdom, and the weakness of God is stronger than human strength" (1 Cor. 1:25). And they are not capable of the higher thinking that even we are given through the Holy Spirit. Apart from God, what God was and is doing is inconceivable for man, or even the heavenly beings, including Satan. However, God has revealed it to us by his Spirit! Further, God has chosen to reveal his wisdom to these powerful forces through us, the church—"His intent was that now, through the church, the manifold wisdom of God should be made known to the rulers and authorities in the heavenly realms" (Eph. 3:10).

The Holy Spirit that is given to us through Christ is the great promise of the new covenant. Certainly God was to accomplish the redemption of sin through Christ's blood, but apparently in view of the coming crucifixion, God was forgiving sins in some way even before, attributing righteousness to those who trusted his promise (Gen. 15:6; Rom. 4:3). God also previously gave his Spirit to certain people, as with King David (Ps. 51:11) and John the Baptist (Luke 1:15). However, up until Christ had ascended back into heaven, the Spirit was not available to all believers (John 7:39, 16:7). But in these last days, because of Christ's resurrection and ascension, the promised Holy Spirit is given to us through him—"Repent and be baptized, every one of you, in the name of Jesus Christ for the forgiveness of your sins. And you will receive the gift of the Holy Spirit. The promise is for you and your children and for all who are far off—for all whom the Lord our God will call" (Acts 2:38–39). And it is by his Spirit that we possess the mind of Christ, as Paul wrote, "We have the mind of Christ" (1 Cor. 2:16). It is ultimately through our possession of his mind—his thinking—that we can see how God sees us.

The prophet Joel foretold of the outpouring of the Holy Spirit, "I will pour out my Spirit on all people" (Joel 2:28). Peter cites this passage in explaining what God was doing on the day of Pentecost when the disciples had experienced the effects of this promised outpouring (Acts 2:16–21). The disciples were speaking in a way that Jews of the dispersion from many foreign places and languages could understand in their own languages! Either the apostles were speaking a universal God-language that everyone could understand, or they were speaking in their own language and the Spirit was translating it directly into each of the listeners' minds. Seemingly inspiration of the Holy Spirit was happening both to those speaking *and* those listening (Acts 2:5–12). It is still happening for us. Those who wrote scripture were led by the Holy Spirit to write it—"Above all, you must understand that no prophecy of Scripture came about by the prophet's own interpretation. For prophecy never had its origin in the will of man, but men spoke from God as they were carried along by the Holy Spirit" (2 Pet. 1:20–21).

In addition, the Holy Spirit also leads believers as we read and listen to it. Paul explains this other side of inspiration, writing, "We have not received the spirit of the world but the Spirit who is from God, that we may understand what God has freely given us. This is what we speak, not in words taught us by human wisdom but *in words taught by the Spirit, expressing spiritual truths in spiritual words*. The man without the Spirit does not accept the things that come from the Spirit of God, for they are foolishness to him, and he cannot understand them, because *they are spiritually discerned*" (1 Cor. 2:12–14, italics added).

God has given us his Spirit so that we may understand the deeper wisdom of God revealed by his Spirit and the words God inspires. Those without the Spirit *can* understand the gospel of Christ, if their hearts are opened to it, but they *cannot* much beyond that. This is why those who are unsaved generally see the wisdom of scripture, especially that of the cross itself, as foolishness, or they just don't get it at all (1 Cor. 1:18). The deep wisdom of God is spiritually discerned and only those with the Holy Spirit can understand.

The Holy Spirit is for the believer as a disk operating system on a computer. Although it operates behind the scenes, the computer would be incapable of working any of the programs without it. It makes sense of and makes usable to the user all the programmed stuff contained within. The programs that most of us operate are read and operated by this system. If the computer didn't have an operating system, the programs would be unreadable and useless. It's the same with God's word—his higher thoughts and wisdom. Without the Holy Spirit within us, we are incapable of interpreting, understanding, and applying God's word. However by the power of the Spirit, the anointing of God, we are enabled to understand the essential thoughts and ways of God in order to operate as Christians! The anointing of the Holy Spirit teaches us inwardly and interprets God's wisdom for us, "But as his anointing teaches you about all things and as that anointing is real, not counterfeit—just as it has taught you, remain in him" (1 John 2:27).

And through God's Holy Spirit, we are given the most amazing gift of all—the mind of Christ! "The spiritual man makes judgments about all things, but he himself is not subject to any man's judgment: 'For who has known the mind of the Lord that he may instruct him?' But we have the mind of Christ" (1 Cor. 2:16–17; Isa. 40:13).

Thus Christians approach the world completely different. What compels us is no longer our own appetites and desires. We process information and experiences with a whole new operating system based on God's wisdom, with Christ as the interpretive benchmark, the divine "weights and measures."

As we learn the word and as the Spirit works within us to reveal the deeper things of God, we are transformed. Paul says that this deepening knowledge of God affects us "missionally"—"Since, then, we know what it is to fear the Lord, we try to persuade others" (2 Cor. 5:11). We come to "fear" the Lord, and our realization causes us to try to lead others to him. Reverent fear is our natural and first response; when in coming face-to-face with the truth, we realize our estrangement from God and the tragic consequences of it—"Therefore, since we are receiving a kingdom that cannot be shaken, let us be thankful, and so worship God acceptably with reverence and awe" (Heb. 10:28). To see just a bit of him and simply get an inkling of God's infinite being and power is to immediately fear him. Those who simply encountered heavenly beings in their angelic form were usually terrified. There is a good reason that the angels often first said to those they appeared to, "Do not be afraid"! Concerning the angelic appearance to the shepherds at the time of Jesus's birth, Luke records, "And there were shepherds living out in the fields nearby, keeping watch over their flocks at night. An angel of the Lord appeared to them, and the glory of the Lord shone around them, and *they were terrified*. But the angel said to them, '*Do not be afraid.* I bring you good news that will cause great joy for all the people'" (Luke 2:8–10, italics added).

They were terrified and had to be comforted by the angels. The Roman soldiers guarding Jesus's tomb had a similar response when the angel rolled the stone away. Matthew tells us, "There was a violent earthquake, for an angel of the Lord came down from heaven and, going to the tomb, rolled back the stone and sat on it. His appearance was like lightning, and his clothes were white as snow. *The guards were so afraid of him that they shook and became like dead men*" (Matt. 28:2–4, italics added).

The guards were scared out of their wits! And these examples are just discussing their seeing angels and not God himself. Imagine the overload of seeing God. I suppose it would be as plugging a lamp directly into the power of a nuclear power plant! Thus, God told Moses that he could not see God's face and live (Ex. 33:20).

As our faith grows and our love for God matures, any fearfulness quickly subsides, leaving only reverence and awe, as John says, "There is no fear in love. But *perfect love drives out fear, because fear has to do with punishment.* The one who fears is not made perfect in love" (1 John 4:8, italics added). Our fear quickly wanes as our awe of his might and mercy take over. Paul continues, "For Christ's love compels us, because we are convinced that one died for all, and therefore all died. And he died for all, that those who live should no longer live for themselves but for him who died for them and was raised again" (2 Cor. 5:14–15).

During my junior year in high school, I was a part of those out-of-control, made-for-movies kinds of classes. I am not exaggerating. This class was literally out of control. I certainly was no perfect student and did plenty of things I am ashamed of now, but there were some guys in our class who did some outrageous things and caused more than one teacher to simply quit teaching altogether. Oh, the stories I can tell! At the start of the school year, we went into

English class to meet our brand-new young teacher. She was sweet, enthusiastic, and all smiles. She told us that she had heard about our class (think, been warned) and that she knew how to handle us. She said that she would "just love us." I remember my immediate cynicism, thinking to myself, "Oh no, you poor woman." I knew she had no idea what was to come! And those guys put this poor teacher through hell. And the rest of the class with her.

The same first day of school, many of the same ones of us went into our typing class for the first time (to explain to those of the younger generation, typing class was the forerunner of keyboarding). The teacher stood up and firmly told us we better not mess with her. Period. She was not new to the school, and she was surely well aware of our class. And she meant business. Suffice it to say, by the end of the school year, she was the favorite teacher of many. Her classes were always under control, and she did not tolerate much tomfoolery from anyone. Man, her glare alone was frightening! Several found out really quickly that she was tough and serious, unafraid of a bunch of rowdy teenagers. And we learned how to type too! My senior year, in two regional curriculum contests among schools of all sizes, we took both the top individual and team awards for Typing II. And we proudly presented her with the team award plaque. She deserved it. She was also a very godly woman, which I would come to recognize only later!

Our typing class started good and got even better. The English class started sweet, went bad from day one, and only got worse. One teacher started out "loving," coddling, and failing to demand respect. She really ended up without respect or love from our class. One started out demanding respect and showing little affection, and ended up both respected and loved. As I type this manuscript, I am reminded of her tremendous impact on me, not just in typing but also in life and character. I would realize later what a wonderful Christian woman she was and that some of her spiritual DNA has long lived in me! Although I was unconverted and too immature to recognize him in her at the time, God, through her, certainly showed himself to me—and, I am sure, to others!

God is that way—he first demands reverence and respect. He speaks the language of unbelieving, arrogant humanity. I personally was there, even though I did not realize it at the time. All humans apart from God start there! I came to God out of fear and reverence, not out of a feeling of love. I think we often build expectations around people hearing the gospel and "falling in love with God." We interpret and communicate faith and the love of God in terms of mere human feelings, when biblical faith is a decision based on evidence and testimony. Whether we can "feel" God's existence and sense his deep love for us when we first hear the gospel is really irrelevant to whether we can and should believe it or not. Similarly, it is ridiculous and completely unrealistic to think someone must *feel* a deep, authentic love for God when they first meet him and get to know him. Perhaps some can indeed come to God initially and feel both faith and love; many simply cannot. I was one of the latter. And God does not ask for or require that. Faith is first a decision about him, and the love of God raises us to live above all our human affections and leads us simply to do what is right according to God regardless of how we might "feel." When I came to Christ as a college student, I was scarred emotionally, dealing with bouts of serious depression, and was generally scared of what lay ahead for me in life. My feelings were completely untrustworthy. And so are everyone else's (Jer. 17:9).

So as a young man, I came to believe in God more from the reality of what I would have to believe in order to *not* believe in God than anything else. My first impressions mainly concerned how big and powerful God was! He and creation were just unbelievably difficult things for me to wrap my mind around. But as I dared approach him, it was as if he was the new teacher on the first day saying, "Don't mess around with me, Ronnie. Do what I tell you and we will get along quite well. Crossing me is a very bad idea, son!" As I had with my typing teacher, I started out respecting and fearing God, and I ended up with a deep abiding love and adoration for him, as well as respecting him even more. I flat out feared him in the beginning, but the only fear I feel anymore is when I realize I may be "crossing" him with my pride and indifference. And that helps me get back on track very fast! And much more than as with my typing teacher, as I write out this manuscript, I realize all that God has done to me and for me and those I love, as well as how much he has taught me about himself, myself, others, and our life purpose here. I also realize that it was he who put that godly teacher in my life at a time when I desperately needed a mother figure and someone to help mold my fragile and vulnerable character. God is so good!

So with God, we best start out our relationships with him in respect, reverence, and holy fear, as Paul wrote, "Therefore, since we know the fear of the Lord [and understand the importance of obedience and worship], we persuade people [to be reconciled to Him]" (2 Cor. 5:11, Amplified Bible, brackets are part of quote). And after coming to him, very quickly what must begin to drive us should not be fear but love (but remember the love of God, not mere human affection), as the apostle went on to say, "Christ's love compels us" (2 Cor. 5:14).

The transition from doubt to faith and from fear to love is powered by our grasp of the compelling truth that Christ died for us to demonstrate his love for us and to pay our death penalty. This compelling love of Christ we experience brings within us a completely new point of view or perspective. The love of Christ brings to us a whole new life paradigm, as Paul further writes, "So from now on *we regard no one from a worldly point of view.* Though we once regarded Christ in this way, we do so no longer" (2 Cor. 5:16, italics added). When we grasp God's incomparable love, our whole perspective of God, others, and ourselves changes completely. Thus, as Paul continues writing, through Christ we are made completely new, "Therefore if anyone is in Christ [that is, grafted in, joined to Him by faith in Him as Savior], *he is* a new creature [reborn and renewed by the Holy Spirit]; the old things [the previous moral and spiritual condition] have passed away. Behold, new things have come [because spiritual awakening brings a new life]" (2 Cor. 5:17, Amplified Bible, brackets and italics part of quote). We are born again by water and the Spirit (John 3:3–5; Eph. 5:26; Tit. 3:4–7; Rom. 6:3–7; Acts 2:36–39).

As we first grasp God's mighty power, which produces awe and reverence (fear), and as our growing love begins to compel us and dispel any negative fear in us, our whole perspective is completely altered into a God-perspective. God gives us the mind of Christ by the work of his Holy Spirit in us. Our new mind—this new perspective—changes everything. We become new creations, not so much outwardly, initially anyway, but on the inside we are made completely new immediately! When we change our minds (repent) about God, we come to trust in God's love and goodness (Mark 1:15). We become "convinced" that Jesus Christ indeed died for the sins of all of us, because all of us are dead in sin until we receive him by faith.

Authentic, biblical faith is based on reason, not blind feelings. Biblical faith is based on historical authorities. Biblical faith is based on good logic, both deductive and inductive reasoning. And such faith changes everything about us. Biblical faith begins with our coming to fear the Lord, and it is fueled and driven by the love of God that we come to know and grow in. Paul says these two things are what matter most—"The only thing that counts is faith expressing itself through love" (Gal. 5:6).

Having the mind of Christ gives us the God-perspective on everything. Thus we no longer live for ourselves. His essence (love and faithfulness) redefines our essence. We are being recreated into Christ's image, which is the exact representation of God's being (Heb. 1:3). "I am the way," Christ definitively declared. He said that he was, in fact, the only way to the father (John 14:6).

Thus we can now "take captive every thought to make it obedient to Christ" (2 Cor. 10:5), rather than our thoughts being captive to our very human and fleshly desires. Paul writes, "Those who live according to the flesh have their minds set on what the flesh desires; but those who live in accordance with the Spirit have their minds set on what the Spirit desires" (Rom. 8:5). We go from minds of the flesh, which are set on fleshly desires, to possessing the mind of Christ given us by the Holy Spirit, which is set on what the Spirit of God desires. We regard no one, including ourselves, others, and Christ himself, from a human point of view—that is, basically, a "what's in it for me" attitude. We go from being takers to being givers! We go from living to die to dying to live.

We have been given the very mind of Christ! We have been given the thoughts, feelings, and ways of God through his Holy Spirit—those thoughts and ways that can be had only through his Holy Spirit. It is through our possession of this most divine gift that we can interpret all the messages of love that God sends our way, through his word, by his Spirit, through blessings and discipline, and through others. Because of this divine ability, the love of God powers us for his purposes rather than our being driven by the desires of our flesh. Through the mind of Christ, most clearly visualized through the gospel account, we can see God seeing us, seeing others, seeing Christ, and seeing himself. We discover truth and reality—the truth that sets us free (John 8:32).

Everything other than the truth and reality of God is a mirage—ruses, lies, and spiritual atrocities—created by the ultimate perpetrator, Satan himself. He is the father of all lies (John 8:44). He is the accuser of the saints (Rev. 12:10). He is the deceiver of the world (Rev. 12:9). He is the "god of this age" who blinds unbelievers' minds (2 Cor. 4:3–4). He is the ruler of this dark world (Eph. 6:12). And without God's Spirit in us, we are beholden to this age-old evil despot.

The apostle Paul writes, concerning the essentiality of the Spirit within us to enable us to truly understand the things of God, "The person without the Spirit does not accept the things that come from the Spirit of God but considers them foolishness, and cannot understand them because they are discerned only through the Spirit. The person with the Spirit makes judgments about all things, but such a person is not subject to merely human judgments, for 'Who has known the mind of the Lord so as to instruct him?' But we have the mind of Christ" (1 Cor. 2:14–16).

It is the Holy Spirit that gives us the mind of Christ. Through him, we have revealed to us all that God has prepared for us, because of how he sees us. Paul writes, "What no eye has seen, what no ear has heard, and what no human mind has conceived"—the things God has prepared for those who love him—these are the things God has revealed to us by his Spirit" (1 Cor. 2:9–10).

God reveals to us how he sees us. Thus we can, by his power, see God seeing us.

Questions and Thoughts for Reflection and Discussion

1. What are some examples of how God's thoughts are not the same as ours? Use the comparison of children to their parents—how what is completely foolish or incomprehensible to a child is most logical from the parents' perspective and vice versa?

2. What does it mean to you that in Christ and through the Holy Spirit you have the mind of Christ? Consider the many implications.

3. Many ask the obvious question from the human perspective, how do you "know" this or that about God. The reality is we "know" nothing in this way, not even of the world here and now. We can be deceived or wrong about anything. Thus, it can only absolutely be said that we "believe" something. When we say we "know," we can really only claim that we most strongly believe it. This kind of belief is based on

evidence and reasoning. With that in mind, why can we strongly believe (know) we have the mind of Christ?

4. Discuss how thinking like Christ changes our views of everything—God, the universe, others, and ourselves.

CHAPTER 14

THE GOD WHO WATCHES AND WAITS FOR US: THE PARABLE OF THE LOST SON

I walked away with all God had given me;
Squandered it away in the ways that he hated.
While I wasted everything he'd given me,
I had no idea that still for me he waited.

And in desperation I turned back to the Father,
With no comprehension of his great love for me.
I returned destitute, broken, and beaten.
I had no idea how me he would see.

He raced to me as soon as he saw me,
Threw his arms around me, ignoring my degradation.
Lovingly and kindly put his robe and ring on me,
And threw for me a joyous celebration!

I understood my watching brother's resentment.
To love like God we were both completely unable.
Still God prepared for me in the midst of my enemies,
A welcoming and bountiful banquet table!

T he Gospel of Luke contains one of the more famous Bible stories, "The Lost Son," a parable Jesus used to demonstrate, among other things, God's love and mercy. It is often better known as "The Prodigal Son" because of the King James Version rendering. The story is about the unconditional love of God, the riches of our inheritance in Christ, the free will and self-determination God gives us, the evil and foolishness that we are capable of, and the lack of love and mercy we often have for others who mess up. Following is the entire story from Luke 15:11–32 (New International Version) as told by Jesus:

There was a man who had two sons. The younger one said to his father, "Father, give me my share of the estate." So he divided his property between them.

Not long after that, the younger son got together all he had, set off for a distant country and there squandered his wealth in wild living. After he had spent everything, there was a severe famine in that whole country, and he began to be in need. So he went and hired himself out to a citizen of that country, who sent him to his fields to feed pigs. He longed to fill his stomach with the pods that the pigs were eating, but no one gave him anything.

When he came to his senses, he said, "How many of my father's hired servants have food to spare, and here I am starving to death! I will set out and go back to my father and say to him: Father, I have sinned against heaven and against you. I am no longer worthy to be called your son; make me like one of your hired servants." So he got up and went to his father.

But while he was still a long way off, his father saw him and was filled with compassion for him; he ran to his son, threw his arms around him and kissed him.

The son said to him, "Father, I have sinned against heaven and against you. I am no longer worthy to be called your son."

But the father said to his servants, "Quick! Bring the best robe and put it on him. Put a ring on his finger and sandals on his feet. Bring the fattened calf and kill it. Let's have a feast and celebrate. For this son of mine was dead and is alive again; he was lost and is found." So they began to celebrate.

Meanwhile, the older son was in the field. When he came near the house, he heard music and dancing. So he called one of the servants and asked him what was going on. "Your brother has come," he replied, "and your father has killed the fattened calf because he has him back safe and sound."

The older brother became angry and refused to go in. So his father went out and pleaded with him. But he answered his father, "Look! All these years I've been slaving for you and never disobeyed your orders. Yet you never gave me even a young goat so I could celebrate with my friends. But when this son of yours who has squandered your property with prostitutes comes home, you kill the fattened calf for him!"

"My son," the father said, "you are always with me, and everything I have is yours. But we had to celebrate and be glad, because this brother of yours was dead and is alive again; he was lost and is found."

The word of God often befuddles us, which of course is inevitable because God's nature and ways are beyond our imagination (Isa. 55:8–9; Eph. 3:20–21). However, the Bible reveals God to us and further explains what God's overarching revelation, the creation, demonstrates to us about his eternal power and divine nature (Rom. 1:20).

Stories such as this are clearly intended to make us think deeply and differently. They force difficult questions and give us opportunity to see the world from God's eternal perspective and not just from our small, self-centered ones. Good stories make us think visually and practically. They help us find practical applications of the deep truths they reveal. They invite us into the imaginary in order to be able to effectively probe what is real. These stories of Jesus are designed to make us consider deeply the nature and ways of God, rather than simply take lazy short-cuts to warmed-over, often inexact, sometimes incorrect conclusions. Jesus often was very direct in his teaching. Sometimes he was not. Certain of his stories he explained, other times he did not. In these, most of all, he challenges us to think, to make spiritual judgments, and to utilize our God-given spiritual faculties.

Just previous to this story, Luke recorded another parable concerning a shepherd from whose flock a single sheep strayed and was lost. The shepherd left the flock unwatched but in the safest place possible and went to rescue a single sheep that had wandered off. Jesus ended the parable with this concluding statement, "I tell you that in the same way there will be more rejoicing in heaven over one sinner who repents than over ninety-nine righteous persons who do not need to repent" (Luke 15:7). The story of the lost son is one more parable Jesus used to drive home to us the nature of our Heavenly Father, and as well to show the value of each of us to him.

Our value to God, even at our worst, is clearly demonstrated in the story of the lost son. A few summary conclusions might be: (1) The father in the story represents God, our heavenly father; (2) the older son represents ones who seemingly remain faithful to God but who all too often feel *entitled by* rather than *indebted to* God for the love and goodness he gives us, becoming "self-righteous." Perhaps they even feel that those who are not so righteous are patently not entitled to anything, but rather should perhaps be saddled with an unforgiveable debt to God, the church, and society; and (3) the younger son represents those who are foolish and take their God-given inheritance—all that God has and will give them—and squander it in selfish, self-serving, foolish, and destructive living, ignoring and disobeying God. The inheritance the boy was given represents the innumerable blessings God gives to each of us—the amazing bodies we live in, the beautiful world we have been given as our home, the loving families and friends we generally have or have access to in abundance, the intelligence we enjoy, the countless positive and joyful experiences that are a part of our story, and the even greater inheritance that lies ahead of us if we remain faithful to God. The pitiful condition the foolish son ends up in represents the spiritual and emotional squalor and pain of the human condition apart from a right conception of and relationship with the God of the Bible. In reality, this is the true inner condition of those who cannot see God seeing them.

Most of us, if we dare be introspective enough, can see the spirit of the younger son roiling within us. Perhaps we can dig deeply enough into our fleshly nature to see the older son sneering out of us. The most difficult part, however, is for us to understand how the father sees us in either condition.

Over the years, I've seen far more accounts of those who behaved as the younger son. These often come limping into counseling, bemoaning the mess they've made of their lives, but often not even correlating much of what has befallen them with their sin and disobedience. It is often unbelievable what we can do and think and the excuses we use to justify outrageously disobedient, destructive lifestyles. So much of counseling is simply helping people deal with the messes they've made of their lives. Paul writes, "Do not be deceived: God cannot be mocked. A man reaps what he sows" (Gal. 6:7). Those who come to visit pastors generally have a Christian faith of some sort or at least a leaning toward it, and thus they are looking to God and the church for answers. It is mind-boggling just how illogical, unspiritual, unfaithful, and self-centered we can become. And a messed-up life grows out of a messed-up belief system.

At the core of foolish belief systems are mostly blatant misunderstandings of God. All false doctrines have at their roots misconceptions of God. From the earliest times, humanity has disfigured the concept of God into human imaginings of gods, mere creations of their own, even though God has made his eternal nature and existence clear through the creation (Rom. 1:20). These physical and mental idols are made in a way either to explain the unexplainable or to answer unanswerable questions. Ultimately, human idols and idolatrous notions are seen variously as possessing whatever traits and roles we desire in them that seem to serve our selfish purposes. This ignorance and idolatry is, and has always been, pervasive. No one is immune. As modern Christians, we may be a little more "sophisticated" in our thinking than some of the earlier more absurd ideas about God or the gods. But still, sometimes we make God and Christ out to be what we *want* them to be in our own minds, and in the name of Christian tolerance, we put up with others doing the same thing—"For [you seem willing to allow it] if one comes and preaches another Jesus whom we have not preached, or if you receive a different spirit from the one you received, or a different gospel from the one you accepted. You tolerate all this beautifully [welcoming the deception]" (2 Cor. 11:4, Amplified Bible, brackets included in quote). In our own misguided hearts and minds, we can all too easily try to define God the way we think he ought to be rather than accepting him as he reveals himself to us and, further, accepting how he sees us!

We impose our will on the idea of "God" in the same way that we impose our will on the scriptures by selective narrow-minded reading, proof-texting, reading only the parts we prefer, and by otherwise overlaying our preconceived paradigms on scriptures as a whole. We can get very good at developing odd scriptural constructs, connecting scriptures that are not meant to be corrected, and not connecting ones that clearly are. Or we simply cherry-pick our preferred notions of God that we have heard over the years, often from other perhaps less than open-minded Christians, and decide that's what we will believe. These approaches to God and the Bible of course lead us to "play god" in our own lives, trying to be "in control" of things and to otherwise do whatever we like rather than making it our aim to please him (2 Cor. 5:9). Although mental and emotional, it is nonetheless idolatrous; in that, the "god" we serve is but a mental construct and not real at all—"it is a different Jesus."

It is simply ludicrous to think God is whoever we want him to be, and the church can seem nearly as guilty as the pagan religions in this regard. But God is who he is; we cannot change him. We get no vote in who God is, what he does, what behaviors and lifestyles he approves of, and whom he accepts as his own. We will be wisest to honestly seek him in order to find out who he really is, rather than making him out in our own foolish minds to be what we want. Idolatry is simply serving and worshiping ourselves—"For although they knew God, they neither glorified him as God nor gave thanks to him, but their thinking became futile and their foolish hearts were darkened. Although they claimed to be wise, they became fools and *exchanged the glory of the immortal God for images made to look like a mortal human being*" (Rom. 1:21–23, italics added).

Ultimately and most unfortunately, in most if not all of the cases I counsel and witness, the "mortal human being" that ends up being worshiped is the person we see in the mirror every morning! Humans are very, very bad actors when it comes to playing "God" in our own lives. We don't even come close to being competent at it. In fact, we come as far from it as possible! This folly is at the heart of the original sin of Adam and Eve in the Garden of Eden played out over and over and over again. I can just hear the serpent whispering his damning lie again to each of us, "You will not certainly die . . . For God knows that when you eat from it your eyes will be opened, and you will be like God, knowing good and evil" (Gen. 3:4–5). As if to say, you will be like God, and you will be a god. How foolish to believe that lie, especially considering the curse it has brought on humanity from its inception. It drove us from God and his life-giving fruit, thus bringing our demise.

Leaders both religious and secular can be caught going way beyond the human assignment and "playing God." It can often be seen when we are determining who should be accepted into our denominations and tribes, both religious and secular. It is exposed at times when we determine who should live and who should die. Or in deciding directly or indirectly who should be blessed and who should not be blessed, as with societies, cultures, and social strata. Or when we decide, based on our own desires and preferences, who is worthy or not worthy of love and acceptance, as with bias, unfairness, and prejudice in families, friend circles, people groups, churches, and other kinds of social groups. The degradation, marginalizing, and devaluing of others, God, and ourselves in attitude and action that is possible when humanity fails to let God be God is tragic for all of us—"And since they did not see fit to acknowledge God *or* consider Him worth knowing [as their Creator], God gave them over to a depraved mind, to do things which are improper *and* repulsive" (Rom. 1:28, Amplified Bible, brackets and italics included in quote).

God's role as the creator and sustainer of our world is utterly impossible for us to attempt to play in our or others' lives. It is a ridiculous charade for us, and we are doomed to gross failure from the outset in any such effort. When we inadvertently try it (and try it we do, when we fail to live by faith in God), we end up like the lost son, squandering all our God-given blessings in foolish, self-serving, destructive living. We all do it to some degree; even those who grew up in church—"The Lord looks down from heaven on all mankind to see if there are any who understand, any who seek God. All have turned away, all have become corrupt; there is no one who does good, not even one" (Ps. 14:2–3; Rom. 3:10–12). But some do it more profoundly and openly than others, and I can think of so many people I have known who acted as the younger lost son. The measure of our wandering and squandering must not be measured simply by the length of time spent in such folly, but rather in the inner depth of faithlessness and selfishness we sunk to. Thus, the list of God's lost sons and daughters includes us all.

And plenty of others come to mind when I think of those I have known who were more like the older, responsible brother. Although still difficult, seeing others and seeing how they see us is much easier than seeing God and seeing how he sees us. Every human struggles most to understand and identify with the father in Jesus's story. We all face the greatest difficulty in relating to him, for such unselfish, extravagant, extraordinary, and selfless love is rarely hinted at among us (Rom. 5:6–8; John 15:13). It is not that none of us ever try to be like God; it is just that we are not God and we are not "gods." And even with our best efforts, we will fall so short of his excellence—"for all have sinned and fall short of the glory of God" (Rom. 3:23). But if we can "get" at the father in the story—seeing how he saw and felt about his wayward son—we can begin to see God seeing us.

Conversely, suffice it to say, if we get God wrong, we have everything wrong. And as with our Garden of Eden ancestors, it always leads to destruction (Matt. 7:13–14). The Bible reveals that it turns out very badly for those who live unrepentantly, failing to change their courses, and end up facing God in self-serving, God-twisting-and-denying conditions. It doesn't matter what we may currently think or say about the destination of our lives, or what people may say about us after our deaths. God is the righteous judge and determiner of our fates (1 Cor. 4:3–5). God knows those who are already his (2 Tim. 2:19), and in the end, God alone will determine the fate of each of us. There is an ultimate story behind each of us that only God knows fully. We can and do often fool others. We can and often do fool ourselves. We cannot, however, fool God. Therefore, our ultimate existential life goal must be that of knowing, trusting, and humbly obeying him.

At the recommendation of my oldest son, Brandon, I read an interesting and a thought-provoking science-fiction book a few years back. It is a sequel to *Ender's Game*[1], a story about a young boy, Ender Wiggins, who was trained early and found to be a technical and tactical genius. The book I am referring to, *Speaker for the Dead*[2], was released the next year. Although it is set some three thousand years after *Ender's Game*, because of the relativism involved in time travel, Ender is only thirty-five years old in the second story. In an advanced society on a planet far away, some such as Ender became "Speakers for the Dead." They were given access to all the information about a deceased person, and at the memorial, the speaker would, without judgment or unnecessary commentary, simply tell the whole truth about the deceased person's life—who they really were and what they had done. No secrets anymore.

We tend to do the opposite when our loved ones die; in that, we sometimes make them out to be much better than they actually were. One's funeral often turns out to be many of our finest hours! I went to a woman's funeral some years ago, whom I had known fairly well. After sitting through the memorial, I remarked to a good friend I was with that I wished I had known the woman they had talked about in the funeral—rather than the one I had actually known. In the real world, only God is qualified to speak for the dead. He has access to all the files, and he knows the complete and true story about each of us. And in the end, he will tell us and everybody else what the truth of our life really was (Matt. 12:36; 1 Cor. 4:5).

---

1 Card, Orson Scott. *Ender's Game.* London: Orbit, 1985.
2 Card, Orson Scott. *Speaker for the Dead.* London: Orbit, 1986.

None of us gets a vote as to truth and reality. It is what it is, and it always will be that way. We don't have to wait though to figure out the critical success factors for us in regard to God. The word of God can judge the thoughts and attitudes of our heart (Heb. 4:12–13). Jesus said it was his words that would be our judge in the end (John 12:47–48). Thus we do well to pay close attention to God's word now, seeking to find God for who he really is, rather than behaving as if he is someone he is not (2 Pet. 1:19–21). None of us will want to find out the hard way, and perhaps too late, that our beliefs and behaviors have been wrong, futile, or otherwise displeasing to God (Matt. 7:21–23).

The rainbow behind the cloud of this initially tragic lesson of the lost son is this: We have a heavenly Father who is waiting and watching for us to awaken from our utterly foolish thinking and living and realize all we are missing when we stray away from him. God wants us to also see all we can have and experience if we will repent and get back to him. He's watching and waiting for each of us. If you are reading this and realize you've wandered off, come home to your Father. If you mess up, call him; if you mess up really badly, call him really fast! Pray fervently. Seek him diligently. Run to him eagerly.

God is generous, as the father in the story was generous. God is good, as the father in the story is good. God frees us, as the father in the story gave freedom to his foolish son. God is loving, as the father in the story was unconditionally loving. And he is merciful, kind, and does not hold grudges against us. And he calls us all to be like him. As the father threw his wayward son a homecoming party, Jesus tells us that God throws each sinner who turns to him a celebration—"I tell you that in the same way there will be more rejoicing in heaven over one sinner who repents than over ninety-nine righteous persons who do not need to repent" (Luke 15:7).

Consider again the homecoming: "So he got up and went to his father. But while he was still a long way off, his father saw him and was filled with compassion for him; he ran to his son, threw his arms around him and kissed him."

This is how God sees each of us. This is how he has promised to be toward each of us. And God is a promise keeper—"The Lord is not slow in keeping his promise, as some understand slowness. Instead he is patient with you, not wanting anyone to perish, but everyone to come to repentance" (2 Pet. 3:9). God wants all of us to be like the lost son and to repent of the foolishness of seeking in the world what can only be found in and through him. He is rooting for us—"[God] wants all people to be saved and to come to a knowledge of the truth" (1 Tim. 2:4, brackets added). God wants all of us to be saved, not just a select few. That includes each of us, those we care about, those we come in contact with, and all the rest, whom we have never met (John 3:16).

The Father sees us from a long way off and responds to our seeking—"Come near to God and he will come near to you" (James 4:8). When we come home to him in humility, repentance, and submission, he will come running to us (Rom. 3:20). There will be a party thrown for us in heaven, even if "the faithful" who witnessed our failure do not seem too excited about our return. God will indeed give us a robe to cover the scars of our hard living and the insignia ring, signaling that we are his child and a part of his family, and not because of our goodness or effort but because of his!

Jesus, reflecting the mercy and goodness of God, gave the great invitation to all: "Come to me, all you who are weary and burdened, and I will give you rest. Take my yoke upon you and learn from me, for I am gentle and humble in heart, and you will find rest for your souls. For my yoke is easy and my burden is light" (Matt. 11:28–30).

That's who is waiting for us at the end of all our wanderings, when we wisely, humbly, and with thanksgiving return home to the true lover of our souls!

Questions and Thoughts for Reflection and Discussion

1. Think of some present-day example of an individual you know or have heard about who walked away from God in a proud, destructive way and discuss how their life resembles or previously resembled the lost son in Jesus's parable.
2. How have you been that lost son? Describe your experience.
3. What hidden parts of your story might be revealed if a Speaker for the Dead wrote and shared your funeral eulogy?
4. How does seeing well God seeing you help mitigate that fearful thought?
5. What attributes of God, suggested in the story of the lost son, might be hard for you to believe?
6. How have you seen yourself act toward another as the older brother acted toward his wayward younger brother?
7. How do you see yourself trying to "play God" in your own life or in the lives of others?
8. How have you seen people trying to do so with themselves and each other?

CHAPTER 15

LUMPS OF CLAY: GOD'S WORK IN US

Yet, O Lord, you are our Father. We are the clay, you are the potter; we are all the work of your hand.

—Isaiah 64:8

My dear children, for whom I am again in the pains of childbirth until Christ is formed in you, how I wish I could be with you now and change my tone, because I am perplexed about you!

—Galatians 4:19–20

Therefore, my dear friends, as you have always obeyed— not only in my presence, but now much more in my absence—continue to work out your salvation with fear and trembling, for it is God who works in you to will and to act according to his good purpose.

—Philippians 2:12–13

LUMP OF CLAY

He handed me a lump of clay,
He had fashioned carefully,
How artfully he'd molded it,
In love so gracefully.

I took it into my own hands,
But then dropped it on the floor.
Seemed incapable of fixing it,
So I handed it back to him once more.

He took it back and smoothed it out.
Again it looked quite good.
His fingerprints were left on the clay,
While repairing the drop it had withstood.

He handed the lump right back to me,
And let me try once more,
But my awkward hands and ineptitude,
Made the effort a daunting chore.

My fingerprints left ugly marks,
Disfiguring my lump of clay,
His own work became unrecognizable,
When I'd done it my own way.

I handed the clay back to him,
As he worked to correct my vanity,
These powerful, artistic hands,
That shaped goodness into humanity.

With persistence he handed it back to me,
With such patience and such wonder.

But each time I messed his beauty up,
In my clumsiness and blunder.

As my eyes gazed out from the clay,
He'd put my spirit in,
I saw his fingers wet with tears,
Smoothing away my sin.

I watched in amazement, looking into his eyes,
Saw my own reflection there, but dim.
Each time he handed it back to me,
I looked a little more like Him!

Are you seeing it yet? Are you seeing God seeing you? Or are you at least seeing it a little better than previously? If you can see how God sees you, then you will see *God* in a completely new and right way. If you can see you as God sees you, you will see *you* in a completely new way. And you will be forever free from the nagging fear and hopelessness that dogs us apart from God—"So if the Son sets you free, you will be free indeed" (John 8:36).

The book of Genesis, the age-old manuscript, is a beautiful depiction of God creating the universe, setting the earth in place, and designing and sustaining it as a home for us. In a brief telling and amazing fashion, the writer, thought by most to be Moses, packs in timeless descriptions of the creation narrative, designed to build faith in the youngest and simplest as well as the oldest and the most knowledgeable. It is equally informative and thought-provoking for both those who are less schooled in the sciences and those who are more knowledgeable scientifically, anthropologically, or philosophically. The creation account dares us stand on the shores of time and look out into infinity, thinking deeply about our origin and purpose. It challenges us to go the limits of our capabilities in knowing and understanding. It summarizes huge swaths of events and ideas into impossibly tight descriptions. Unlike any of the other early accounts of our origin however, Genesis reveals and expresses things no mere human could know, understand, or contrive.

From the outset, the Bible boldly asserts and assumes God's existence and power: "In the beginning, God created . . ." Thus, the Bible concludes that "The fool says in his heart, 'There is no God'" (Ps. 14:1). The Bible makes amazingly and seemingly "unbelievable" claims concerning creation and the ordering of the cosmos out of chaos. However, in my own view, whatever one believes about our origins will seem "unbelievable"—in fact, logically impossible. In spite of that, I believe we have sound reasons to believe in the creator and creation account as depicted in the book of Genesis. And I personally believe that science's proposal that matter and the universe are self-generated through chemical and organic evolution to be utterly and utterly and ridiculously impossible. But I also believe that the positions of Christian fundamentalism and conservatism are generally unfair with their unnecessary rigidity in understanding the Genesis creation story, reading it as if it were written to twenty-first century humanity in modern scientific jargon! Given that the creation itself is the primary revelation of God's eternal power and divine nature, and that humankind was seemingly given dominion over it and responsibility for it, those who insist on completely and scientifically literalizing such narratives as Genesis are likely using it in a way it was not written to be used.

Rather it seems that we should reconcile and understand the biblical revelation first through how the original readers would have seen it, and secondarily, through what we can observe, measure, and understand through human knowledge and the conventions of history, science, anthropology, and logic. I believe a biblically defined faith is a reasonable faith, reaching its conclusions based on solid premises and ideas using valid logic and sensibility, both inductive and deductive. I believe that once we come to recognize our universe's divine origin as described in the Bible, we can then reconcile the best theories and hypotheses of science (science's faith) back to the Bible's creation account. The correlations will at best be inexact, as Genesis is not written to moderns with modern scientific discoveries and notions. But the earliest humans were a lot smarter than we give them credit for, and we moderns are obviously not nearly as smart as we like to think we are. Most still remain "east of Eden" rather than find readmission to the Garden and its life-giving Tree of Life (Gen. 3:24).

The fact is that everyone lives by faith. The only question is: faith in what? Everything we can assert about the greater concerns of our origin and purpose is simply what we believe, not really what we may claim to "know." What we call knowledge is simply a matter of *what* we believe most strongly as being true, be it our beliefs about the divine or our beliefs about the material world, as studied and interpreted by the scientific process and human logic. All of the science that deals with origins is rooted in theories, conjecture, and hypotheses—science vernacular for "faith." Strongly held theories are a part of science's "statement of faith." My opinion is that many, especially humanists, hold tenaciously to scientific theory more as religion than as an academic endeavor. Then they often become aghast that others might not agree with their premises, let alone their firmly held conclusions. Although they would be loath to admit it themselves, I believe that at their roots, atheism, agnosticism, and humanism have as strong of underlying emotional motives as a lot of religion often does.

Science's theories of origin are just that—what science believes, not what science actually knows. Yet many blindly accept their beliefs assuming that they have already proven all they posit. I believe the unwitting are sometimes intentionally and often unintentionally misled by many humanistic proponents of modern scientific theory in this regard. And these authorities mislead the uninformed every bit as much as religious leaders have often done with their followers in the past (and still do I believe). But I still grant that what science believes—its faith—is indeed mostly based on substance, measurements, observation, evidence, and reason. But I also believe, contrary to what many scientists and philosophers claim, that the faith revealed in scripture can and should also be based on substance, evidence, and reason (Heb. 11:1). In my opinion, science, anthropology, and philosophy all can be said to, in various ways, bear great testimony to the veracity of the general descriptions of Genesis. I believe that the truth behind each of the two "faiths"—religion and science—will ultimately not end in disagreement but will only and finally explain how the creator created and ordered the universe we live in and are a part of, as well as how he continues to sustain it by his divine power. It is as if to say, true science and true religion are not in disagreement; the disagreements are between scientists and their proponents and theologians and theirs, all who too often disregard the evidence found in the other in order to make their own bold claims of "rightness."

Genesis depicts God as a potter, not a scientist. He is like an artisan, building and molding a creation that reflects his own heart, perspective, and purposes. God is an artist designing a work of art sculpted with reason and heart, mind and emotion. Therefore, the creation must first be interpreted as such. It was God's energy that became the matter—the clay, so to speak—that has been formed into our universe, as even science's "big bang" theory suggests. It was his ingenuity and design that ordered it, as described in the first verses of Genesis. It was his artistic hands that formed the "clay" planet we call earth and orchestrated earth to possess the perfect blend of operating systems so as to be an ideal home for humankind. He designed evolutionary processes that shaped our planet, plants, animals, and microbes. It was by his loving design that the divine potter sculpted humankind from clay—"Then the LORD God formed a man from the dust of the ground and breathed into his nostrils the breath of life, and the man became a living being" (Gen. 2:7). By his power, he crafted the processes that ultimately culminated in the sudden explosive growth of humanity around 200,000 years ago, as currently accepted by science. It was his Spirit that breathed into the human species the breath of spiritual life, giving humankind, unlike all other living species, a living soul. Whatever can be discovered in science (and scientific theories are just that—theories), will ultimately only turn out to be descriptions of what God has done and how he has done it.

Genesis weaves a beautiful, descriptive, poetic tapestry of the design and development of creation—time, matter, light, heavenly bodies, rotation, night, day, seasons, and space itself. It depicts it as having been created and ordered in "six days" of creation followed by a "seventh day" when God rested from his work ("sabbath" means to *stop, rest, or desist*). On the first day came matter, time, light, and darkness (although some would assert that the Genesis story is not about the creation of the matter but only the ordering or it). But the account seems to indicate that the first thing God did was create time itself, with the lights to mark it out. And God *saw* the light as "good" (Gen. 1:4). On the second day, interstellar space or the heliosphere was made as the stars, planets, and other objects took shape and hurtled away from the center of the world's original point of formation. The universe began to take shape. On the third day, water (seas) and dry ground (land) appeared. Earth took shape as the home of humankind. Again the creator "*saw* that it was good" (Gen. 1:10). The third day also saw the development of the earth's vegetation, which was also seen as good (Gen. 1:12).

Creation continued, and on the fourth day, God made the sun to hold our planet in place and to provide the energy for life's growth and continuation, and he set the moon in place that would be seen in its phases, variously lighting the night sky. God saw that too as good (Gen. 1:18). The fifth day is described as the period of the development of sea and water animals as well as the production of birds. God saw it all was good as well (Gen. 1:21). He blessed the life he had produced and ordered it to be fruitful in the sea and on the earth. On the sixth day came the land creatures of all kinds, which God saw also as good (Gen. 1:25). During that same period, he created humankind, God's crown of creation. Genesis says that God made us in his own image as male and female and commanded us to multiply, fill the earth, and take care of our world. God gave all the other living plants and creatures to us as food. As the sixth day ended, Genesis tells us that God saw all he had made, including humanity, and concluded only at this point that it was more than just good; "it was *very* good" (Gen. 1:31).

In Genesis we see the story of God molding his creation. It is as a temple for him, and his "resting" in it on the seventh day expresses the ancient notion of temples. The story of creation, the world, and humanity's role in it is God's story. And it reveals that God has seen us from the very start as "very good." Apart from the corrupting evil that coats the whole cosmos, as rust coats new iron, we are beautiful to God. The Bible promises that the time is coming when the creator will remove the corruption and the very elements that cause evil and its sinful consequences and that he will redeem his cosmos, bringing about a "new heaven and a new earth" (Isa. 65:17, 66:22; 2 Pet. 3:13; Rev. 21:1).

Because it is God's story, the Genesis account is also our story. It is a prophetic message, written by an ordinary person or ordinary people, not modern academics, scientists, or philosophers. It's a poem, even a song—the song of the ages—written in the words of its time. It is "sung" to the tune of the legions of the nameless who care little about how smart we moderns think we are in "figuring" creation out. The Genesis creation account is a looking back in time and space to what was and how it came to be. It is patently not an account of scientific processes, but rather is communicating to us the soul of the universe. It is a story that has been corrupted in spirit and purpose by believers who have literalized it in such a way as to invite and even dare empirical scrutiny by unbelievers who might seek to cast doubt on its scientific "accuracy." I believe that Christian "creationists" who somehow see themselves as the lone defenders of truth and the sole proponents of the creator and our creation story have in fact corrupted the spirit and purpose of the creation account's message, and thus have unnecessarily damaged the Bible's reputation before an unbelieving world.

Therefore the artistry and majesty of the creation narrative has been dashed by science on its graphite tables and squashed in the test tubes of laboratories, senselessly analyzed as if one can scientifically and empirically measure the message of a sculpture that in fact is about heart and soul, and that emerges from and exists in infinity. From my humble perspective, the Genesis creation account is an artistic, divine message lost somewhere between the two unholy purposes of Christian fundamentalist control and academic elitism. When it is in fact purely and simply an original, ancient depiction that is older than human existence and observation and ageless beyond contemporary notions. To deny the creation is to deny the soul of humanity. To deny the soul of humanity is to deny the very soul of the universe. A travesty indeed!

Religion's misuse of the Genesis story, as a wholly literal and scientific account of creation, has unnecessarily turned away countless people. Just as unnecessary, I believe, are the senseless attacks on the creation story by modern science and unbelievers who have blinded too many against its ultimate reality! The ignorance and arrogance on the one side is every bit as deadly as the arrogance and ignorance on the other. The elementary but ageless account ought to humble us, to let us be free once and for all of our destructive tendency to try to play God, when the centuries past have clearly shown us how utterly unqualified we are to do so. Beholding the cosmos ought to awe and humble all of us, as we see our "smallness" in respect to the universe's vastness. It ought as well to encourage us, as we come to see how unique and special we are within all we can see and know.

Religious and unreligious, believer and unbeliever, educated and uneducated, all seemingly prefer still, as our ancient ancestors Eve and Adam, to gorge at the fruit bowl of the Tree of the Knowledge of Good and Evil, seeking to defend what needs no defense or to destroy truth that cannot be destroyed. We ought, I believe, to be humble in regard to our own power and intellect and, conversely, confident in our acceptance of the Creator God's. To move forward, believers, as Christ's ambassadors and peacemakers, must find a way to convert the swords of hatred, selfish agendas, and arrogant self-promotion into plows with which we can sow, as one race—the human race—the seeds of true knowledge that produce life in us all! This is the life the creator breathed into us. Creation is after all about life. We need no longer try to "prove" something that needs no proving, nor do we need to disprove something that cannot be disproved. Yes, what we may presently *believe* about creation may be disproved, but the real truth about creation can never be disproven.

All this has been said to make the point that God is an artist—a potter—and we are his pottery, made from the clay he selected. We are designed for a reason and for a purpose—his. God illustrated this to the prophet Jeremiah in a personal experience. Jeremiah wrote, "This is the word that came to Jeremiah from the LORD: 'Go down to the potter's house, and there I will give you my message.' So I went down to the potter's house, and I saw him working at the wheel. But the pot he was shaping from the clay was marred in his hands; so the potter formed it into another pot, shaping it as seemed best to him" (Jer. 18:1–4). Note the phrases: "there I [God] will give you my message" and the potter [God] "was shaping it as seemed best to him." God is the potter, and he shapes us the way that seems is best to him. Isaiah wrote it this way, "Yet you, LORD, are our Father. We are the clay, you are the potter; we are all the work of your hand" (Isa. 64:8). It is as the creation account tells us, "The LORD God formed a man from the dust of the ground and breathed into his nostrils the breath of life . . ." (Gen. 2:7).

The apostle John tells us that Christ was in fact the Creator God, "Through him [Christ] all things were made; without him nothing was made that has been made" (John 1:3). Paul says that God created it all for himself, writing, "For in him all things were created: things in heaven and on earth, visible and invisible, whether thrones or powers or rulers or authorities; *all things have been created through him and for him*" (Col. 1:16, italics added). Thus Paul admonishes, "Do not conform to the pattern of this world, but be transformed by the renewing of your mind" (Rom. 12:2).

God formed creation with his powerful yet gentle hands, as an artist sculpting his fine work of art. We, along with all creation, were formed out of his own creativity and purpose. We are *still* being formed. Creation continues on. He made us and sustains us for himself "as seemed best to him." Another translation of Paul's admonition reads, "Don't let the world around you squeeze you into its own mould [sic], but *let God re-mould [sic] your minds from within*, so that you may prove in practice that the plan of God for you is good, meets all his demands and moves towards the goal of true maturity" (Rom. 12:2, J. B. Phillips Translation of the New Testament, italics added). God molded us in the first place by his power and for his purpose, and he remolds us inwardly as a part of his new creation.

God made us in a specific way for a special purpose, but evil has distorted this shape and purpose. Thus when we are born again into Christ, God does not want us again to let the world squeeze us into the mold of another potter! After he originally created humankind, he saw us as "very good" in our original condition. And in the end, he promises to put it all back that way.

In the birth of babies around the world, we daily witness the ingenuity of God's artwork in the miracle human reproduction. David celebrated how God had lovingly and skillfully molded him, saying, "For you created my inmost being; you knit me together in my mother's womb. I praise you because I am fearfully and wonderfully made; your works are wonderful, I know that full well. My frame was not hidden from you when I was made in the secret place, when I was woven together in the depths of the earth. Your eyes saw my unformed body; all the days ordained for me were written in your book before one of them came to be" (Ps. 139:13–16). He describes in poetic words God's sculpting of each of us from conception. God sees our unformed bodies inside the womb. God ordains the very length of the life we are designed to live.

In creating us, God shaped humankind into our original form and breathed into us the breath of life to make us living souls. He engineered the DNA that would not only uniquely define us as a species but also define us as individuals! He made us as body, soul, and spirit, and he wants all of it conformed to him. God makes our original form, and then, because of the fall, he recreates us and reforms us again to our original shape "in his image." Paul's prayer for all of us is this, "May the God of peace make you holy through and through. May you be kept in soul and mind and body in spotless integrity until the coming of our Lord Jesus Christ. He who calls you is utterly faithful and he will finish what he has set out to do" (1 Thess. 5:23–24, J. B. Phillips New Testament).

God sees each of us in our conception beginning, and he breathes into each of us the breath of life that makes us a living spirit. He retrieves us from our fallen state as we respond in belief to his gospel call to us. His Spirit then begins the process of totally restoring—sanctifying—us to our original, intended form (2 Cor. 3:18). He sanctifies us—sets us apart—for his own original purpose for us. And he sees us all along the way as "very good," as Paul writes, "He chose us in Christ [actually selected us for Himself as His own] before the foundation of the world, so that we would be holy [that is, consecrated, set apart for Him, purpose-driven] and blameless in His sight. In love He predestined *and* lovingly planned for us to be adopted to Himself as [His own] children through Jesus Christ, in accordance with the kind intention *and* good pleasure of His will" (Eph. 1:4–5, Amplified Bible, brackets and italics are part of quote).

The infinite, loving, and all-powerful God sees us in Christ in our intended state. In Christ, God sees us as "holy and blameless" as we originally were—made in his image. He gave himself as a model for us to be able to see in our mind's eye what humanity "done-right-looks-like." He planned what we would look like originally, and he planned what we would look like made anew in Christ. He planned what we would live for and do originally, and he planned what we would be used for and do when we were made anew—"For we are God's handiwork, created in Christ Jesus to do good works, which God prepared in advance for us to do" (Eph. 2:10). God prepared in advance, from the foundations of creation, for our re-creation in Christ. And he planned in advance the works we are to do. He gives us in the gospel the model we are to be fashioned after, "For those God foreknew he also predestined to be conformed to the image of his Son" (Rom. 8:29).

We were made by Christ and for Christ. In fact, God made us intending us to "look" like Christ.

And by his own power and goodness that's how God sees us as Christians throughout our lives—like Christ!

Questions and Thoughts for Reflection and Discussion

1. Take time to relate your own life and development to the poem at the beginning of this chapter, "Lump of Clay."
2. Why do you believe in God?

3. What have previously been your views on creation and the Genesis account? Why? How might that have changed recently or over the years? How might rethinking it from other perspectives help us?
4. How do see God's hands shaping and molding us in our physical births, our rebirths, and Christian growth?
5. What do you think your life would look like in the present if you were mature and perfectly conformed to Christ's image?

CHAPTER 16

SEEING GOD SEEING YOU

*For Christ's love compels us, because we are convinced that
one died for all, and therefore all died. And he died for
all, that those who live should no longer live for themselves
but for him who died for them and was raised again. So
from now on we regard no one from a worldly point of
view. Though we once regarded Christ in this way, we do
so no longer. Therefore, if anyone is in Christ, he is a new
creation; the old has gone, the new has come!*

—2 Corinthians 5:14–17

*The eyes looking at me became my own,
And I saw the world completely anew.
I now saw it through the eyes of God's love;
I see me now from the Father's point of view!*

When I was young, I was mainly scared of my dad. He was the
oldest son of an alcoholic father. Born around the time of
World War I, my dad grew up during the Great Depression, lived

through the Dust Bowl on a farm in Oklahoma, lived through World War II, and finally left the farm to work in the oil field long before there was OSHA and anyone was really watching how common workers were being treated. His father had been very hard on him and had taught him to be the classic country tough guy, working hard, drinking hard, and fighting well. Thankfully my dad had stopped drinking around the time I was born and didn't drink at all until after my mom died and I was in my last years in high school.

Not only was I afraid of him, I also felt a lot of other negative emotions toward him, especially anger and resentment at the way he treated my mom and my older siblings a lot of the time. I also resented him for relentlessly teasing me, as he said, "to toughen me up." I resented his selfish behavior around the house, where we were all to be at his beck and call. We watched what he wanted on television, when he wanted to watch it, and often we weren't allowed to watch TV if he wasn't in the mood. I resented his seemingly merciless attitude toward all of us. I resented how unfair and duplicitous he could be and how he would regularly claim he never disciplined us when he was angry and how untrue that obviously was. I resented the way he often seemingly hated everyone outside of his own family. I came to resent his prejudice toward anyone different than we were. I resented his domination of us all. He generally treated my mom like one of the kids. She had to get the same permission on so many things as we did. In my own recollection, he frequently told her "no" about things she wanted to do. I have countless negative memories of him. And after she died, it all got much worse for the younger four of us still living at home.

However, I did feel love toward him. I guess it was simply family love (*storge*, Greek). Although most of the time I didn't want to, I sometimes even liked him. He could be funny. He could be kind. He could be generous. He could even be encouraging. I watched our favorite football teams with him, and that was fun as long as we were winning. He'd angrily turn the game off though if he didn't like what was going on. He wouldn't watch it anymore, and he wouldn't let me watch it. Ironically, I suppose it to be, I do the same thing now, not angrily, but I see no need to watch my teams play badly and lose. He played board games with me. I was very competitive and liked playing the games. My older siblings wouldn't play with me much, probably because they didn't like that I was so competitive, and in the games I played all the time with my dad, such as checkers, I could generally beat them. But my dad's anger and controlling nature cast a dark pall over all of that for me as a child and then as an adolescent and young adult. I mainly saw my dad negatively, and in my own mind, I saw him as seeing me through a negative lens as well. And that is really, in fact, an understatement.

Frankly, I thought he didn't like me very well. I felt he didn't like my personality. I was not "tough enough" for him, even though I was in reality a pretty tough, rough-and-tumble kind of kid. I was too sensitive for his tastes. He interpreted my interests in things he had no interest in as feminine—sissy behavior as he called it. He interpreted my sensitivity to and concern for others as weakness. He resented that I was close to my sisters, spending time actually conversing with them about various topics, which, by the way, I also did with my brothers when they would engage me. Perhaps he had even resented my being born at all and the fact that I, being her youngest, was a momma's boy. He resented my intellect and could sense how often I inwardly disagreed with him. I rarely would dare disagree with him outwardly, but he had a way of exposing my disagreement nonetheless. He was generally harder on me than he was on my brother just older than I, who was my best friend and buddy. He seemingly favored my brother over me, and it did not go unnoticed by either of us. We actually used it in our favor as we grew up. But the reality was still sad for me.

After all my seven other siblings had left home for college and on to adult life, and my mom had been dead for five years, I was left alone with my father for my last year of high school. I often felt like a hostage or prisoner. I still groan inwardly to remember how miserable and unhappy I mostly was living alone with him in that empty shell that had once been full of such a big, often boisterous family. It was bad enough just being there without my siblings, after having grown up in a home that originally had ten people in it, but being the only one there to take the brunt of his angry, controlling, and manipulative behavior nearly did me in. I often wished to be dead. At least once, as best I can remember, I held an unloaded gun to my head. I had suicide fantasies. I had a lot of hatred in my heart toward him. Suffice it to say, I was always conflicted in regard to him! And it left me with a lifelong off and on, nagging death wish of sorts, often feeling the world would be better off without me and wishing I could just go to sleep and avoid further hurt.

However, it finally came my time to leave home and go away to college, and even though I bore a massive load of resentment, I felt sorry for him as I drove away and left him alone. I knew how lonely that house had been with two of us in it; I could just imagine how he would feel all by himself in it. Since we had constantly taken care of him around the house, I had no idea how he would make it alone. And in fact he didn't stay there alone; instead he went and stayed with his own parents, who were still alive, and let his mom take care of him, as he had insisted we do. But still, even when I went for a visit, I was treated about the same as I had been growing up. I had to do housework and take care of him, unlike my friends who went home and had moms to take care of them.

As the years went on by though, and I moved on into full adulthood (although my wife might argue that it has still never happened!) and was further removed from those early painful years, I was able to come to peace with my dad. I could finally separate the good from the bad and see how some of the things that I resented were actually wise and bold parenting. In fact, I came to wonder how he had figured out some of the things he did that were pretty extraordinary. I could see he tried his best to teach us character, that he drove us to be our best, and that he certainly didn't spoil us, allowing us to feel somehow entitled, like so many of our generation. I for sure had it better than he had!

When I was in my later twenties or early thirties, I saw a quote attributed to Mark Twain that said, "When I was a boy of fourteen, my father was so ignorant I could hardly stand to have the old man around. But when I got to be twenty-one, I was astonished at how much he had learned in seven years." There is a debate over whether Mark Twain actually said it, but regardless of who the author was, it resonated with me. I guess as a sign I had come to peace with the man who was my father, I bought him a plaque with the quote on it and gave it to him. I wrote him a note on the back and I could tell it meant something special to him. Kelley and Treva were my parents, for good and bad. She was sick much of my life, but her fingerprints are all over my heart and life. She was so sweet, affable, and generous. She loved her children dearly. She was extraordinary as a mother and as a person in many ways. My dad was mentally unstable a lot of the time, and he lost it when my mother died, but for good and bad and whether I like it or not, he lives on in me. God designed it that way.

I could go on and on about my dad and his impact on me early on and then later on. I have spent quite a few hours in counseling trying to "right-size" all that I had experienced with him, directly and indirectly. I still have to mentally work my way through certain bad thought patterns after being forty years removed from living in his household. I have what seems to be a mild form of PTSD that recurs, occasionally waking me from sleep in the middle of the night after fearful or anxious dreams related to my early life. Many scars have remained. But these scars that we all have are not meant to destroy us; they are meant to drive us to our Heavenly Father, where we are completely safe and through whom we will finally be eternally healed!

My dad was a strict disciplinarian. I have found many of his adages and axioms to be priceless, even though many were originally laced with expletives. My dad believed that if something was worth saying once, it should be repeated constantly. He drove us as kids to better ourselves, generally denigrating all he was and did, telling us not to be like him (of course, he generally just denigrated everyone anyway). There were countless things he said to us over and over and over. However, when you look at what he produced, the results are enviable to the most learned parenting experts. Seven of his kids got college degrees, the first generation of his family to ever go to college. Sadly he was the cause of the one who did not finish her degree. To get away from him and his abuse, she married early and went to a trade school, becoming a lifelong beautician, doing what she had loved and wanted to do anyway. She owned her own shop for years and was very successful at that. Five of his kids have master's degrees as well. All of his kids are Christians, all are married with children and grandchildren, and there are at this writing no divorces among his eight kids. We love each other and have learned how to say and show it. We have learned over the years to get along well and avoid silly sibling squabbles. Most would see all of us as fairly respected people in our various communities. Most of his grandkids are Christians, most have college degrees, and most are still married to their original mates. And in the end, we all loved our dad, respected him, and treated him well, in spite of any baggage we might have had concerning him. We were able to bury him together when his long life ended, all of us at peace with him and each other.

As I grew on into adulthood, I got to have quite a few conversations with him over the next twenty plus years he was still alive. These were conversations that could go quite deep and be at least somewhat personal. I learned about him as a human. I, as a young minister, was able to actually pastor him, although I don't think he recognized it as that. I even baptized my dad while he was probably in his late sixties, although the exact date I've forgotten. I suppose he softened and tempered with age, and I suppose I matured both as a person and as a Christian. It was during these years, I came to see my dad seeing me. And frankly, seeing what I saw, I don't think my previous views could have been much more incorrect!

My dad was proud of me. My dad cared as deeply for me as any father ever could. His passion for me and his other kids drove him. Sometimes seemingly driving him a bit crazy. When we were kids, he would drag us out of bed in the middle of the night to go sit out a storm in the dirt storm cellar he had dug in our yard. It was not popular with us, but he said he did it because he could not imagine a tornado striking our home and our bodies being spread out all over the place. He did it for us out of his love for us, and after we all left home, he never went to the storm cellar again. Frankly, we stopped going to the cellar during storms after our mom died, I think because a big part of him died with her. And I believe he often wished and maybe in his twisted mind thought it best if all of us had already been dead.

He told me about his upbringing and the tough life he had lived. I realized how much better he had actually made it for us than what he grew up with. He talked endearingly about my mom and my siblings. My youthful struggles with his human weaknesses and failings and how they played out in his control and discipline had obscured the loving, merciful, and concerned side that was ultimately what drove him. I officiated his funeral twenty years ago as of this writing. He had asked me some time before he died if I would do that for him. It was difficult. It was one of the harder things I have ever done, as I was quite conflicted with all the competing feelings that flowed through my mind and as I looked out into the faces of my dear family.

For his eulogy, I wrote a piece in his honor that I called "Bridge Over Troubled Waters," taken from the Simon and Garfunkel song released in 1970 by that name. My point was that he had served as a bridge from the troubled, challenging time he came from to where he wanted his family to end up. The years he lived through were very troubled times in our world—troubled waters. His was the Great Generation. In the world at large, in our country, and in the world he had grown up in, there had been constant turmoil—"war, severe economic depression, and extreme drought, as well as rapid, massive social, cultural, and economic changes. As with most decent parents I suppose, he along with my mother dreamed of a different and better world for their children than they had experienced. My dad willed it so, even though in his imperfections his way of getting us there was at times downright painful, unfair, unwise, and so forth. But still he got us from a troubled shore across the seas of life to a better place. He got us there over some very troubled waters. I concluded my eulogy with, "We made it, Dad." Tears well up in my eyes as I write it. I think he died at least with that satisfaction. He was proud of all of us. I only hope somewhere in his troubled heart and mind he finally saw his own father seeing him.

Seeing my dad seeing me, as he had in his heart all along, changed everything. All in all, it made me a much better person. It gave me a measure of peace. It made me a better dad. It made me a better minister and pastor.

I think many of us are with God as I was as a youth with my dad. We feel as if he doesn't like us. We think he's being mean to us. We think he doesn't understand us. We think he's being selfish. Of course, unlike our heavenly Father, my dad was quite imperfect, and there were lots of things he did that were not righteous. Of course, it's that way with all of our dads or other caregivers. But as I said, some of what he did I found to be fairly brilliant and in the end found out he did his best. Sadly, as with our own earthly fathers, too few people really take the time to get to know their Heavenly Father. We go to church, maybe listen to some Christian music and sermons, perhaps read our Bibles or a book or two, and otherwise just "go with our gut feeling" concerning who God is and what he wants. But our searches, if they can be called searches at all, are often lukewarm and half-hearted at best. And thus fairly futile.

Little can be accomplished that way in this present world. That kind of effort will yield no success in seeing God. It will in fact ultimately prove counterproductive. God said to the Jews in exile, "You will seek me and find me when you seek me with all your heart" (Jer. 29:13). Jesus cited a statement from Moses when he said in regard to our relationships with God, "Love the Lord your God with all your heart and with all your soul and with all your mind" (Matt. 22:37). Jesus also pronounced a blessing on those who would be single-minded in their hearts before God, saying, "Blessed are the pure in heart, for they will see God" (Matt. 5:8). Being pure in heart is not really about being sinless per se; it is about our hearts being only about one thing—God. Pure means that something contains only one thing and nothing else. God has made it so that we will find him—see him—when we wholeheartedly seek him. He wants us to find peace with him and the world as he made it. He wants us to learn the secret of contentment in the midst of a tumultuous world, and then for us to be laid to rest in peace to live on in eternal bliss with him and all who call on his name!

When we see God seeing us, everything changes. It is indeed an eternal "game changer"!

Questions and Thoughts for Reflection and Discussion

1. How might negative attitudes you carry with you about your own father, mother, or other caregivers negatively affect how you see God seeing you?
2. What negative traits or behaviors that you saw in your parents might you be imposing unnecessarily on God?

3. Why are we prone to spend so little time and put such little effort in seeking God?
4. What mental, emotional, or relational issues might it be wise for you to work on clearing up in order to see God more clearly?
5. The name of this book, *Seeing God Seeing You*, is a double entendre, meaning it has two interpretations. How would you describe the two interpretations that may be made of it, and why is each important?

CONCLUSION

I suppose that it can honestly be said that I have been writing this book my whole life. I certainly have over the forty-five-plus years of my life as a Christian. I came from a sometimes fundamentalist, always conservative, church background. Grass-roots Christianity where I lived and grew up was about being right and keeping the rules. There wasn't a lot of talk about a personal relationship with God, and sadly, there often seemed too little practice of it. Little was said about God's mercy and grace in my personal world; less was known about it. My parents, from the Great Generation, were generally stoics. There was little or no belief in any literal presence or work of the Holy Spirit in us. Lukewarmness and complacency were rampant in the churches. Repetitive traditionalism was strictly adhered to. Change was resisted and resented. It seemed generally accepted that everything was already correctly believed and practiced; therefore, any change was a departure from *the* truth.

However, from the very start of my search for God and then walk with him, I felt the need for change and reform. I was completely green though. I knew nothing. I had never read the Bible. I had not a clue what all I didn't know. I did however know I didn't know much. What I did know is it just didn't all seem to reconcile very well.

What was missing for me was at its core truly seeking out and seeing God—simply, purely, and wholly. Just God. In my early church experience though, it was so much about doing church right. It was so much about having the correct interpretations. It was too much about correcting ("saving") everybody else, while often ignoring obvious and gross issues within our own selves and churches. It seemed to be the prevailing thought that *we* were right because we *were* right!

Perhaps it was just me. Perhaps I was just projecting myself or everybody else. But in retrospect I don't think it was so then, and I don't think so now. This is not about guilt; it is about opportunity—the opportunity to get out of our own private little self-serving bubbles. It is about stopping seeing the world, and especially ourselves, through our own cracked and dirty lens. It is about repenting (changing our minds) and simply believing the gospel. It is about yielding to God's continuous transformation of us. It is about giving up our addiction to the sweet but toxic fruit of the Tree of the Knowledge of Good and Evil and exchanging it for the nourishing and life-giving fruit of the Tree of Life.

God loved us before we were, and he loves us still because we are. His love for us is completely independent of our performance or perfection. He loves because he is love. Many of us likely still need to go through our own forms of "counseling" to "right size" our views of God—to correct the misperceptions we carry with us. We need to try to understand the purposes behind things that have happened or are presently happening to us. Perhaps some, rather than just needing a minor correction, need to undergo a massive correction in their views of God. No, it is not easy. In fact, it is the hardest work of all, but the work God wants us doing—truly believing in Christ (John 6:29).

It is most certainly worth it.

It is not easy because it is about going down the narrow road to life. It takes intentionality. It takes determination. It takes bold honesty. It costs everything. It will at least sometimes evoke in others around us misunderstanding, resentment, rejection, or even hatred of us. It forces us to reject the world's and even the church's demand for slavish conformity. In seeing God seeing us, we will from the inside out become less and less like the world around us, in many surprising ways. We will be as different as Christ is different. We in fact become holy—completely set apart for God's use alone.

All in all, if we will let this world be about God, as it truly is, we will find that in reality he has made it all about us. And it is designed to lead us straight to eternal life!

And all that I have written herein is indeed designed to describe "my gospel." Yes, this is my gospel. My prayer for each and every one of us is that we can indeed finally and fully see God seeing us! Amen!

Questions and Thoughts for Reflection and Discussion

1. What are your five greatest takeaways, ideas, challenges, and so forth, from reading this book?
2. What are two or three changes you will begin to make immediately to help you better see how God sees you?
3. Who in your sphere of influence might you seek to help in this journey as well?
4. To whom would you recommend this or a similar book in order to help them grow in seeing God seeing them?

Other Books by Ronnie Worsham

Fighting and Beating Depression
Forty Days on the Mountain with God
Discovering Jesus
Reflections on Faith
A Funny Little Cow Ponders Pain (coauthored with Kristen Wilemon)
God Thoughts
Glowing Embers

Visit on Facebook @RonnieWorsham

Made in the USA
Columbia, SC
23 April 2019